All Their Days

All Their Days

Linda Sole

PIATKUS

Set in 11/12 pt Times by
Datix International Limited, Bungay, Suffolk
Printed and bound in Great Britain by
Biddles Ltd, Guildford and King's Lynn.

Chapter One

'Nellie, where are you? I'm warning you – if you don't get yourself up here fast there's going to be trouble!'

I could hear my mother's voice calling to me from the back yard of our terraced cottage; she sounded frustrated and angry. Standing in Grandfather's allotment, which was tucked behind a sheltering wall and out of sight, I was for the moment safe from her wrath and continued to eat the large, fat gooseberries, relishing their tart but delicious flavour as the juice spilled over and dribbled down my chin. The warmth of the sun made me reluctant to answer her call, even though failure to do so would bring swift retribution.

Mother's name was Rose Pearce and she was a sharp-tongued woman in her early-thirties; tall, thin and attractive in her way, she nevertheless had a hard, unforgiving manner, seldom smiling unless it was at my younger brother Bob who was still only eight and the darling of her heart. For me there was never a smile nor yet a word of praise; I might have been swifter to answer her summons if there had been.

I ought to have gone up to the house when she called me, of course, but she had been at me all morning, sniping and carping, and I'd sneaked away when her back was turned.

Even as I struggled with my conscience I saw Grandfather open the wooden gate that connected the allotment to our tiny yard and was spiked with guilt as I saw the way he was hobbling. His rheumatism had been playing him up for days; it showed in his face as he shuffled painfully towards me, his scuffed boots dragging over the rough paving stones.

Wilf Barnes had worked down the coal mines for most of

his life but every spare moment he'd had once his shift down the pit was finished had been spent here in his allotment. My beloved grandfather was famed for his vegetables and soft fruits, never failing to carry off half the prizes at the annual village shows. He had hoped to spend all his days working his small plot when he retired but the miseries had caught up with him too soon and now he could hardly walk. My father had taken over from him but everyone said that Sam Pearce did not have Grandfather's green fingers; it was true but neither Grandfather or I would have dreamed of repeating such talk within his hearing: we two kept our secrets to ourselves.

'Hello, Grandad,' I called to him. 'What are you doing down here then?'

As if I didn't know: he had come to look for me, of course. He was a quiet man, saying very little when my mother's temper got the better of her, but whenever he could he tried to shield me from the worst of it. He never said or did anything to indicate that he cared for me more than my brother but sometimes there was a special warmth in his eyes as he looked at me, and we had this understanding between us: a feeling that needed no words. When I was younger he had often carried me around the village on his shoulders, and I loved the warm, peppery smell of him.

'Didn't you hear your mother calling?' he asked, a faint reproach in his voice. 'She's on the war-path now, lass. You'd best get yourself up there and do what she wants.'

'Yes, Grandad.'

There was no escaping now, not after he had hauled himself from his chair and made what must have been a tiring journey in search of me.

'I'm sorry,' I said, and darted at him, kissing his cheek with lips still moist and sticky from the gooseberries. 'I'll go straight up – and thank you.'

He leaned on his stick, his eyes following my progress as I ran towards the yard. He would rest for a while before himself returning, dreaming in the sun of the days when he was a young man and courting my grandmother. He had told me so many stories of her that I felt I knew Dolly Barnes even though she had died before I was born. She had

2

been a kind, good woman and sometimes I wept because I had never felt the warmth of her arms about me.

I knew why my mother had been calling me. I hadn't responded because if there was one chore I hated it was helping with the washing. I hated washday altogether, hated the smell of the soda and the steam coming out of the dirty clothes as they boiled in the old-fashioned copper in the scullery: it stung my eyes and throat, making my head ache if I was in there too long.

Mother said it was only an excuse to get out of helping but that wasn't true. I didn't mind work; I rather liked peeling potatoes and cleaning the vegetables Father brought in from the allotment; I would quite happily peg the clothes on the line or wash the dishes; making beds and beating rugs weren't high on my list because the dust got up my nose and made me sneeze but I didn't complain when I was asked to do these things. It was the washing I hated and my mother knew that.

Today was Monday, 6 May 1935 and a special school holiday – in London King George and Queen Mary were celebrating their Silver Jubilee and there were to be street parties all over the country – but for me there was to be no escape and no idleness. I was a girl and girls were expected to help in the house. Sometimes I envied Bob his freedom; occasionally he helped with the allotment but most of the time he was allowed to run free in the village streets with his friends, getting into all kinds of scrapes. My mother turned a blind eye to his wildness, except for the time he came home with a bruised face from fighting with the tinkers on the common, and then she had made my father take his belt to him.

'I won't have you mixing with that trash,' she had said, her face grim as he screamed and wept for the pain. 'Let this be a lesson to you.'

Afterwards he had been sent to bed without any supper, but she had relented and taken him up a slice of his favourite cake later. Now and then I wondered why she liked Bob so much more than she liked me.

When I reached the wash-house Mother had rinsed the sheets and was ringing them out by hand. She looked up as I

3

entered but didn't say anything, simply thrusting one end of a sheet at me. I took it and in silence we folded and refolded the wet linen, then I pressed the ends close to the great wooden rollers of the heavy mangle and began to wind the handle. It was hard work and I had to use two hands before the water started to drip into the tin bath beneath, splashing at first, then reducing to a trickle as the sheet was put through for a second time.

There were four singles as well as a double – Mother put top to bottom each week and washed the bottom sheet – and five pillow cases as well as the bolster covers, several towels, vests, longjohns, shirts and Grandad's combinations, all of which had been boiled until they were white.

'That's the lot then,' she sighed with satisfaction. 'Help me carry the basket out to the yard.'

The rush basket was heavy with so many damp clothes packed into it but I was tall and strong for my thirteen years and people often thought I was older.

Once outside in the sunshine I could breathe more easily. I bent down to take my end of the sheet as we pegged it on one of the lines that ran the full length of the yard; soon the rows of spotless washing were flapping lazily in the breeze.

Mother's expression was a mixture of triumph and tiredness; it was always a battle on washday with three men in the house and for a moment I felt sorry that I had deserted her.

'Are you going to the party this afternoon, Ma?' I asked. 'Everyone will be there.'

'Then they won't miss me, will they?' she replied sourly. 'I haven't got time for gallivanting – though I suppose you'll have to go or there will be sulks?'

'They gave us a holiday so that we could.' My cheeks were burning as I looked at her. It wasn't fair of her to be so harsh; I helped her most evenings when I came home from school and I'd cleaned the bedrooms before escaping to the allotment that morning.

'You'll be leaving school soon,' she said, a speculative expression in her eyes. 'Fourteen next month, Nellie.'

'Yes, Ma.' Her eyes were greenish in colour – very like my own. We were alike in some ways, both tall and stubborn – though I was much heavier than her and she made me very

4

aware of my size. 'I'll be able to help you more then, won't I?'

I spoke appeasingly, wanting to take that tired, strained look from her face: she seemed to have so little joy in life and I sometimes wondered what had made her the way she was. It wasn't that she had an especially hard life, for my father was a gentle man and good to her. In the scullery the whitewash was peeling off the walls because of the damp but the rest of the house was comfortable enough: we weren't rich but we certainly weren't poor and most women in our village would have been grateful for what she had, but there was always a downturn to her mouth and a bitterness that spilled out when she was tired or angry.

'That's as maybe,' she said now, her eyes flicking away. She scooped up the empty basket, tucking it under her arm. 'You can go to the baker's for me – and take a message to your dad at the same time.'

I nodded, saying nothing as I followed her inside; that kind of chore was much more to my liking. Most days Mother made her own bread but not on washday; for just that one day she grudgingly bought from the small bakery at the bottom of the hill. Mr Robinson delivered to all his regular customers free of charge but we did not belong to those privileged few: Mother would have thought it wasteful to buy when she could make. She took some coins from her purse in the dresser and pressed them into my hand.

'A large white, and make sure you don't lose the change.'

'Of course not.' I felt resentful as I pocketed the money. Did she think I was so foolish that I could not be trusted to do a simple errand? 'What shall I say to Dad?'

'Tell him not to forget his promise,' she said, and once again her eyes slid away from mine. 'He'll know what I mean.'

I wondered what all the mystery was about. She usually said what she meant straight out and I sensed something hidden, almost furtive, in her manner.

Once I was out of the house, though, I soon forgot the small mystery. Walking down the road my spirits began to lift and I hummed a tune from the music halls. Grandad had taught me several and they made me laugh inside.

5

'I'm Burlington Bertie ... I rise at ten-thirty and saunter along ... ' I too sauntered along as if I had all the time in the world.

The village was grouped into two huddles of terraced grey houses by the steep hill that divided Lower Stonckton from Upper Stonckton. Set in the shelter of the impressive Pennines the houses were mostly built of tough, abrasive stone with slate roofs and small, perpetually closed windows through which the cold winds penetrated in winter but the sun seemed never to shine, making the rooms dark and cheerless – even now, in early summer.

The sun was warm out of the wind, birds sang in back gardens that had just begun to burst with colour after the long winter, and all was right with the world as I hummed my songs and thought about the likelihood of my father giving me a penny or two to spend at the shop. He did now and then when my mother wasn't around to remind him that sweets were a waste of money and ruined your appetite for proper food.

I thought about something she had said at breakfast that morning; it was what had upset me, the real reason I had taken refuge in the allotment.

'You're a great lump of a thing,' she had grumbled as I spread strawberry jam on my toast. 'Is that the third round or the fourth you've had?'

It was only my second and I had left it uneaten on the plate.

'It's puppy fat,' Grandad had defended me. 'She'll grow out of it. Besides, there's many a man prefers an armful in bed on a cold night to a bag of bones. Our Nellie won't go short of offers when she's older, you take my word for it.'

'You just wash your mouth out with carbolic!' Mother's reply was predictable. 'Giving the girl ideas ... whatever next?'

I knew what they were both referring to, you couldn't live in a small village like ours and not know the facts of life. Mother was a good neighbour; she helped out with births, sicknesses and deaths, and I often had to run errands, boil water and be prepared to fetch the doctor or the undertaker, whichever proved necessary. So I had a good idea of what

6

went on when babies were born even if I wasn't quite so sure of how they got started, but I didn't see why Grandad's remarks should give me ideas. Like most girls of my age I dreamed vaguely of marriage and a home of my own one day, but took little notice of the opposite sex except for my family – which may be why I didn't notice the young man until he planted himself firmly in the middle of the path, preventing me from walking on.

'Where are you off to then, young Nell?'

I looked at him consideringly, a little annoyed at the cheeky note in his voice. Just who did he think he was? Talking to me like that!

'You're back then,' I said flatly. 'I thought your family had gone for good.'

Tom Herries was one of the tinker family; it was fighting with one of his younger brothers that had got Bob into such hot water with Mother.

'Hoped you'd seen the last of me, eh?' He grinned. 'Can't stop a bad penny turning up – that's what they say, ain't it?'

I supposed he was a bad penny; my mother would certainly say so. She had no time for the Herries family and nor had most of the local people. Tom's father was a surly-looking man who had come and gone over the years; living quietly in his horse-drawn caravan, he'd mended pots and pans, undertaken odd jobs and then wandered off again with his pasty-faced wife and brood of noisy, dirty children, but the previous winter there had been trouble. One of Tom's elder brothers had become involved with a local girl – a girl who had hitherto been highly respectable. Her father had warned the tinker off but he wouldn't be told and they'd fought, the older man ending up with a broken head and the girl running off with her lover, her father's curses ringing in her ears. The incident had turned folk against the tinkers and several of the men got together to warn the Herries family that they were no longer welcome.

'You weren't the cause of the trouble,' I said after some deliberation. I hadn't thought about it before but in the past I'd found Tom good company. We had gone fishing for frogs and newts in the pond some years back and he'd once beaten off some bullies who were pulling my hair as I walked home from school. I supposed I quite liked him. 'The quarrel wasn't your fault, was it?'

Tom's dark eyes sparkled with humour as he gazed down at me from his superior height. He was taller than most lads his age – which was a little over eighteen – broad-shouldered and handsome despite the way his black hair straggled from under a filthy cap and his threadbare trousers were tied around his waist with string, his black boots worn down at the heels and cracked beneath their layers of mud.

'Your ma wouldn't agree with that,' he remarked cheerfully.

'No, I don't suppose she would – but Ma doesn't agree with much I say.'

That made him laugh out loud. He had very bold eyes and they roved over me, bringing a flush to my cheeks and making me uneasy.

'You're all right, young Nell,' he said, a quirk to his mouth. 'When I'm rich I might come back and marry you.'

'Who says I'd have you?'

Tom chuckled deep in his throat. At that moment something in his eyes made me want to slap him but I was afraid that he might hit me back. I had heard somewhere that the Herries were a violent lot, though I had never seen any evidence of it in Tom: still, it wasn't worth taking the risk.

'You'd have me all right – that's if I asked.'

'You'll never be rich.' His self-confidence was irritating. Anyone would think he was the son of a lord rather than a tinker's lad.

'Now that's what you think.' His mouth curved in a cocky smile. 'Tinker's blood might flow in my veins but I've got what it takes up here.' He tapped one finger against the side of his head. 'I'm not going to live the way my folks do. I've got brains and I'm going to use them to make a better life for myself.'

'How?' I fixed him with a straight look. 'Not by thieving, I hope?'

'There's more than one way to skin a cat – and more than one way to get rich.'

'Not for the likes of you, Tom Herries! You'll end up in prison or at the end of a rope, that's what you'll do.'

'Then I'll be in good company.' His eyes mocked me. 'There's been many a gent caught with his fingers in the pie, but I shan't get caught.'

'Sez you! Rogues always pay for their sins in the end.'

'You're still wet behind the ears if you believe that. You can get away with anything if you go about it in the right way.' His cheeky grin was back. 'You remember me, Nell Pearce – one day you'll know I was right.'

I stared after him as he strolled off. 'I'll never marry you, Tom Herries!'

He glanced back over his shoulder, an infuriating gleam in his eyes, but didn't say anything. I threw him a look of disgust. He was like the rest of his family after all; thieves and rogues, that was what Mother said, and for once I was inclined to agree. I had thought Tom might be different but there was no way for a man like that to get rich – not honestly.

My father was the local shoemaker; he had his own small shop and he earned decent money, enough to keep us all in clothes and food and to put a bit by, but he wasn't rich, not like the gentry, not in the way Tom had meant.

My only experience of the gentry was the Harrington family. They lived in a big, ugly slate grey house near Malham. I knew that because Father had taken me to the sheep sales in Malham a couple of times; these sales had been held there for nearly two hundred years and they attracted ordinary folk as well as the farmers who came to buy and sell stock. Once, Father had called at the Harringtons' house on the way to the sale, to deliver some shoes he had made for a member of the family. I'd sat outside in the van he had borrowed for the day and waited for him, knowing he was pleased because they had asked him to make the shoes.

'It was a pleasure to make something from the very finest leather,' he had told me afterwards. 'And they're a good family, an old, local family.'

Sometimes, when my father had the use of a van, which belonged to another of his regular customers and could only be borrowed occasionally, he took me for a ride with him, showing me things I would otherwise never have seen.

9

All around Malham was an area of extreme natural beauty, with the Pennine Way and, eastward, Gordale Scar, where waterfalls plunged down a ravine so deep that it had made me dizzy just to look at it. Then, high on the fells, there was Malham Tarn, its waters cold and mysterious, sometimes even threatening, which might be why the author Charles Kingsley had been inspired to write *The Water Babies* – one of my favourite stories at school – while staying at Malham Tarn House.

For some reason I was thinking of that day at the sales as I completed the last few yards to my father's shop at the end of the street and wondered if he had made any more shoes for the Harrington family; if he had, I hadn't heard him mention it.

As I entered the shop with its clutter of tools, boots and shoes in various stages of repair I inhaled the strong but pleasing odour of fresh cut leather and smiled at my father sitting behind his workbench, feeling the familiar warmth inside as he greeted me with his serious gaze.

'Well then, our Nellie,' he said, glancing at me over the top of the gold-rimmed spectacles he wore for his work. 'Why aren't you at school – not playing truant, I hope?'

'It's a holiday. Surely you haven't forgotten – for the jubilee?'

'Ah, yes.' He removed the glasses and rubbed his nose. 'I mustn't forget the party this afternoon, I'll see if I can get along. So what have you been doing with yourself then?'

'I've been helping Ma with the washing. Now I've come with a message. She said to tell you not to forget your promise . . . whatever that means?'

I was hopeful that he might enlighten me but his expression closed up and it seemed as if the message had touched a sore spot, reminding him of something he would rather have forgotten.

'As if I'm likely to forget after she went on about it the way she did,' he muttered to himself. 'She would never let me hear the last of it.'

His gentle brown eyes dwelt on my face and his expression puzzled me; it was as if he were regretting something, as if his thoughts were causing him distress.

10

'Here you are, lass.' His hand went to his rusty black waistcoat. 'Take this and buy yourself a treat.'

'Thanks, Da.' I held out my hand, exclaiming as I saw what he had given me. 'It's a shilling!'

'Aye, I know.' He shifted uncomfortably on his stool. 'You're a good lass, you deserve it – but don't tell your mother.'

'No fear of that,' I said. She might have taken it away from me! 'Thanks, Da. Is there anything I can do for you, an errand?'

'No.' His eyes seemed glued to the bench in front of him. 'Get off and enjoy yourself while you can.'

'I'll be away then.'

I was filled with a warm glow of gratitude as I left the shop. My da was that good to me! I loved both my father and grandfather so much that sometimes it hurt; I wanted to love my mother that way but she was too sharp-tongued, too ready to slap first and ask after. Bob was a little pest at times but he was my brother and I felt protective towards him – as long as he wasn't telling tales to Mother.

I wouldn't spend the whole shilling on sweets, I decided, though Bob would get a penny's worth of licorice bootlaces. Most of it would go on a few Woodbines or some baccy for Grandad, if Mr Brown at the corner shop would let me buy them. He often refused requests for single cigarettes from young lads of around my age, but he usually let me have them because he knew they were for Grandad.

I was happy as I walked into the dim interior of the tiny corner shop with its curious mixture of smells – soaps and parrafin warring with spices, fresh cut flowers, fruit, vegetables and strong cheeses – pleased that I could take home a surprise for my grandfather.

The village women had been busy baking and preparing from early that morning, most of them putting the jubilee celebrations before their usual routine of washing and ironing. Gay strings of flags were fluttering from the lamp-posts; long tables crowded with food, bottles of beer and lemonade, had been set up by the green and children were already playing ball games when I arrived with the plate of fairy cakes Mother had grudgingly sent.

11

'You're to watch out for your brother,' she'd told me before we left. 'Don't let him fall in the pond – and don't let him mix with that tinker trash!'

I wondered how she knew that the Herries family had come back. As far as I knew she hadn't been out of the house or yard all day, but perhaps she had had a visitor while I was on my errands. News travelled fast in a small village like ours.

'Why don't you come with us, Ma?' I asked. 'Couldn't the ironing wait for another day? Why don't you relax and have some fun for once?'

'It's easy for you to talk,' she replied. 'Get off with you, Nellie. Sitting out in a breeze listening to a lot of noisy brats screaming their heads off – when they're not stuffing their faces or being sick – isn't my idea of having fun.'

What was her idea of fun? It was difficult to imagine her ever having been young. Had she and my father ever gone to dances or to the pictures? Unless he fell asleep by the fire my father spent his evenings reading the newspaper or listening to the wireless; Mother sometimes sat down to listen with him but always with a bit of mending or knitting in her hands. I couldn't remember seeing her completely idle; she had always to be doing something.

'Now remember what Ma said,' I warned Bob as he ran off to join some of his friends. 'You're to stay away from the tinkers.'

'Aw, Nellie,' he grumbled. 'Give over do. You're worse than Ma.'

I shook my head but didn't try to argue with him – what harm could he come to when we were surrounded by people we knew? If he fell in the pond a dozen hands would be there to pull him out. Seeing some of my own friends, I went to join them.

'Sit here, Nellie,' Mary Hopkin called and gestured to a chair beside her. 'I've been saving this for you.'

Mary was a slight, fragile-looking girl with fair hair and pale blue eyes. She was sometimes bullied by other children at school and I had tended to protect her, clipping the ear of cheeky lads who tugged at her plaits; because of that we had become very close, telling each other all our secrets.

Mary's father was a farmer, not rich but comfortable. He had a small car and had taken us both to the picture house in town for her birthday; we had seen a new musical with Fred Astaire and Ginger Rogers. Mary was an only child and her parents made a great fuss of her. She complained that they were over-protective, but I couldn't help thinking how lucky she was as she showed me the new dress her mother had made specially for the party.

'It's really pretty,' I said. 'Have a fairy cake – Mother made them.'

'You try one of these cream horns,' Mary countered. 'Mother bought them from a shop in town – they're fresh cream. I've been saving these two for us in case you came.'

'Ooh, lovely,' I enthused as I took one of the cakes and bit into the crisp pastry and the cream with its oozing centre of raspberry jam. 'I suppose it's fattening but it does taste good.'

People were chattering all around us and at the far side of the green the local brass band had begun to play a marching song; they made a couple of false starts but then they were away, drums and trumpets competing in an attempt to see who could make the most noise. I thought it was a shame my mother hadn't come. All the other women seemed to be having a good time – and she was at home ironing!

The men had gathered together at the beer table and the sound of their laughter grew louder and louder as the contents of bottles and barrels of ale were gradually emptied into glasses and tipped down their throats. I saw my father arrive and waved to him; he waved back but just as he was about to come over to me one of the other men pushed a glass of beer into his hand. I glanced away as Mary spoke to me and when I looked back I saw that Da was laughing with the others at some joke or other. He seldom laughed like that and it surprised me to see him accept another beer, drinking half of it down in one go as if he relished it.

The brass band had retired for some refreshment and someone had begun to play an accordion; the music was lighter, catchy, and feet started tapping all around me, then a few of the women got up and began to dance together. One or two of the younger men joined them and then ten or twelve couples were dancing a kind of Irish jig that made everyone else clap and encourage them.

'Dance with me, Nellie,' Mary begged, pulling at my sleeve with eager hands. 'Go on, it's fun.'

We got up and joined the others, throwing ourselves into the dance with more enthusiasm than skill. We were both giggling when we found ourselves being parted by two young men – Mary's partner was a lad from the village but the hand that grabbed mine belonged to Tom Herries. With my mother's warning still fresh in my mind I tried to pull away from him but he whirled me around so fast that I could scarcely catch my breath. He let me go only when the music had finished and I was panting.

'You might have asked me,' I muttered resentfully. 'Instead of taking it for . . . ' My words were lost as we heard the angry shouting behind us and turned to look at the fight that had started. 'Isn't that . . . '

'That's my father, damn him,' muttered Tom. 'I might have known he would ruin everything. It's the drink. He can't hold his drink.'

Tinker Herries was blind, roaring drunk. I supposed he must have had a first name but if he did I had never heard it; he was Tinker Herries to everyone and generally spoken of with scorn or derision, especially since the incident the previous winter. Now for the first time I understood why my mother was so against the family.

Clothed in filthy rags, unwashed and unshaven, Tinker stood in the middle of a group of men who were eyeing him warily, his fists clenched and held before him in an attitude of defiance.

'Who among you weak-arsed donkeys is man enough to take me on?' he roared while swaying on his feet. 'Sure the lot of you are cowards . . . cowards, white-livered rats . . . '

Tom had left my side and was making his way through the stunned crowd towards his father.

'Stop making a fool of yourself, Tinker,' he said. 'No one wants to fight you, it's a party.'

'And who asked you to poke your nose in, runt?' Tinker turned on his son in a blaze of fury. 'Get out of me way before I thrash you.'

14

'Now then, Tink,' Tom said, laying his hand persuasively on his father's arm. 'Come away home . . . '

Tinker's answer was to lash out at him with his huge hands. The blow took Tom off guard and felled him. He lay on the ground, blood seeping from his nose as he shook his head; before he could get up Tinker kicked him in the side and he gave a scream of pain. A man moved forward from the crowd and to my dismay I saw it was my father – my mild-mannered, soft-spoken father who rarely raised his voice in the house.

'Behave yourself, Tinker,' he said in an authoritative tone. 'If you touch that lad again I'll have the law on you. You'll find yourself in the cells before you can draw breath.' He knelt down beside Tom, who had doubled over and was vomiting on the grass. 'Are you all right, lad?'

With a great roar of rage Tinker sprang at him, catching Father a blow in the back with his boot. For a moment he went sprawling and I screamed. Mary grabbed my hand and we clung to each other as my father recovered and threw himself at the tinker. In another moment they were at it hammer and tongs, slugging it out like a pair of bare knuckle fighters.

'Sam Pearce was a rare one for a fist fight before he married that sourpuss,' I heard a man's voice say, and a second agreed with a laugh. I glanced round but could not see who had spoken. Every man present was calling out encouragement to my da, yelling their heads off in a fever of excitement as the fight went on and on.

'Go on, Sam!' they roared. 'Teach the bastard a lesson he'll not forget in a hurry.'

To my amazement my father seemed to be doing just that. I let go of Mary's hand and started to scream encouragement at him.

'Go on, Da – give him one! Give him a bloody nose.'

The fight ended as abruptly as it had begun as my father's fist connected with the tinker's chin, laying him out cold; he lay twitching and moaning but unable to get up again. Then Tom and one of his brothers were hauling their father to his feet, wrapping his arms around their necks and dragging him away. Only when they had moved off did I become aware of

15

the unnatural silence; everyone had stopped shouting and there was an expectant hush. As I looked towards my father, now panting and wiping a smear of blood from his mouth, I saw the reason for the hush that had fallen over the men.

My mother was standing alone, staring at my father as if she had seen a ghost. The look on her face was so strange and shocking that I left Mary's side and went to join her. She did not even glance at me, nor at Bob as he came to slip his hand into mine and look up at me anxiously; her eyes were fixed on my father's face. He walked towards us, then reached out and took her hand.

'We'll go home now, Rose,' he said, and she went without a word.

She had plenty to say when she had recovered from the shock, however. Bob and I got off lightly compared to the tongue lashing she gave Da after we had been sent supperless to bed. It wasn't possible to hear the words but her voice was shrill and accusing downstairs and I covered my ears with my hands, wishing it would stop.

It wasn't a row. It couldn't be a row because my father never raised his voice to her once. I could hear him answering her in a slow, soft tone that never varied and it made the memory of his fighting on the village green all the more impossible to believe. If I hadn't seen it with my own eyes I should never have given it credence.

It was ten minutes or so before Bob came and asked if he could get into bed with me. I pulled back the covers and let him; he snuggled against me as he had when he was a toddler and I cuddled up to him, sensing his need for comfort.

'Da really gave it to him, didn't he?'

'Yes, he did.'

'Do you reckon Ma will ever forgive him?'

'I expect so – when she gets over it.'

'It wasn't his fault. He couldn't let Tom get kicked again, and no one else did anything.'

'She ought to be proud of him.'

I was proud of my da, proud of the way he had stood up for what was right and of the way he had put the tinker down. I thought about what the men behind me had said

16

about my da being a rare one for a fist fight before he was married, and it made me wonder again just why he had married my mother. She must have been pretty enough when she was young but there was no joy in her.

Had she always been that way?

I was downstairs before my father left for work the next day and told him I was proud of him. He shook his head and looked grave.

'It was a damn' fool thing to do, Nellie,' he said. 'I'm old enough to know better.'

'But you stood up to him, Da – you were the only one brave enough to do it.'

'The only one daft enough according to your ma.' There was a rueful smile in his eyes as he touched his ribs. 'And this morning I think she's right!'

'It's time you were getting ready for school, Nellie.'

Mother had come into the room without us realizing it. She glared at me and I knew she had heard us talking; she always seemed angry if my father paid me any attention.

'Can I set the table for you, Ma?'

'If you want,' she said grudgingly. 'What do you fancy this morning, Sam?'

'The same as the rest of you,' he said. 'I think I'll just walk out to the allotment while the tea's brewing. Fancy a breath of air, Nellie?'

'I'd best do the table for Ma,' I said, and watched him leave with regret.

She turned on me the moment the door closed behind him, her eyes stabbing at me angrily. 'You were dancing with one of those tinker trash when I arrived,' she said, and as I stared at her in silence she slapped me across the face. 'If ever I catch you with one of them again I'll get your father to take his belt to you! I've warned Bob and now I'm warning you you're to have nothing to do with that family, any of them. Do you understand me?'

I pressed my hand to my burning flesh, feeling the sting of tears. 'It was just a dance, Ma – and he didn't ask, he just grabbed me.'

'Do you understand me?'

'Yes, Ma,' I whispered and blinked back my tears, determined not to cry in front of her.

'Just remember what I've told you.'

She went out into the back kitchen and I heard her banging the enamel pots on the gas stove. I spread a white cloth on the table and began to lay it with four places – Grandad never came down to breakfast these days, it took him too long to get out of bed in the mornings.

It had been fun at the party; it had been fun dancing with Tom, even though I had been annoyed with him for just grabbing me like that. In its own way even the fight had been fun once I'd seen my da was getting the better of the tinker – but my mother's sudden arrival had spoilt everything.

I was angry with her until I remembered the look in her eyes as she stood staring at Da . . . she had looked frightened, lost, lonely, and that had upset me.

She had slapped me before; it wasn't the end of the world. She was still my mother and I loved her even if she didn't seem to care for me that much.

'I've done scrambled eggs the way you like them,' she said, making me jump as she came into the room behind me. 'Fetch your father in, Nellie, while I call that lazy young scamp down.'

'Yes, Ma.'

I ran off joyfully to fetch my father in to his breakfast. My mother's words had been as near to an apology as I was ever likely to get from her.

'You can't always judge a book by its cover,' Grandad said to me that afternoon when I brought him a cup of tea and sat with my knees hunched up on the stool at his feet. 'Some folk might think Sam Pearce weak because he lets your mother rule the roost, but slow-flowing rivers often run deep, lass. It's not the first time your father has thrashed a man, and it doesn't surprise me.'

'He's never seemed like one for a fight before.'

'Mebbe he's never had reason that you know of.' Grandad took out his heavy gold watch and opened the cover to look at the white enamel dial. 'Will you pop down to the shop for me before they close, Nellie?'

'You know I will,' I said and sprang to my feet. 'What can I get for you?'

'An ounce of baccy – and one of those walnut cakes you like. We'll have it for tea.'

My mother would say it was a waste of money buying cakes from the baker's shop, but sometimes Grandad liked to give us all a treat and what she didn't know wouldn't hurt her. I took the money, kissed him and ran before she could come in from the scullery and ask where I was going.

The warm weather was changing and there was a cool breeze as I set off down the street. I walked quickly because it was chilly and I wanted to get back home as soon as I could; it was only as I got to the corner that I saw Tom Herries come out of my father's shop. He waved and called to me to wait. I hesitated because of my mother's warning but then realized I couldn't ignore him. He ran across the road to join me.

His face was covered with bruises ranging from yellow to a dark purple – far more of them than he had had the previous afternoon.

'What happened to your face?'

'It was Tinker,' he said. 'He thrashed me, but it was for the last time. I'm never going back to the van. I've only stayed this long for my mother's sake but I won't stay now. She should have left him years ago. If she hasn't the sense to get out it's her own fault. One of these days he'll kill her – if I don't kill him first.'

His words sent a coldness down my spine.

'You don't mean that?'

'I'll kill him if I stay. That's why I'm leaving. I just wanted to say goodbye, and to tell you I was sorry.'

'Sorry   for what?'

'For what happened yesterday. Your da getting into that fight with mine . . . '

'Da couldn't see you get hurt. It wasn't your fault.'

'Tinker isn't so bad when he's sober,' Tom said. 'When he was younger he was halfway decent. It's the drink that's dragged him down. A man's a fool to drink, especially if he can't hold it.'

'I think my da had had a couple of drinks too.'

'That's different, he can take it. Tinker can't. He gets nasty when he's drunk. He's an evil devil then, I can tell you. He's thrashed every one of us in his time – but he won't touch me again.'

'Where will you go, Tom?'

'Here and there. I'll find myself a job somewhere in the Dales. Father's going south and I hope he stays there for good.'

'Well, goodbye then, Tom.'

'See you around,' he said and went off whistling.

I stared after him for a moment, then set off at a run for the corner shop. It was just as well Tom and his family were going. Ma would skin me alive if she knew I had been talking to him. We couldn't be friends and I wasn't much of a liar.

'Your last day at school,' Mary Hopkin said as we left the playground together. 'Aren't you the lucky one then? I've got another whole term to go just because I was born a few weeks later than you.'

It was seven weeks after the street party and my fourteenth birthday. That morning I had received cards from my parents, Bob, and a special one with five shillings in from my grandad. Mother had given me some lisle and wool stockings and a sensible nightdress, and from Mary I had received a bottle of Evening in Paris scent.

She had been moaning for days about the fact that I was leaving school before her. I was torn two ways; a part of me wanted to stay in the safe familiar world of childhood, but it was exciting to be on the threshold of a whole new world. Not that I expected my life to change very much. Nothing had been said about my finding a job and I thought my mother wanted me to stay at home and help in the house as many girls still did, even though there were more opportunities for jobs these days. I had thought about going into a factory or a shop but there was plenty of time to make up my mind during the long school holidays.

'It will be your turn next,' I replied. I lingered, somehow unwilling to part from my friend. 'I'm going to miss you, Mary.'

20

'We'll see each other at weekends.'

'It won't be the same though.'

'You're not regretting being through with school?'

I hesitated, thinking of something our Headmistress had said to me during break that morning. She'd stopped me on my way back to class after I'd seen some of the younger children in from the playground.

'I'd like a word, Nellie.'

'Yes, Miss Browne.'

I'd stared at her with fast-beating heart, wondering what I'd done to attract her notice, but she smiled at me for once, her stern features softening.

'So you're leaving us today, Nellie?'

'Yes, Miss Browne.'

'That's a pity. You are an intelligent girl. I'd hoped you might stay on, take further education and make something of yourself. You have a way with the younger children . . . ' She pursed her thin lips. 'Haven't you ever considered becoming a teacher?'

'No, miss.'

It was true that I liked looking after the young ones, but didn't all girls feel that way? It was surely just a part of preparing for womanhood and a family.

'My mother has always said I should leave when I was fourteen,' I said as Miss Browne frowned. 'It might have been nice though . . . '

Perhaps there was a wistful note in my voice for she hesitated and said, 'Well, if ever you want help with furthering your education, come and see me.'

'Yes, miss. Thank you. I shall.'

It had given me a warm feeling to know that she thought me intelligent. I'd done well enough, coming near to the top of the class in several subjects, but I was used to Mother's treating me as if I were an idiot at home and had never thought of myself as bright – certainly not clever enough to be a teacher.

Now as I looked at Mary I felt uneasy, though I didn't know why. Perhaps it was the odd looks Mother had been giving me recently.

'No, I suppose I won't miss school,' I said. 'See you on Saturday then.'

My feet dragged all the way home. There was no reason for the peculiar sensation of dread at the pit of my stomach but it had been there all day, nagging at me, making me nervous.

When I saw the large black car parked outside my home the sickness churned inside me, rising to a lump in my throat. So few people had cars round here – don't let it be the doctor! Don't let Grandad be ill!

I flew down the covered passage to the back door, my heart racing. I couldn't bear it if anything happened to Grandad, I couldn't! He had seemed a bit quiet these last couple of days but I hadn't realized he was ill . . .

I threw the back door wide and went rushing in, then stopped and stared at the two women sitting in the kitchen. One was older than my mother with a plain, straight look about her, the other several years younger, well-dressed and attractive but somehow dowdy despite the quality of her clothes. Neither of them was known to me but their eyes were bright with curiosity as they looked at me. For a while there was silence while I tried to gather my wits, then one of them – the eldest – spoke.

'So this is Nellie,' she said and gave a decisive nod. 'She looks strong and healthy. Very well, Mrs Pearce, we'll take her.' She got to her feet and began to pull on a pair of grey cotton gloves. 'No need to stop for anything, Nellie. Your mother has packed your things.'

'Packed my things?' I was stunned, disbelieving as I looked at my mother. 'Ma? What does she mean?'

'Mind your manners, girl.' Mother looked through me, her eyes refusing to meet mine. 'Whatever will these good ladies think of you? This is Miss Alice Harrington . . . ' She indicated the younger woman, who smiled at me. 'And this is Mrs Jermyns – she's housekeeper at Beaumont House out Malham way. She has come to fetch you. You're to work for her – for the family – now.'

'Work for her?' There was a tightness in my chest. I still couldn't believe this was happening. 'You mean, I'm to go into service? That is what you're saying, isn't it?'

'Yes.' Mother's mouth was thin and white-edged. 'It has all been arranged. Don't make a fuss, Nellie. You're to go with Mrs Jermyns now.'

I was stunned. I hadn't given much consideration to my future but the last thing I would ever have thought of doing was entering domestic service.

'But you never said!' The words burst out of me. 'What about Da – and Grandad? When shall I see them?'

'You'll come home when you have a day off,' Mother said, so cold and ungiving. 'Do as you're told, Nellie. It's a good place. You should be grateful to your father for arranging it.'

Da had arranged it himself! I recoiled as if I had been struck and the fight drained out of me: if my father had agreed to my being sent away like this it was useless to appeal. It was my birthday and I was being sent off without even being allowed to have my tea. The callous cruelty of it was numbing.

'Don't be too harsh with her.' The younger woman spoke for the first time, her voice soft and appealing. 'It's all right, Nellie. I'm sure you will be happy with us – and you'll be able to come home every month; there's always someone coming this way to give you a lift.'

She was trying to be kind but I was too numbed to appreciate it, all I knew was that my safe, happy world had suddenly fallen apart.

'Of course Nellie will be happy with us – if she behaves properly and works hard. You really must leave this to me, Miss Alice, if you please.'

Mrs Jermyns spoke appeasingly to her companion but there was a hint of annoyance in her voice, as if she resented the interference.

I looked at her properly for the first time and swallowed hard. She had iron grey hair scraped back into a bun beneath her plain black felt hat, and her lips were thin and pale. She seemed formidable and I thought she might be as sharp-tongued as my mother. A wave of rebellion swept over me. I wanted to scream and shout but held the misery inside me. It wasn't fair! I hadn't even been told what was going on.

For one moment my eyes met the hard, unforgiving stab of my mother's icy gaze, then I turned away. Why did she hate me so much? What had I ever done to deserve this from my own mother?

23

Chapter Two

'Cheer up, Nellie, going into service ain't the end of the world. It's hard work but you'll get used to it – and it has its perks now and then.'

I stared at the girl with whom I was to share a bed for the foreseeable future, curiosity beginning to overcome the feeling of misery which had stayed with me during the journey to Beaumont House. We were in an attic room that was even smaller than my own bedroom at home; it was barely big enough to hold the brass and iron bed, scratched single wardrobe and marble-topped washstand – and I had to share it with Iris.

'Like what?' I asked. 'What kind of perks?'

'Miss Alice gives us things when she feels like it, and Cook ain't stingy with our food. We eat as well as them upstairs.'

I had already been given my tea in the kitchen, which was about three times the size of ours at home. The walls were painted a dark cream and lined with pine dressers on three sides, the fourth almost entirely taken up by the black iron cooking range. There were lots of copper pans everywhere and the room smelt deliciously of spices and baking. The meal itself had consisted of bread and butter, homemade jams, and three kinds of cakes – far more than I was used to at home.

'Leave even a crumb and you'll get less next time,' Iris had whispered. 'If you can't manage the cake put it in your pocket for later.'

Iris had devoured every scrap of her own food with a hungry concentration that made me think she must be half-starved. She was a tall, thin girl with a pale complexion and straight dark hair she wore scraped back beneath a white cap, but she was talkative and friendly and her careless chatter had begun to ease the ache inside me.

'Miss Alice came with Mrs Jermyns to fetch me,' I said as I began to unpack my things from the battered trunk Mother had sent over by carrier. 'She drove the car herself.'

Iris nodded, lowering her voice confidentially. 'It didn't go down too well at first with them upstairs – Sir Charles and Lady Amelia, that is – not ladylike, you see. Leastways, that's what 'er highness says.'

'You mean Lady Amelia?' I smiled inwardly as I heard the note of disrespect in her voice. 'Don't you like her?'

'Not much.' Iris pulled a face. 'Never a smile or so much as a thank you from her, no matter what you do, not even if you've sat up half the night waiting for 'er to come home – now Miss Alice is different, she's what I call a real lady, and she's got guts. She stuck to 'er guns even though they tried to bully 'er into giving up 'er lessons. Says she needs to drive for 'er charity work – does a lot of that since ... ' Iris coloured and looked self-conscious, as if she had said too much.

'Since what? Go on, tell me. You can't stop now.'

'You won't say as I told you?'

'No, of course not. Cross my heart and hope to die.'

Iris giggled as I made the sign of the cross dramatically across my breast. 'I'm not sure if that counts if you ain't a Catholic. You ain't, are you?'

'No. Go on do, Iris. Tell me about Miss Alice.'

'Blighted in love she were, poor woman.' Iris drew a sighing breath. 'He were ever so handsome so I've heard but not good enough for 'er highness upstairs – some sort of scandal in his family – so he was sent packing and Miss Alice broke 'er heart over him and vowed she would devote 'erself to good works and never marry.'

'That's sad. How old is she?'

'Thirty-three if she's a day,' Iris replied and pulled a face. 'She's an old maid and sure to die one now – shame, ain't it?'

25

'When did this happen?'

'Must be more than ten years now. I heard as he went off abroad to make his fortune.'

'Maybe he'll come back and marry her one day.'

'Not if that old sourpuss upstairs has 'er way.'

'Is Miss Alice Lady Amelia's daughter?'

Iris shook her head. 'She's Sir Charles's youngest sister. He had another one but she died five years ago, of scarlet fever, poor thing. Near broke Miss Alice's heart again that did.'

'Do they have any children – them upstairs?'

'Don't let Mrs Jermyns hear you call them that.' Iris looked guilty. 'I'm getting you into bad ways and you not here a couple of hours.'

'I know better than to make that mistake.'

I hung a dark blue wool dress in the wardrobe next to the two that already hung there and were seemingly all Iris possessed besides her uniforms.

'That's a nice dress,' she remarked, a wistful note in her voice. 'Your Sunday best?' She stroked the soft material as I nodded. 'Pity you won't be able to wear it – 'cept on your days off.'

'Not even on Sunday? You mean we have to wear these horrible things all the time?'

'The uniforms ain't so bad,' Iris said. 'Better than what I had afore I came here anyway. My mother were left a widow with eight kids to feed and clothe. I never had a dress like yours, not once.'

'I'm sorry,' I said, and felt guilty. 'I didn't know, I didn't realize.'

'It's all right. I've got dresses of me own now. Miss Alice gave me that brown one there – it fits me a treat.'

'It's very nice,' I said, though I thought the colour a bit dull for Iris's complexion.

I could hear a wireless playing; it sounded like Nelson Eddy yodelling and must be rather loud for it to reach all the way up here. I was trying to listen and not paying much attention when Iris suddenly said, 'They've got one son, Mr Lucas . . .'

There was such a peculiar note in her voice then that I

turned to look at her. 'What's wrong with Mr Lucas? Is he like his mother?'

Her cheeks stained with fiery colour. 'No, he's . . . he's just a bit odd, that's all.'

'What do you mean?'

Iris was obviously determined to say no more on the subject. 'You'll find out for yourself,' she muttered. 'If you've finished we had better go down to the kitchen and see what needs doing. They'll have had dinner upstairs by now. I'd have been helping serve it only it's my night off, but I give it up to see you settled in.'

'That was kind of you. I'm glad you're here, Iris. It won't seem so bad now that I've met you.'

'You'll be all right,' Iris said. 'I expect you'll be helping in the kitchens for a start. Cook's a decent soul – providing you don't upset her; she can be a right tartar if she likes, but that ain't often. I'm the parlour maid . . . ' A look of pride came into Iris's face. 'But now and then I help Miss Alice dress when she goes out. She won't have a maid of 'er own and she don't like Mabel – that's 'er highness's personal dresser – so I help out, just now and then; she don't go out socially that often, says it's a waste of time.' Iris looked wistful. 'That's what I'd like to be one day, a lady's maid . . . or maybe I'll work in a posh dress shop.'

'Don't you want to marry and have a family?'

'No thanks!' Iris exclaimed. 'You wouldn't catch me living the way my ma does, never enough money to go round, working day and night to make ends meet, and a houseful of screaming kids to take care of when she comes back after wearing 'erself out scrubbing and washing for others.'

'I suppose it must be hard if you have to go out charring and then take care of a family as well – but surely it doesn't have to be like that? Your ma was unlucky. If your father hadn't died . . . '

Iris gave a snort of derision. 'That's all you know! The day he kicked the bucket was 'er lucky day. The lazy beggar spent all his time drinking when he had money and taking it out on 'er when he didn't. She was well rid of him.'

'But all men aren't like that.'

I thought of my silent grandfather keeping his thoughts to

27

himself to avoid causing trouble in the house and my soft-spoken father giving into my mother more often than not. I'd only heard him raise his voice to her twice and that was when she'd been on at me or Bob. Tears sprang to my eyes as I realized I would not see either Da or Grandad very often in future, but I brushed them away. Iris gave me a look of understanding.

'Thinking about your family?' she asked softly and slipped an arm about my waist, giving me a quick squeeze. 'It won't be so bad here, honest.'

'Thanks.' I cleared my throat. 'I don't suppose it will – be interesting anyway. I might even like it.'

When Iris and I went downstairs that first evening we found the kitchen a hive of frantic activity. There had been a delay with dinner – some kind of ructions upstairs apparently – and Cook was muttering darkly about giving her notice if this went on. She was a big woman with a double chin, sharp intelligent eyes which mostly held a twinkle – except when she was upset, as now – and thick short fingers which were surprisingly dexterous when rolling pastry or shaping mountains of delicious food.

'I'll not stand for my dinner being ruined,' she said and shook her chins at the butler, a tall, thin man with a long nose and an air of hauteur. 'I'm warning you, Mr Sands, if there's much more of this I shall leave. My sister in Bournemouth has been after me to go into a hotel with her – and I'll do it, I vow I will.'

'Now, now, Mrs Jones,' he soothed, obviously used to her and not in the least ruffled by her threats. 'No real harm's been done. Besides, it's only the family tonight, and if the beef is a little overdone it's their own fault.'

'Indeed it is,' she muttered. 'But it's my reputation at stake here, Mr Sands. My reputation . . . '

'Not in the least,' he reassured her. 'Everyone knows it isn't your fault.'

'You, girl!' Cook's eyes suddenly lighted on me. 'Strain that broccoli for me and be quick about it – put it in the large tureen.'

'Yes, Mrs Jones – that one warming by the range?'

28

'Yes – and don't break it! I want every drop of water out, mind. One thing I won't put up with is water in my vegetables.'

'Nor will my da,' I replied without thinking. 'He can't abide soggy greens.'

'My broccoli is never soggy.' Cook glared at me. 'I hope you weren't implying it?'

'No, ma'am. I can see it's just right, just as it should be.'

In the middle of the careful operation of straining the broccoli I was unaware of the sudden hush until I turned to find Cook's baleful eyes on me.

'And what would you know about it, miss?'

Iris was pulling frantic faces at me. I swallowed hard, not wanting to make an enemy of the woman who ruled supreme in the kitchens.

'Nothing very much,' I mumbled, 'but I like cooking and broccoli should be crisp, just like this. Some people make it soggy but then it's awful . . . '

For one dreadful moment I thought Cook was angry, but then I caught a twinkle in her eyes and guessed she was testing me.

'Most new girls don't even know what broccoli is,' she observed. 'You've been brought up right, girl. Like cooking, do you?'

'Yes, ma'am. I know about broccoli because Grandad used to grow it, but Da's not very successful, hasn't got the same touch.'

'Let me look at that tureen.' Cook lifted the lid as I placed it on the table before her. Her eyes narrowed as she looked suspiciously for any sign of water, then she wiped the narrow rim with her cloth and replaced the fitted lid. 'Always use a clean cloth to wipe the rim,' she instructed. 'Not bad though, not bad. So you like cooking then?' She turned back to me as Mr Sands and one of the other maids whom I had not yet met carried away trays of steaming hot food in silver dishes. 'Well, tell me your name then!'

'It's Nellie, ma'am.'

'Mrs Jones will do,' Cook said, a definite sparkle in her eyes now. 'It's ma'am for her ladyship, remember that – if you see her and she stops you, which isn't likely unless you're doing something you shouldn't.'

'I'll try not to – do something I shouldn't.'

'So I should hope!'

Cook's tone was still sharp but her mood had obviously mellowed. 'There's a pile of washing up in the scullery for you to make a start on,' she said. 'Iris will show you where before she goes off.'

I followed her into the back kitchen where mounds of dirty dishes had already been stacked in deep stone sinks.

'Make sure you rinse the glasses in cold water,' Iris warned, 'and wash everything well. You'll be in for it if Mrs Jones finds grease on her dishes.'

'She won't,' I promised. 'I like her.'

'She's not a bad sort,' Iris agreed. 'I think she liked you and that's a good start.' She hesitated for a moment. 'I'd give you a hand but there's choir practice at the church this evening and I'm already late.'

'You get off,' I said. 'It was good of you to stay for my sake, Iris, but I can manage now.'

'I shan't be long,' she replied with a smile. 'We'll talk later.'

Turning back to the sink, I plunged my hands into the hot water and began to wash the fine china plates that had been left to soak. It wasn't the way I'd expected to spend my first evening after leaving school but it wasn't so bad.

I was busy all weekend, washing dishes, helping Mrs Jones by preparing the vegetables, sweeping the back stairs and scrubbing the kitchen floor – and getting to know the other servants. Besides Iris, Mrs Jones and Mr Sands, there was Henry Brooks, who waited at table and doubled as Sir Charles's valet, the under parlour maid Janet – a shy girl who had little to say for herself and was in awe of Iris – another maid who helped in the kitchens and was called Doris, and a woman who came in to do most of the rough jobs; there were also three gardeners who did all the outside work, including chopping kindling for the kitchen. They were always in trouble with Mrs Jones for bringing mud in on their boots. Of Mabel – or Miss Parkinson as she was officially known to everyone below stairs – I caught only a fleeting glimpse that weekend. Miss Parkinson ate with Mrs Jermyns and seldom showed herself in the servants' hall.

Both Saturday and Sunday passed peacefully enough and it was not until I came downstairs on Monday morning that I had a rude awakening. Instead of remaining in the kitchen to help Cook, I was told to join Doris in the laundry room.

'The laundry room?' I hadn't given a thought to the masses of washing that must accumulate in a household this size. 'You mean I've got to help in the laundry, too?'

'You an' me both,' Doris said and shrugged. 'Mrs Briggs comes in on Mondays to give us a hand, but Tuesday to Fridays it's just you and me in the mornings.'

'You and me . . . we have to wash clothes every day?' I groaned. 'Every day of the week?'

'There's a lot of washing in a house like this,' Doris said. 'Sir Charles changes his shirt at least twice a day, sometimes more, and their sheets are done three times a week. Ours are done just once, top to bottom, same as at home, but they like fresh sheets, top and bottom.'

'It's a pity they don't have to wash them!'

'You're a lark, you are,' Doris said, screwing up her snub nose. 'What do you think you're here for?'

'I didn't know it was to help out in the laundry room!'

'Did you think you wus going straight into the parlour then?' Doris derided. 'I've bin here eighteen months and I've never bin upstairs yet.'

'I – I thought I might be a cook's helper.'

'You'll get to do that too,' Doris said, 'when you've finished with the washing. It's laundry six 'til eight most days then a break for our breakfast, then back to the laundry 'til half-one, then dinner. After that it's preparing vegetables, tea – and the washing up. Supper comes whenever it suits Cook. Weekends we do a bit of scrubbing below stairs.'

'When do we ever stop?'

'You'll get a day off a month same as the rest of us – and there's church on Sundays if you're religious, or an hour to yourself if not, but Lady Amelia don't like it if you don't go to church at least once in a while.'

'I like church,' I said, 'but I hate washing, especially every day.'

31

'You'll get used to it.' Doris shrugged. 'Same as me.'

I would never like working in the laundry room, but for the moment I didn't have much choice.

It was so cool and fresh outside in the gardens. Sometimes over the past few days I'd felt my chest grow so tight I'd thought I was dying. Away from the steam and stink of washing soda I could breathe again, let my lungs fill with air and feel that I was alive once more. I knew I ought to go straight to the kitchen but after five days incarcerated in the overpowering heat of the laundry room I was desperate to escape for a few minutes.

My eyes were stinging but I wasn't sure if it was from the soda or tears. I hated being in this house, I hated helping with the laundry and I missed my home and my family. I wanted to see my grandad and da, though I was still too angry with my mother for doing this to me to miss her. Sometimes I was so miserable that I wanted to crawl away and die but I was too stubborn to give way; crying wouldn't help. I'd been sent away from my home to a life of hell and it was no accident that I'd been put to work in the laundry, my mother must have arranged it that way. But why had she been so deliberately cruel?

'She knew . . . she knew I hate it so . . . '

The tears were very close, but I refused to let them fall. No one cared how awful I felt, no one would help me.

My wanderings had taken me through the kitchen gardens to a high wall. I hesitated. I ought to turn back, they would be waiting for me, my work would be waiting, but I was so tired . . . A gate stood open, propped back by a wheelbarrow filled with trowels, bits of string and sticks. Beyond the wall was what seemed to be a wild garden, tangled and overgrown with straggling roses, holly bushes and yew hedges; it looked as if no one cared much what happened there.

Why didn't the gardeners look after this part of the grounds? The day I'd arrived I'd glimpsed the front and side lawns and shrubberies, which were immaculate – why this wilderness? For a moment I hovered uncertainly, then walked through the gate and into the neglected garden. A path seemed to lead through the bushes and I followed it, my curiosity aroused. I was aware of a tingling sensation at the base of my neck. I knew I had no business being here but I could not turn back. Birds were singing all around me and the whole place seemed to have an air of enchantment, like a secret wood from one of the fairy tales I'd loved at school.

The path led eventually to a little wooden summerhouse; this did not look quite as neglected as the garden, though it could certainly have done with some attention. I stared in fascination for a moment then walked towards it, climbing the three front steps to peer inside through a dusty window. I could see very little even though I pressed my face against the panes and squinted.

'What do you think you're doing?' The man's harsh voice made me jump and I swung round. 'This is my private place, servants are forbidden to come here. I dislike being spied on.'

I was speechless with dismay, my startled gaze drawn to his face and the livid scar which ran from his left brow to his chin.

'The result of an unfortunate fall,' he drawled, his dark grey eyes narrowed and angry. 'If you don't like it, run away like all the rest. No one asked you to come here, you're not wanted – this place belongs to me.'

'I – I'm sorry, sir,' I whispered. He was a man of twenty-five or so and obviously gentry. 'I wanted a breath of fresh air after the laundry room, and the gate was open . . . '

'You were curious about the monster who inhabits the haunted woods, is that it?' His right eyebrow rose in a wry expression. 'Well, at least you're braver than most of them – who are you?'

'Nellie Pearce, sir. I've just come to work at the house – and I didn't know I wasn't allowed to come here. It – it's so wild I thought no one would mind.'

'Well, I mind, Nellie Pearce.' His left eye was dragged down slightly by the scar, giving him an odd squinting expression. 'Didn't anyone tell you about me?'

'No, sir.'

'I'm Lucas Harrington. Are you sure no one told you anything?'

'Just . . . that you were Sir Charles's only son.'

'Nothing more?'

'Nothing more, sir.'

'So you didn't come to spy on me?'

'Oh, no, sir. I just wanted a breath of fresh air after the laundry. It's so hot in there and I can't breathe!'

My pitiful cry seemed to amuse him for he gave a harsh laugh. 'Is it so bad in the laundry then?'

'It's like the pit of Hell for me,' I said vehemently. 'I hate washing. I always have, even at home.'

'Why work there then?'

'I don't have any choice. I was put there.'

His good eye narrowed as he studied me thoughtfully, and when he turned his head so that I could no longer see the scar I realized he must once have been attractive.

'So what would you rather do?' he asked, suddenly turning back to face me. 'Be a lady's maid, I suppose?'

'No, sir.' I sighed wistfully. 'I should like to learn to cook.'

'Wouldn't you find that rather demanding?'

'I should like it. I like food.'

His eyes sparked with interest. 'So do I,' he said. 'It is one of my few consolations these days – that and my dabblings.'

'Your dabblings, sir?'

'My dabblings.' His good humour evaporated suddenly. 'None of your business, Nellie Pearce! Go back where you belong and stop bothering me.'

He looked so fierce that I was alarmed. Backing away from him, I turned and fled through the tangled shrubbery, catching my dress on straggling roses and tearing the skirt.

'And don't come here again,' Lucas Harrington called after me. 'I might gobble you up, Nellie Pearce.'

I gave a little shriek of fear; not because I imagined he meant his threat, but because I had made him angry and he was one of the family. I hadn't seen any of the others, except Miss Alice – and that only when she had driven me to the house on the first day.

'Where is it? Where is it?' I muttered feverishly. Oh, where was the gate? Surely it should be here somewhere?

At last I found it but it had been shut and locked from the other side.

'Let me in! Let me in!'

For a few moments I hammered uselessly on the gate but then I realized that there was no one to hear. I could not return the way I'd come – and I certainly wasn't going back to the summerhouse. There must be another way to approach the house . . . yes, up there to the right there was a narrow path. I would follow that and see where it led.

When I came to another high wall I was afraid that I would after all have to go back to the summerhouse and beg Mr Lucas to show me the way out, but after some searching I found the gate that he must have used earlier. He had left it carelessly unlatched and it stood slightly ajar, inviting me to pass through.

Realizing that I was in the formal gardens at the front of the house I felt a tingle of apprehension: I was not allowed to come here unless sent on an errand for the family. I hesitated, unwilling to break more rules than I already had – but what else could I do? Time was passing and I would be sure to receive a scolding from either Cook or Mrs Jermyns: I dare not waste any more precious seconds. I would have to risk it and pray that no one saw me. Taking a deep breath I began to run across the lawns as fast as I could; I was about halfway when I saw the small group of people come out of the front door.

It was the family themselves and I became flustered as I saw they had noticed me; I stepped on something slippery, tripped and fell flat on my face. For a moment I lay winded, too surprised and shocked to move, then I felt a hand on my shoulder and looked up into a face I recognized. I sat up hastily, my cheeks on fire.

'Begging your pardon, Miss Alice,' I cried. 'I know I shouldn't be here but I got lost and the gate was shut – and it won't happen again . . . '

'Have you hurt yourself?' Alice Harrington asked, a note of concern in her voice. 'You fell very hard.'

Getting to my feet I brushed at the grass stains and debris on my white apron. The palm of my hand was stinging where I'd grazed it but I shook my head.

'It was my own fault, miss.'

'You were nervous of something – or someone?' Alice

35

glanced towards the high wall. 'You were in the wild garden . . . my nephew . . . '

'Oh, no, miss, I wasn't frightened of Mr Lucas,' I said, understanding the look in her eyes. 'I was scared because I knew I shouldn't be here. I went for a walk because it was so hot in the laundry and my eyes stung and then the gate was locked and I couldn't get back . . . '

'You met Mr Lucas?'

'Yes, miss. He told me I wasn't to go to his special place again but . . . ' I faltered. 'It was just so hot in the laundry room and I . . . '

'He spoke to you?'

'Yes, miss, for a few minutes. He was a bit cross but he didn't seem too angry, he just teased me a little . . . '

'My nephew teased you?' Alice's eyes narrowed intently. 'Please tell me what he said to you?'

'He asked if I'd come to spy on him and said I was braver than most, but then when I asked about his dabblings he got cross and told me to stop bothering him. He said if I went there again he would gobble me up – but of course he was only teasing me.'

Alice looked peculiar and I caught my breath.

'I'm sorry if I've done something awful, miss.'

She shook her head. 'No, not at all. It's just that my nephew seldom speaks to anyone – and never to strangers.'

'I'm not lying, miss. He did say those things to me.'

'I believe you, Nellie.' A smile flickered in her gentle eyes. 'So how are you getting on here? It's not as bad as you feared, I hope?' She frowned as I did not answer at once. 'Are you unhappy with us?'

'No, miss. At least . . . '

'Please go on, Nellie.'

'It's just that I don't like being in the laundry room all the time. The smell of soda makes my eyes water and sometimes I feel as if I can't breathe; it was always like that at home too. I like helping Cook, miss, and I don't mind what else I do – I'll do anything but that!'

'Yes, I understand. I had no idea that's where you had been put. I shall speak to Mrs Jermyns about it and see what can be done.'

36

'Oh, thank you, Miss Alice,' I cried. 'I should be ever so grateful to you. I'll do anything for you – anything!'

'Will you indeed?' Alice's eyes sparkled with amusement. 'Well, perhaps one day I'll remind you of that.'

'What do you mean?'

'Nothing. Nothing at all,' she said. 'Run along now. I'm sure you must have work to do.'

I had been dismissed. I turned and walked swiftly towards a covered walk that must lead eventually to the kitchen – and a scolding! But I didn't care, I didn't care. Miss Alice had promised to speak to the housekeeper about my working in the laundry and that was all that mattered.

Chapter Three

'What you going to do on your day off then?'

The question took me by surprise. Since the morning after my adventure in the wild garden, when I'd come downstairs to be told by Mrs Jermyns that I was not to go to the laundry but would help Cook instead, the days had just flown by without my noticing. I still missed my home, of course, and sometimes I felt upset as I wondered what I'd done to make my mother turn against me, but I was no longer desperately unhappy.

'I don't know,' I said now. 'I could go home, I suppose, but it's a long way to walk, especially if it rains.'

It had been raining continuously for days now, preventing further exploration of the gardens even if I'd been tempted to return to the summerhouse. Not that I had either the intention or the inclination to risk another confrontation with Mr Lucas! I was content in the kitchens, especially now that Cook had taken an interest in me and was teaching me how to make delicious flaky pastry.

'Always keep your dough cool and slightly dry,' Mrs Jones told me. 'But with flaky pastry the secret is in the layers and the rolling – you need a light touch for pastry.'

'I've never tasted any as good as yours,' I replied and received a beam of approval. 'Mary Hopkin's mother's pastry was good, but yours just melts on the tongue.'

'I do have a reputation for it,' Cook replied, her chins waggling complacently. 'It takes years to learn how to do things properly, but I think you might have a calling for it – and cooking is a calling, Nellie. You should remember that and don't let anyone tell you different.'

'Oh, I won't, I promise you I won't,' I cried fervently. 'I want to learn everything from you, Mrs Jones.'

'Well, we'll see, we'll see – get off to the scullery and peel those potatoes now. First things first, you have to learn to walk before you can run, and preparation is important – don't forget what I told you about putting them in cold water with a pinch of salt!'

Cook did go on about things sometimes, but she was easy to be with if you kept on the right side of her and I'd been happy these past weeks, much happier than I'd expected. I hadn't given much thought to going home and now that Iris had raised the subject I wasn't sure what I wanted. By the time I'd walked there and back it wouldn't leave much time for visiting.

'Do we have to have a day off every month?' I asked when Iris joined me later.

'Don't say you don't want your day off!' Iris rolled her eyes then went into peals of laughter, her thin face lighting up from inside, making her look more attractive than usual. 'You're the funny one, Nellie Pearce. When you came here you were like a Christian slave thrown to the lions. Now you don't want to go home.'

Iris went to choir practice one evening a week – a special dispensation granted by Lady Amelia herself at the vicar's request, because Iris had a good voice and never missed church on Sundays. I'd gone with her the previous week and I knew the curate had been discussing the story of Daniel in the lions' den with her when they stopped to talk after the service. The curate was a young man in his early-twenties and quite good-looking; I suspected that Iris might be a little sweet on him despite all her protestations about never getting married.

'Well, do we? Couldn't I work three months say, then have three days off all at once?'

'You and your fancy ideas! Whatever next?'

'It would be worth going home then, for three days.'

'You'd better ask Mrs Jermyns.'

'Right, I will then.'

Iris stared at me as I dried my hands on the kitchen towel,

then smoothed my hair to make sure there were no straggling wisps escaping from beneath my cap.

'Do I look all right?'

'You're never going to ask 'er?'

'Why not?'

'I didn't mean it, Nellie. She'll never agree to you going off for three days at a go.'

'Maybe she will if I ask her.'

'Rather you than me.'

I shrugged. 'You never get anything if you don't ask.'

Iris watched as I walked from the kitchen. I stuck my head in the air, unwilling to let on that I was shaking in my shoes at the prospect of bearding Mrs Jermyns in her den, but just as loath to let go of the idea now that it had occurred to me. Why shouldn't I have three days all at once if I was willing to give up my regular day?

Mrs Jermyns' sitting-room was at the top of the stairway leading up from the servants' hall and just a few steps away from where the family's part of the house began. As yet I'd never been there or into the upper regions of Beaumont House, except by the back stairs which led to the attic nest I shared with Iris. My heart was pounding as I walked up the last few stairs and turned right. Taking a deep breath I stopped outside the first door and raised my hand to knock, then hesitated as I saw it was slightly ajar.

'Do you expect me to believe you haven't been meeting him?'

The sharp voice made me jump back. That wasn't Mrs Jermyns; I must have come to the wrong door! I was about to turn away when a voice I recognized answered the first and something made me linger, despite knowing full well that I had no right to eavesdrop.

'I really don't mind what you believe, Amelia. If I wanted to meet Gerald that would be my business . . . '

'I'm not sure that Charles would agree.'

'I am no longer a child. Not that I was a child then,' Alice Harrington went on in the same steady tone. 'I was however young enough to believe that my brother might know best – and to consider it my duty to obey him.'

'It is still your duty to listen to him.' The sharp voice I

40

now realized must belong to Lady Amelia rose higher. 'You may be in possession of your own income but you still live under our roof, and while you do you owe us both a duty to behave respectably.'

'I shall of course listen to my brother, if he chooses to speak to me on any reasonable subject – but since I have not spoken to Gerald since ... ' There was a catch in Alice's voice. 'Please excuse me, Amelia. I have business elsewhere.'

'Alice!'

There was a rattle as if Alice had seized the door handle, but she must have attended to her sister-in-law's cry because she did not open it immediately. Startled, I turned and fled the way I'd come before I could be discovered in the act of listening to their conversation.

In the small, dark hall at the bottom of the stairs I paused to catch my breath, my thoughts whirling in confusion. I'd had no right to listen to the argument between Miss Alice and Lady Harrington, but remembering what Iris had told me the night I'd arrived I had no doubt that Miss Alice's sweetheart had turned up out of the blue – and was putting the cat among the pigeons by the sound of it!

Hearing a shriek of laughter, I turned and saw Iris come out of the kitchen with Henry Brooks close behind her. He appeared to be patting Iris on the bottom and whispering something in her ear; they both stopped and looked guilty as they saw me.

Iris frowned. 'Did you speak to Mrs Jermyns?'

'I think I turned the wrong way – her room was to the right at the top of the stairs, wasn't it?'

'You daft thing!' Iris cried, her frown disappearing. 'Mrs Jermyns's sitting-room is on the left – right's the flower room, don't say you went in there? You probably found Miss Alice there, did you?'

'I didn't go in, but she was in there and – and I think Lady Amelia was with her.'

'You don't say!' Iris looked curious as she gave Henry Brooks a push to send him on his way. 'What was she doing there? Miss Alice always does the flowers, 'er ladyship never ventures this far below stairs – what were they saying?'

'I'm not sure . . . ' I felt myself blushing as I told the small lie. 'I didn't listen, I just ran back down here quick.'

'I would have listened,' Iris said, a gleam in her eyes. 'I bet they were arguing about something. That's usually why 'er highness follows poor Miss Alice down here. She goes on to 'er something rotten at times, I don't know how Miss Alice stands it. I wouldn't! If I had 'er money I'd be off like a shot.'

'Has Miss Alice got money then?'

'More than her brother. She's only Sir Charles's half-sister really, and her mother was an heiress so most of it was left in trust for her until she was thirty. He had charge of it until then; you know the way these families tie every penny up. Well, she couldn't touch it without his say-so until about three years ago . . . '

'That's not fair,' I said. 'Is that why she didn't go off with her sweetheart?'

Iris shrugged. 'It might have had something to do with it, but she's got a strong sense of duty, probably thought she ought to do as her brother told her.'

'Yes . . . ' I'd heard Miss Alice say something like that a moment or two ago. 'But she's older now and independent. She might act differently this time, mightn't she?'

'You did hear something – tell me!' Iris grabbed my arm, her fingers digging into my flesh. 'Go on, be fair. I tell you everything.'

I glanced over my shoulder. 'Well . . . if you promise not to tell anyone else?'

'Go on!'

'What are you two doing whispering out here? Don't you have any work to do?'

The sharp note in Mrs Jermyns's voice made us both jump guiltily. Iris gave me an agonized look, then turned to the housekeeper.

'I was just on my way upstairs, Mrs Jermyns.'

'Get off with you then.' The older woman's gaze came to rest on me. 'What about you?'

'I was looking for you, Mrs Jermyns,' I said. 'I wanted to ask you something.'

'Indeed?'

42

'It's . . . it's about my day off.'

'Ah, yes, you're due one this weekend – have you made arrangements for a lift?'

'No.' I licked my lips nervously. 'I was wondering if I could put it off . . . '

'You don't want to go home?'

'No – at least, not yet. I would like to wait until nearer Christmas then have three days at home, if that would be all right? I mean I would work until then . . . '

'You want three days all at once?' Mrs Jermyns sounded incredulous. 'I've never heard such a request. Ridiculous!'

'It would be easier for the journey,' I persisted. 'I'd have time to see my family instead of rushing there and back and I'd work every off day until then.'

'That's four months.' Mrs Jermyns stared at me hard. 'You will give up four days to have three at home?'

'Yes, please.'

'You don't get your wages until you have a day off.'

'I don't need anything,' I said, desperate to succeed now. 'It would be so much easier for me.'

'It would save Henry the bother of taking you there in the car certainly.' Mrs Jermyns nodded. 'Three days instead of four – very well, but don't expect such favours every time.'

'Was Henry going to take me this weekend?'

'Miss Alice had requested it,' Mrs Jermyns replied. 'But since you've asked for three days before Christmas you can go with the carrier. I'll arrange it for you myself – now get on with your work.'

I watched as she walked up the stairs and turned to her left. Henry Brooks had been asked to take me home so I wouldn't have had to walk in the rain. I'd given up four days for three. My triumph was washed away by a wave of disappointment and I felt let down; I'd made a fool of myself and Mrs Jermyns must be laughing at me.

I felt despondent as I went into the kitchen, but my mood lifted as I saw Cook shaping a mound of profiteroles which would be filled with cream and trickled with warm chocolate sauce.

'They look good.' I went to stand and watch those short, stubby fingers work a culinary miracle. 'Can I have a go?'

43

'Not with these, they're for the family,' Cook replied. 'But I made extra for us – you can use mock cream and practise if you like.' She gave me a severe look. 'That doesn't mean I'll accept less than excellence, though. Now watch how I pipe the cream and then you can try for yourself . . .'

'That's the last of the honey – now what am I to do?' Cook grumbled as she scraped out the glass jar. 'Someone is going to have to fetch it – where's Henry?'

'Gone out with Sir Charles in the car,' Doris ventured with her mouth full. 'I saw him cleaning it when I came from the laundry room earlier.'

'I can't make honey cake without honey.' Cook glanced round the kitchen. 'Her ladyship requested it 'specially for this afternoon – you'll have to go, Nellie.'

'Yes, Mrs Jones.' I hurriedly swallowed the last of my breakfast toast and jumped up. 'Who should I see – the head gardener or Dick?'

'Neither, that's the pity of it.' Cook looked annoyed. 'We don't have our own hives, that's why I'm forever running out of the wretched stuff. You'll have to go to the vicarage – Mrs Roberts promised me three jars of her best.'

I was glad that I'd walked to church with Iris a couple of times; we had passed the vicarage on our way and I knew where to go without having to ask.

'Don't waste time gossiping,' Mrs Jones warned. 'They've got guests upstairs this evening and I shall need you to help me.'

I accepted the money I was given, promised not to be longer than necessary, and slipped out of the back door, hardly believing my luck. The rain had stopped at last and it was a beautiful day, the sun beating down from a cloudless sky. It felt good to be alive.

Whatever I did it was bound to take half an hour or more to walk to the vicarage, buy the honey and walk back – half an hour of glorious freedom! I hadn't had that much time to myself since I'd left home.

The air smelt fresh and clean, a welcome breeze floating in from the top of the dark, distant smudge of the Pennines. It would be so good if I could go walking on the fells! The

44

moors around Malham were wild, open, lonely places criss-crossed by tracks that had once been used as monastic routes or by pack horses.

During the long summer holidays of my childhood my father had sometimes taken me walking on the fells and we had visited places of interest like the beautiful Fountains Abbey near Rippon and some of the granges and priories which had served it centuries ago; he had told me stories about the monks who had walked the ancient ways; together we had visited the prehistoric stone circle and the Tarn which had so caught my imagination.

My father was a quiet man but thoughtful and proud of his native Yorkshire; he had taught me to appreciate the beauty of my surroundings. Looking briefly away towards the moors I felt an urge to explore the countryside around Beaumont House, so much of which was unknown to me, but then kept my eyes fixed firmly on the road which led down to the village, smiling to myself at the wickedness of my thoughts. I couldn't possibly play truant when Mrs Jones was desperate for her honey but it would be wonderful to slip away one day . . .

Lost in daydreams I was startled by the sound of laughter; it had a high, light trill, as if whoever was laughing was very happy, and came from behind a clump of bushes near the kitchen garden gate, just where the land sloped sharply, hiding whoever was there from view.

'Oh, Gerald!' My ears pricked at the sound of Miss Alice's voice; it was hers but different, excited, tremulous, as if she were nervous. 'You shouldn't – you shouldn't have kissed me!'

'Why not?'

'Someone might come . . . '

'Let them.' The man's voice was warm and strong, full of confidence. 'I love you, Alice. I've always loved you. I was a fool to go and leave you, but I'm back now – and this time I'll stand up to him.'

I hesitated. I had to pass through the gate but I didn't want to intrude on what was obviously a private moment. I couldn't just barge in on them, they might be kissing again! I would sing, sing at the top of my voice.

'My old man said follow the van and don't dilly dally on the way . . . ' I belted out an old music hall tune that Grandfather had taught me. 'But I dillied and dallied . . . dallied and dillied, lost my way and don't know where to go . . . Off went the van with my old man in it . . . '

Alice emerged from the bushes looking oddly flustered. She smoothed a few wisps of dark hair from her face, then glanced to her right.

'It was good of you to call Mr Simpson. I'll speak to my brother . . . Oh, Nellie, where are you off to?'

'To buy honey for Cook,' I replied innocently. 'Isn't it a lovely day, miss?'

'Yes, lovely,' Alice replied.

Her eyes shone and she looked beautiful. Her hair had fallen out of its usual strict confines and was trailing down her back, and the faint air of sadness had gone, taking with it the old-maid dowdiness that had made Alice look older than her years.

The man was still standing in the shelter of the bushes which prevented him from being observed from the house. I could see that he was tall and dark-haired with a pleasant, tanned face, blue eyes and a strong, generous mouth. I rather liked the look of him and smiled warmly, wanting him to know that I approved of his coming for Miss Alice.

'I'll be off then,' I said. 'Mustn't keep Cook waiting for her honey.'

'No, of course not,' Alice replied, the corners of her mouth curving upward in a smile of happiness she could not repress. 'It is such a beautiful day, Nellie!'

I whistled cheerfully, resisting the temptation to look back over my shoulder. Let Miss Alice keep her secret if she wanted; I certainly wouldn't whisper it to anyone, not even Iris, but I was glad I knew. Miss Alice had been good to me, and I was happy things were turning out well for her.

Lost in my own thoughts I took no notice of the man standing at the end of the lane as I left the vicarage and turned homewards. Mrs Roberts had been telling me about the school she ran for the children of the 'Wandering People' as she called them.

'Gipsies, tinkers, landworkers, who come and go with the seasons,' she said as I inquired about some posters she was making. 'They are so often neglected. The regular schools can't cope with the children because they disappear without trace then turn up again out of the blue. I try to do what I can – sometimes for the women as well. They often have no idea how to do simple things like cooking or sewing . . .'

I'd taken to Anne Roberts immediately. She was a cheerful, busy woman and, before I knew what I was at, I found myself telling her that my Headmistress had said I ought to have been a teacher.

'Well, if ever you have time to spare, you can come and help me,' she said with a laugh.

I promised I would but there wasn't much chance of that. Life was too busy up at the house. I didn't resent my situation so much now but I sometimes wondered if I could have done something different if Mother hadn't been in such a hurry to get rid of me.

Perhaps it was because I was in a bit of a mood that I didn't notice Tom Herries until he called my name.

'Getting too proud to know me then?'

'Oh, Tom . . . ' I stared at him, surprised to see him there, though I shouldn't have been because he was one of the Wandering People Mrs Roberts had been talking about. 'What are you doing here then?'

'Going to see Mrs Roberts,' he said. 'She taught me to read and write when I was a nipper. Learnt the adding up from her, too, and a lot more. I want to ask if she'll do the same for our Jerry.'

I nodded then said, 'I thought you were going to find yourself a job?'

'I've had a couple but they didn't suit me. I'm still looking.'

I noticed that his clothes were slightly more respectable than the last time we'd met.

'Been buying honey then?' he asked, looking at the jars I was carrying.

'Cook is always running out. She can't get enough . . . ' I bit my lip. 'I'm working at Beaumont House now.'

'Yes, I'd heard.' He grinned at me. 'I keep my ear to the

47

ground. Cook's help – that'll come in useful when we get married.'

'That will be the day,' I scoffed. 'Get off with you, Tom! I can't stand here talking to you. I've got work to do even if you haven't.'

'I'll have a job soon, one that leads somewhere,' he called after me. 'Don't be surprised if you see me sooner than you think, Nell Pearce.'

I didn't stop to look back. I'd been delayed too much already and Cook would be getting impatient. There was no sign of Miss Alice or her friend when I reached the kitchen gardens. I hurried up to the back door.

'I'm back and I've got four jars . . . '

All at once I was aware of the strained atmosphere in the kitchen. I glanced at Doris who had come from the scullery and was still wiping her hands, then at Iris, and finally at Mrs Jones, chilled by the expressions on their faces.

'What's wrong? What have I done?'

'Nothing.' Cook frowned at Iris. 'You'll take this tray up, my girl, or I'll know the reason why.'

'I can't.' Iris's face was deathly white. 'Please don't ask me. I just can't – why can't Mr Sands do it?'

'Because he's busy. Besides, it's your job, Iris – with Henry out it's your place to take it.'

'I can't,' she repeated, a note of desperation in her voice. 'Not after what happened the last time . . . '

I looked from one to the other in astonishment. I'd never heard Iris defy Mrs Jones like this before. 'What's wrong, Iris? Why don't you want to take the tray?'

'It's for Mr Lucas,' she whispered. 'He's lying down with a headache – and I've got to go to his room. The last time he had a bad head he shouted at me and I dropped tea all over the carpet.'

'Mr Lucas suffers terrible with his headaches,' Cook said severely. 'You should be ashamed of yourself, Iris. The poor man needs sympathy not a silly girl like you shrieking at him! He asked for some of my barley water; it takes away the nasty taste in his mouth after he's had one of his do's – and you'll take it up or . . . '

48

'I'll take the tray for you,' I said, then blushed as they all stared. 'If someone will please tell me where to go?'

'You?' Cook hesitated, then nodded. 'Very well. Iris can go with you. Knock first, take the tray in, place it on the bedside chest then come straight out again – do you hear?'

'I'll take you up,' Iris said, looking relieved. 'It's good of you, Nellie. I shan't forget this.'

'I don't mind.'

'I shan't come in,' she said as she led the way upstairs. 'You don't mind, do you?'

'I said I didn't.'

'Only I can't bear to look at him. That scar of his gives me the shivers . . . '

'It's all right. I'm not bothered.'

It was light and airy in the upstairs passage, the sunlight filtering through a pretty stained glass window and casting a rainbow of colour on the silk wallpaper; it made me feel as if I were walking through a field of flowers and I could almost smell their perfume.

'I've never been up here before, it's nice – much nicer than I'd expected.'

The house looked bleak and cheerless from outside and the servants' quarters were painted in dull greens and a dark cream, but here there was an air of softness and charm that appealed to me.

'Yes, it's all right, I suppose,' Iris said, 'but not as posh as their London house.'

'Do they have a house in London?'

'Oh, yes, they go there quite often. At least Sir Charles, Lady Amelia and Miss Alice do – Mr Lucas doesn't go anywhere, not since . . . ' She stopped and pointed to a door at the end of the hall. 'That's his room, just there. You don't need me any more, do you?'

'No – but there's nothing to be frightened of, you know.'

'No.' Iris looked ashamed. 'It's just that I seem to annoy him, and it upsets me when he glares at me . . . '

'Get off then, I can manage.'

I paused in front of the solid oak door. How Cook thought I was going to knock with a heavy tray in my hands was beyond me. It took a lot of wiggling and a complicated balancing act to get the door open, which made enough noise to warn anyone I was coming.

'Your tray, sir.'

As I glanced towards the bed I saw that he was lying with his eyes closed. The scarred side of his face was buried in the pillows and I thought no one would guess there was anything the matter with him if they didn't know, though as I got closer I saw that his skin looked very pale and there were purplish shadows around his eyes; he was wearing a gold crucifix around his neck and his hair was damp.

He hadn't moved or shown that he had heard me. Setting down the tray I glanced at him again. He looked exhausted, the headache must have taken a lot out of him. He must be sleeping; well, I wouldn't disturb him. I noticed that the covers had slipped back and gently drew them up over his naked chest, then hesitated before laying my hand on his forehead. He felt cold despite the heat of the day. Was he all right? Looking round the room, which was sparsely furnished with just the necessary items of heavy dark wood furniture but no ornaments or mirrors, I saw a candlewick coverlet. Should I put it over him?

As I walked towards the blanket chest on which the cover lay neatly folded, my eye was caught by a painting propped up against a chair. I stopped to have a closer look, catching my breath as I saw my own image gazing out from the deep blue-black waters of a lake; it looked as if I'd been drowned and was lying just beneath the surface with my hair floating about my face.

'Leave that alone. What are you doing here?'

I jumped and swung round to face him. He had thrown back the covers and pushed himself up against the pillows, revealing a thin line of dark hair which trailed down his chest to where the sheet still covered his modesty.

'I was fetching a quilt to put over you – you were cold.'

'I'm hot – and you were touching my picture. Who told you you could?'

'I wasn't doing any harm,' I said defensively. 'She – she looks like me.'

'Does she?' His eyes gleamed suddenly. 'Perhaps she is you.'

'I'm not drowned.'

'Who says she is?'

'She looks as if she is.' I moved towards the bed. 'Why did you want me drowned – because I intruded on your special place?'

He gave a harsh crack of laughter. 'Scared you that day, didn't I?'

'No.' I inched closer. 'I like the picture – but I wish I wasn't drowned. I wouldn't like to be lost under the water like the Water Babies.'

'What a mind the girl has! You're a romantic, Nellie. I never took you for a romantic.'

'It looks as if I fell in the Tarn and drowned.'

'It isn't you – it's a figment of my imagination, a woman of mythology, a poet's mad dream. Nothing more.'

'Why does she look like me then?'

'Because your face was in my mind. I've been thinking about you, Nellie Pearce, wondering how you were getting on.'

'I'm helping Cook now. It's much better than the laundry.'

'So I should imagine.'

Had his face lost its look of strain or was that my imagination playing tricks?

'Miss Alice spoke to Mrs Jermyns for me, you know. That's why I don't have to go to the laundry any more.'

'Did she now?' He looked as if he were laughing at me, though I couldn't be sure because of the way his left eye dragged at the corner, giving him a slightly satirical expression. 'I hope you thanked her properly?'

'Oh, I did . . . Why are you laughing at me?'

'Am I?'

'I think so. I can't be sure because . . . '

'It's the scar,' he said in a flat, conversational tone. 'Most people can't bear to look at me at all.'

'I don't mind it. Sometimes I don't know it's there.'

'You've only seen me twice, hardly enough time to make such an adjustment.'

'But I've thought about you, and sometimes I see you as you must have been before – before it made such a mess . . . '

'Are you always so outspoken?'

51

My cheeks flamed. 'Shouldn't I have said that? My da always taught me it was best to face the truth straight on, but I'm sorry if I was rude. I didn't mean to be.'

'Not rude. Honest. I like that, Nellie, I like it that you don't pretend it isn't there. In fact, I like you, Nellie Pearce. Perhaps you would ... ' Lucas broke off as the door was pushed open and someone came in. 'Damn!'

'That's a nice way to greet me!' Alice laughed and came swiftly towards the bed, bending to kiss him on the mouth. 'My poor darling. You've had one of your awful heads. Was it very bad?'

'Bad enough, but it's better now. I thought you were Mother, that's why I swore.' His mouth softened into a smile of affection and I thought that if Lucas Harrington loved anyone it was Alice.

'You came at a bad moment,' he said, a devilish light in his eyes. 'I was about to proposition Nellie.'

'Lucas! For shame,' Alice scolded, and shook her head. 'She's a baby – just fourteen.'

'I don't want to ravish her,' he said. 'I want to paint her properly. I want her to sit for me. Please persuade her, Alice. She'll listen to you – you spoke to Mrs Jermyns about getting her out of Hell ... '

'Did I?' Alice looked startled as he nodded. 'Oh, you mean the laundry thing – yes, of course.' She turned her bright gaze on me. 'You must have realized by now that this wretched nephew of mine is quite, quite impossible ... but he does paint nicely.'

'I do not!' Lucas cried, seriously affronted. 'Call my work pretentious rubbish or a waste of time as Father does, but for heaven's sake don't call it nice!'

'I don't think it's nice. I don't want to be drowned,' I said.

'Oh, that's the Lady of Shalott,' Alice said with a laugh. 'She does look a bit like you, I noticed it myself – but don't you remember the poem from school, Nellie?'

'Of course she doesn't,' Mr Lucas muttered. 'She's probably never heard of it.'

'Yes, I have. I was the best in the class for learning poetry and I know that one by heart.' I glared at him.

'Well, then, you know the story,' he said, amusement

52

lurking in his eyes. 'So you know what happened to the poor lady.'

'Yes – but if it's her, why does it look like me?'

'Nonsense . . . '

Alice glanced across the room to the picture and nodded. 'I agree that it is you, Nellie. Why don't you let him paint a nice picture of you in your best dress to make up for it?'

'I don't want her in her best dress!' Lucas scowled at us both. 'I want her as she is now – a virtuous working girl in all her youthful innocence, fresh and dewlike, untouched by corruption, on the verge of discovery . . . '

'You sound like a lascivious old man!'

I giggled, enjoying myself. I wasn't sure what some of their long words meant or what was behind their banter, but it was fun to listen and watch, though it made me cross when Mr Lucas thought I was ignorant. Why shouldn't I know about poetry, even if I was just a servant?

'You will give the child ideas,' Lucas said, and sighed. 'Please, please, Nellie Pearce, will you sit for me?'

'When? I've got my work to do. Cook will be waiting for me now.' I glanced uneasily over my shoulder, belatedly remembering Mrs Jones's instructions to deposit the tray and leave.

'Alice will speak to Mrs Jermyns,' Lucas said. 'You will be given an hour off every morning. From ten to eleven might be best for the light.'

'Run along now, Nellie,' Alice said. 'I'll see what can be done about all this . . . go on, before you get into trouble with Cook.'

'Yes, miss, thank you.' I walked to the door then glanced back. 'I would like to sit for you, sir – as long as you don't make me look drowned.'

He laughed as I went out and a warm glow spread through me: Mr Lucas had a nice laugh even if he was a bit arrogant and thoughtless sometimes.

Chapter Four

'Whatever next? I never heard the like. First it's one asking for her to be let off the laundry work, then the other demanding she be allowed to sit for him – what do they think she's here for, that's what I ask myself?'

I was preparing vegetables in the scullery and could hear Cook and Mrs Jermyns talking about me in the kitchen. They were having a cup of tea together and Cook had made some almond macaroons 'specially: Mrs Jermyns was partial to the crisp but soft-centred cakes and I suspected that Cook was trying to get round her for my sake.

'It's not quite the thing,' she agreed now, 'but I don't see how we can refuse, being as the request came from Mr Lucas. He doesn't ask for much and I wouldn't feel right in myself if I set against him.'

There was a tantalising pause, then, 'Well, if you think you can manage without her. I dare say no good will come of it, but Miss Alice was very persuasive. She says the girl has broken down barriers she'd thought insurmountable – though what she means by that I'm sure I don't know.'

My ears pricked. I'd guessed there was some mystery in Mr Lucas's past and wondered if I was about to hear something interesting.

'If it brings him out of himself it must be for the better. After he had that nasty accident I thought he would fret himself into the grave.'

'If it was an accident . . . '

'Surely you don't think . . . ' Mrs Jones sounded upset. 'He wouldn't try to do away with himself, not Mr Lucas, that I won't believe, not if I sit here 'til doomsday.'

'You couldn't blame him if he had,' Mrs Jermyns observed. 'Not after what happened.'

'You mean when that flighty piece from London did the dirty on him?' During her infrequent visits to her sister in Bournemouth, Cook was a devoted filmgoer and a fan of the new American talking stars, like Edward G. Robinson and James Cagney. 'If I could only have got my hands on her!'

'I should have liked a few words myself.'

I wondered who the flighty piece from London was and just what she had done to Mr Lucas, but they had lapsed into an irritating silence and when they spoke again it was of me.

'We're agreed then,' Mrs Jermyns said at last. 'She's to have an hour off each morning for as long as Mr Lucas wants her.'

'I think so, don't you? Have another macaroon, Mrs Jermyns, I know they're your favourites. Well, it can't do much harm, can it? She's a good girl, works hard and does what she's told without a grumble – which is more than I can say for some. Let's see how it goes on, shall we?'

'If you're happy I don't mind, but be sure you don't let her get above herself. We don't want all this going to her head.'

As if it would! I burned with indignation but I wasn't supposed to be listening.

'I'll soon bring her down if she gets uppitty, don't you worry,' Cook said soothingly.

'That's settled then. I'll just have another cup of tea, then I'll get on . . . '

After she had gone Cook called me into the kitchen and told me of their decision, a mischievous twinkle in her eye.

'In case you missed any of that, Nellie, you're to have an hour off to sit for Mr Lucas every morning.'

She had known I was there all the time!

'Thank you,' I said and blushed scarlet. 'I never thought Mrs Jermyns would let me but you persuaded her. I'll get up earlier to make up for it if you like?'

'That won't be necessary. We don't want you wearing yourself out, Nellie. Just don't expect too much, that's all.'

'What do you mean?' I was struck by the warning note in her voice. 'I'm just going to have my picture done.'

'As long as you understand that. Gentry are odd in their ways, Nellie lass. When you're useful to them they make out you're wonderful, then . . . well, sometimes they just forget you afterwards. Keep your head on your shoulders and remember your place.'

'She'll be giving herself airs, thinking she's one of them.'

Doris had come in and sat down at the table without my noticing; I was startled to see the expression of jealous spite on her face.

'I shan't do that,' I said. 'I'm quite happy as I am, thank you.'

'Some folk have all the luck.' She took the last macaroon and began to stuff it into her mouth. 'You be careful, Nellie Pearce. He don't want to paint you for nuffing. He'll have your knickers off afore you know where you are.'

'Doris!' Cook gave her a baleful stare. 'I won't have dirty talk in my kitchen. And don't speak with your mouth full: it's bad manners. You won't see Nellie doing it, she's been brought up right.'

Doris scowled sullenly. She threw me a look of dislike but kept her mouth shut as she swallowed the last few bites of cake. When she had finished she gathered some of the dirty plates and took them into the scullery.

'Doris was being spiteful,' Iris had come in for her tea in time to hear what was being said, 'but she might have something. You want to be careful, Nellie. It ain't just gentry – all men are as bad as one another.'

'You will not be disrespectful to Mr Lucas,' Cook said, but she looked thoughtful. 'I'm sure he only wants to paint Nellie – though you're right as a general rule. Girls should be wary of men. It doesn't do to be too trusting. And you ought to take your own advice, Iris. I've seen the way Henry looks at you!'

'I can handle Henry,' Iris exclaimed, and then blushed as he came into the kitchen followed by Janet. They had been serving tea in the parlour upstairs, because it was Iris's day off. She had been home to visit her mother but wouldn't stay for tea because it took food from the mouths of her brothers and sisters. 'Is there any more cake, Mrs Jones? Doris ate the last one.'

Iris was still pink in the cheeks. I glanced from her to Henry and wondered if anything was going on between them. I'd thought she was interested in the curate, but perhaps I was wrong.

'They left half of theirs upstairs,' Henry said, and set a dish of cakes on the table. 'You might as well tuck into them, they won't want them – they're off to London this evening.'

'To London?' Iris's eyes gleamed. 'Miss Alice, too?'

'Just the master and her ladyship,' Henry said. 'I'm to have the car ready in an hour.'

'Did you know they were going?'

'No.' Henry scratched behind his ear while he thought it over. He was of medium height, thin with sandy hair and curiously light eyes. 'It was something to do with a telephone call, I think.'

'If Miss Alice was going she might have taken me,' Iris said.

'Well, she ain't, so you'll have to make the best of it.' Henry grinned at her. 'If you're sweet to me I might bring you a present back – perhaps some silk stockings?'

'Get off with you!' Iris pushed back her chair and stood up. 'I'd better go up and see if Miss Alice wants anything.'

'I told you, she ain't going,' Henry called after her, but she ignored him and went out.

'Strange them going off all of a sudden,' Cook said. 'You don't happen to know why?'

'Some sort of business, I reckon.' He looked at me suddenly. 'Shall I bring you a present from town then?'

'No, thanks – not unless it's some magazines. Any old thing will do, anything with pictures for me ma's scrapbook.'

'I'll see what I can do.' He winked and went out.

I finished my tea then gathered the rest of the dirty plates and took them out to the scullery. Doris was up to her elbows in hot water; she turned her head away as I deposited the dishes on the sink drainer and then began to wipe up those she had already washed.

I hadn't thought about it before but now I realized that Doris's attitude had changed since I'd stopped working in the laundry. We had got on well enough at the start but she

57

was obviously jealous. I was sorry about that, but not enough to let it spoil things.

I was looking forward to having my picture painted.

I might not have felt so happy about that if I'd understood then just what a hard taskmaster Lucas would be. Not that he was demanding during our first session, when he allowed me to wander about his large, airy studio at will, picking up brushes, wooden spatulas and tubes of paint to examine them closely. He smiled as I sniffed doubtfully at the oils he used, and he made a few sketches with a pencil.

'Don't you want me to sit down?' I asked when he told me to have a look around and amuse myself.

'Not particularly. At least not yet. I want to watch you, see how you move, observe your expressions.' He crossed one long leg over the other. 'Tell me about yourself, Nellie – what do you want from life?'

His interest surprised me, making me shy and unsure; my cherished dream of a cottage with roses beneath the windows, a husband who loved me, and children, seemed too vague, not exciting enough to tell him about.

'I don't know.' I blushed. 'Maybe I'll be a cook in a house like this.'

'Wouldn't you like to become famous for your culinary arts – maybe earn a lot of money and travel to strange, exotic lands? Wouldn't you like to see the wonders of the earth, Nellie?'

'Don't put ideas into her head,' Alice said, walking into the studio; the autumn sun was shining in through the big windows, making it warm and light. 'Nellie is quite happy as she is, aren't you?'

'Yes, miss.' I went to peer over Lucas's shoulder at the sketches but was disappointed to see that he had only drawn bits of me. 'I like being here – especially now.' I touched my finger to a line. 'My nose isn't like that.'

'Sometimes it is.' Lucas glared at me. 'Stop peering over my shoulder. You're not supposed to look unless I tell you.'

'He's such a grouch,' Alice said. 'He wouldn't let me see my portrait until the last minute. Anyway, your time is up for this morning, Lucas. I've come to fetch Nellie. I want her for a few minutes before she goes back to the kitchen.'

'What for?' He looked annoyed. 'I haven't finished yet.'

'An hour soon goes,' Alice replied with an understanding smile. 'You'll have to be patient until tomorrow – come on, Nellie.'

I was sorry in a way that my time was over, yet in another I was relieved. Mr Lucas could be very demanding and I wasn't quite sure how to take some of the things he'd said to me.

I followed Alice from the room. Instead of turning in the expected direction she led the way upstairs to what turned out to be her own bedroom. It was decorated in shades of green, ivory and pale rose, and furnished with delicate inlaid satinwood furniture that made me gasp in wonder.

'I've never seen anything as pretty as this,' I said, running my fingers over the top of a delicate table.

'It is nice, isn't it? I shall miss it in a way.' Alice gave me a direct look. 'You know I'm going away soon – with Gerald – don't you?'

She was talking to me as an equal, not as a servant. I answered in the same way. 'Well . . . I thought you might. He's a nice young man, miss.'

'You haven't mentioned what you saw or heard to anyone?'

'Oh, no, miss. I wouldn't do that.'

'No, I didn't think you would.' Her smile was warm and friendly. 'I had to ask, because for the moment it must be our secret. Until I'm ready – you do understand?'

'Yes, miss.'

It gave me a warm glow to feel that I had been admitted into her confidence. I liked Miss Alice just as I liked Mr Lucas, but in a different way; it was easier to know what was going on in her thoughts.

'I want you to have this,' she said, and picked up a blue silk headscarf from her dressing-table. 'It's just a little present but I thought you might like it.'

'It's lovely – but you don't have to give me anything.'

'It isn't a bribe, Nellie, just a present.'

'Thank you. I'll wear it for church.'

She nodded, her expression thoughtful. 'I wanted to have a word with you about my nephew.'

'About Mr Lucas?'

'Yes. I'm very fond of him, as I'm sure you've realized – but he can be difficult. Since his accident he has suffered from terrible migraines and he can be so moody . . . wanting to be alone, almost a recluse.'

'That scar . . . ' I met her serious gaze. 'It doesn't worry me, miss, but I just wondered what caused it?'

'He was out walking on the moors and fell into a disused quarry. It happened just after the girl he was engaged to had broken it off between them. He was very much in love with her. That's why we all thought . . . ' Alice broke off. 'He . . . he was unconscious when he was found, his face badly cut and his left leg broken. That healed well but his face . . . '

'You thought he might have tried . . . surely not, miss! He doesn't seem the sort to take his own life, and if he did he would make a proper job of it.'

'That's exactly what he said, but . . . the scar's made him desperately self-conscious. Afterwards, he wouldn't go out in company, wouldn't see anyone if they visited . . . '

'You can understand how he feels, miss. He must have been a right smasher before it happened.'

Her laughter burst out and I blushed.

'I shouldn't have said that. I meant, handsome.'

'You put it very well the first time,' Alice said. 'Lucas had everything anyone could want, or so it seemed. He was and is very intelligent; he has talent; his paintings are really very good and he was about to hold his own show at a famous London gallery – afterwards, he simply refused to show anything. For a long time he wouldn't paint, wouldn't even speak to anyone but me.'

'He doesn't seem too bad now, miss.'

'No. ' Alice looked thoughtful, as if wondering how much more to say. 'He has come out of his shell a little more lately . . . ' She glanced at her wristwatch and exclaimed, 'Look at the time! You must go or we shall all be in trouble with Cook; she'll be threatening to leave us again.'

'That won't do,' I said. 'Thanks for the scarf, miss.'

My thoughts were chasing round and round in my head as

I hurried away. Much of what Miss Alice had just told me I had already gleaned from things I'd heard or observed, but I hadn't known about the broken engagement. Not that it was any of my business, but it might explain why Mr Lucas got so angry sometimes.

I ran all the way to the kitchen, arriving breathless and expecting a scolding for being late, but Cook merely told me to get on with the vegetables.

I'd always suspected that Mr Lucas was a bit of a favourite with Mrs Jones, and now I felt sure of it. Providing I didn't abuse her good nature, Cook wouldn't scold me if I was a few minutes late, which was a good thing because I had an idea that Mr Lucas might forget all about time when he really got down to work.

'Why don't you ever have a day off?' asked Mr Lucas, a note of irritation in his voice. He wiped his brushes and scowled at me. 'An hour simply isn't long enough. I need you for three or four hours at a time.'

'I'm saving my days to go home before Christmas.'

'You really are a tiresome girl, Nellie.'

'Yes, sir. I'm sorry, sir.'

He stared at my face, then gave a harsh laugh. 'That innocent look doesn't fool me, you know. I can see beyond it, Nellie Pearce. I can see right into your soul.'

'You never can!'

'Artists see much more than other people.' He gave me one of his mocking stares. 'Why don't you ever complain, Nellie? I treat you shamefully, making you sit here for my benefit when you'd much rather be somewhere else.'

'I like being with you – you make me laugh. Inside.' Over the past weeks I'd learned not to vary my facial expression without permission: Mr Lucas had a temper on him when I forgot and changed my pose.

'So you laugh at me, do you?' His brows met in the middle as if he were annoyed.

'No, sir! Not at you, never at you. It just makes me laugh to hear the things you do say.'

He laid his brush down and came out from behind the easel. 'Then why won't you take a day off for me?'

61

'I can't, sir, not yet. I asked Mrs Jermyns . . . ' I broke off as I saw Miss Alice hesitate in the doorway. She looked upset, and sensing something was wrong, I jumped up.

'Sit still! I haven't finished with you yet.'

'I'm afraid you will have to be.' Alice's voice echoed the distress on her face. 'I'm sorry, Lucas, but I'm going to take Nellie away from you. She has to go home . . . at once.'

'Is it me grandad?' I had begun to shake and knew the answer before she spoke.

'Your father telephoned. Mr Barnes has been taken ill; he wants to see you.'

'How will I get there? How bad is he? Is he dying?'

I knew the answer to the last question, too. I wouldn't have been summoned like this if it were not desperate. Tears were burning behind my eyes and there was a crushing pain in my breast.

'I'll take you myself,' Alice said. 'Do you want to fetch anything from your room first?'

'No. Please, can we go straight away?'

'Yes, of course. We'll be there in an hour . . . less.'

'Nellie.' Mr Lucas caught my arm as I passed him. 'It will be all right, you know.'

'No.' I choked back a sob. 'It won't.'

'Nellie . . . '

I pulled away from him. 'Let me go. I have to go to me grandad!'

I was praying the whole time during that nightmare drive to my home. Don't let it be too late! Please don't let it be too late! The words echoed in my mind like a litany, over and over again. This couldn't be happening! Grandad had always been there, silent, loving, a permanent presence in my life. I couldn't bear to think of him dying.

Why hadn't I gone home on my days off? Four months I'd been at the house now; that was four days I could have spent with my grandfather. I'd thought it would be better to have them all at once and planned the treats I would buy for him, but now I was filled with a sense of loss; four days . . . but I'd wasted them and now it was too late.

62

The drive seemed to take forever. Glancing out across the winter bleakness of the moors I wanted to scream in frustration. Why had I ever come to this isolated place? Why had I ever left my own village where I knew everyone, every nook, every cranny, every street that Grandad and I had walked together? The answer was of course that I'd been given no choice. Mother had sent me away.

Why? Why? Why?

The question drummed in my head. If I'd been at home I could have been with Grandad all the time, sat with him, held his hand, comforted him. If he died before I saw him I didn't think I would ever forgive my mother.

'We're almost there now.' Alice's voice seemed to come from a long way off. 'A few more minutes . . . '

It might as well have been hours. There was a lead weight in my chest and I knew it was too late; it had been too late before we started.

'It doesn't matter now.'

Alice glanced at me. 'You can't be sure, Nellie.'

'I know. I've felt it for a while.'

She was silent as she drew up outside the terraced house, its curtains shut tightly against the grey morning, then she turned to look at me. 'Shall I come in with you?'

'No, miss. Thank you for bringing me but – but there's nothing you can do.'

'Telephone when you're ready to come back. Someone will fetch you.' She touched my hand in sympathy. 'I'm very sorry, Nellie.'

'Yes, miss. I know.'

I got out of the car, my courage almost failing, then I walked down the covered passage to the back door. I wasn't wearing a coat and the chill bit into my flesh, nipping at my nose and hands. The kitchen door opened as I got there and my father came out.

'Da . . . ' My voice cracked as he opened his arms. 'Oh, Da . . . '

'I'm sorry, lass.' He held me tightly. 'Wilf wanted to see you so bad but he couldn't hold on . . . he just couldn't hold on.'

I wept into his hard shoulder, inhaling the scents of musk,

leather and glue that clung about him. Despite the feeling inside me I had hoped against hope that I might see Grandad alive, if only for a few moments.

'When – when was he taken bad?' I asked at last. 'How long did he suffer?'

'It started in the night, though he hadn't been himself for a while. Not since . . . ' Father's voice trailed off. 'We had the doctor out to him and he thought he might rally.'

'Why didn't you send for me sooner?'

'Your ma . . . we didn't want to upset you unless . . . ' My father looked guilty. 'I thought he would linger for a few days. I'm sorry, lass. It was very sudden. Better for him that way. He didn't lay and suffer.'

'No, I suppose not.' I swallowed hard. 'Can I see him?'

'Yes, of course. If you want.'

'He's me grandad. I love him.'

'He loved you, Nellie. Didn't let on, but you were the apple of his eye. Always. He thought the world of you from the day you were born.'

'I know.' I lifted my chin. 'Where's Ma?'

'Seeing to him. She'll be finished by now, I reckon.'

'I'll go up then.'

'Aye, lass. You do that. I'll just bide by the fire until you come down.'

I gave him a watery smile, then started up the narrow stairs. It was funny but I'd never realized how musty the house smelled before, or how small it was. At the top of the staircase I hesitated, then turned towards the tiny room where Grandad had spent his last years; it was little more than a boxroom really but he'd been glad of it.

'It's good of Sam to have me here,' he'd told me once. 'I couldn't manage me own place no more – not after Dolly died – and I'd no mind to go into the workhouse.'

The workhouse was an old folks' home these days, but my grandfather remembered it as it had been when he was young, and dreaded it. I was glad he had never had to go there; at least he'd had a comfortable bed of his own to die in and his family around him – except me. Tears stung my eyes as I thought of him looking for me, hoping I would come before it was too late.

64

I went into the bedroom and found my mother sitting in a chair by the bed. She glanced up as I walked in, her face expressionless.

'He's gone,' she said. 'It was a waste of time sending for you – you couldn't have done anything. He went sudden.'

'I could have said goodbye.'

'What good would that have done? If you'd been here the last few months when you were due, you'd have seen him . . . '

'I was saving my days for Christmas, to have them all at once with him.'

'Don't blame me then.' She shrugged. 'We none of us knew it would happen so quick.'

'Da said he'd been ill.'

I approached the bed and gazed down at Grandad's face. He looked peaceful, much younger than when he was alive, and some of the hurt eased out of me.

'Not that you'd notice,' Mother said. 'He was just quiet . . . moody like. Hardly spoke to me. You'd think I'd done something evil . . . ' She went still as I looked at her. 'You think it's because I sent you away . . . you're blaming me for his death?'

The guilt was in her eyes. Whatever I thought or felt I could see my mother believed it was her fault, and that it had hurt her in some way, had somehow pierced the armour around her heart.

'No, I don't blame you for that,' I replied. 'Grandad was old; it would have happened sooner or later. You couldn't change that, no one could.'

'But you blame me for sending you off the way I did?'

'You could have told me sooner, Ma. Prepared me.'

'You'd have made a fuss,' she said. 'Worked on them both, got them on your side. It was the best way.'

'But why? Why did I have to go the minute I left school? We aren't poor, not like some. Da always gives you whatever you ask for, doesn't he?'

'Your da's wonderful in your eyes, isn't he?' Her mouth twisted in a bitter smile. 'I wonder what you'd say if you knew the truth . . . '

'What do you mean?' I was chilled by the look in her eyes.

'What's wrong with me da? He's a good man. Grandad always said he was a good man.'

'Sam's all right.' She paused deliberately, an odd, malicious expression in her eyes. 'But he's not your da.'

I felt as if a bucket of icy water had been thrown over me. 'Of course he's my da . . . '

'No,' she said. 'I was carrying you when I married him, and you weren't his.'

I felt sick and began to tremble. It couldn't be true. It couldn't! I wanted to scream at her, to shake her and force her to confess it was all a lie, a cruel wicked lie to hurt me, but I couldn't move or speak.

'Does – does he know?' The words came at last. 'Does he know I'm not . . . '

'He knows. You don't think I'd have married him else, do you? I've always been honest. Sam was mad for me. I was pretty enough when I was your age, and I wasn't much more than seventeen when it happened . . . '

'When what happened?'

None of this was real. It was a nightmare. Surely I would wake up soon and it would all be over! I had imagined so many reasons why my mother might have sent me away but never this. Never this . . .

'I was raped,' she said, not a flicker of emotion in her face or voice. 'Raped, beaten and left for dead. My father raised the alarm when I didn't come back that day. It was Sam who found me. He knew from the start what had happened – and asked me to marry him a few days later.'

My legs felt weak and I sat down on the edge of the bed. No wonder Ma hated the very sight of me.

'I'm sorry,' I said in a strangled tone. 'I didn't know – I didn't understand.'

'My father made me promise never to tell you,' she went on in the same flat voice. 'He thought it would hurt you. And Sam was like a father to you – better than most would be in the circumstances.'

'Not me da . . . ' I repeated the words. They didn't make sense even though I knew they must be true. I was a bastard born of a brutal rape. I felt as if my roots had been torn up and nothing was real or safe any more. 'I can't blame you if you hate me.'

'I always have,' Mother said, almost as if she were talking to herself. 'Sam's a good man but it's always been there between us. I've felt the shame of having you all my life.'

'Please . . . ' I couldn't bear any more of this. 'I'd like a little while with me grandad.'

'Yes. I'll go down then,' she said. 'Will you be staying for the funeral?'

'Yes, yes, I shall. After that I'll go. You won't have to see me again, Ma. I'll not trouble you or – or me da – again.' I was hurting so much that I just wanted to be alone with my grief.

Mother looked uncertain. 'You'll not tell Sam I told you? He's a soft fool; he'll blame me for blurting it out – especially now.' She glanced at the stiffening figure on the bed. 'Maybe I should have waited . . . '

'Maybe you should,' I said, 'but it doesn't matter. Don't go soft on me now, Ma. I don't think I could stand that.'

'You'll thank me one day,' she said suddenly. 'For the place I got you at Beaumont House. It's a chance for you – a chance I never had.'

She walked out of the room before I could reply. Once she had gone I turned to the still, silent form of my beloved grandad. I touched his cold hand, then lay down beside him and rested my face against his.

'Oh, Grandad,' I choked as the tears began to flow. 'Oh, Grandad, I need you so much . . . so much. Why did you have to go and leave me?'

I'd thought there was still my da but now I felt as if I had been cast out into the wilderness. Sam Pearce had been good to me. I knew he was fond of me, but he wasn't me da . . . he wasn't me da. My heart was breaking with the pain of it. I loved him but I couldn't expect him to love me, not now, not after what my mother had told me. How could he love the child of a rapist? How could he bear to look at me, knowing what he did?

How I got through the agony of the next few days I shall never know. I answered when spoken to, walked, ate and breathed, but I felt as if I were dead inside. Everything I had

67

ever loved or believed in had been ripped away from me, leaving me bereft and alone.

I was aware of my brother sniffing beside me in the church as we listened to the funeral service. I held his hand to comfort him, but nothing could penetrate the awful misery that surrounded me like a mist. Even when we followed the coffin to its final resting place and I felt Sam touch my arm, I could not rouse myself enough to acknowledge him.

How could I ever look him in the face again? I was ashamed of being the child of a rapist and hurt that my mother had chosen to fling the truth at me at this time – when I was more vulnerable than ever before.

There was no one I could turn to for comfort, no one to ease the pain inside me as I wept bitter tears into my pillow.

'Oh, Grandad,' I whispered into the darkness. 'Oh, Da . . . oh, Da . . . I can't bear it. I can't . . . '

I hadn't known anything could hurt this much.

Chapter Five

'So you've made up your mind to go back then?' Sam looked at me as I came downstairs carrying a small bag and a coat over my arm. 'I'm glad the coat fitted you, lass. I bought it in the market last time I was over, thought it was better than your old one – and now it has come in useful.'

His smile was as warm as ever. Never once in his life had he said or done anything to make me feel I was not his daughter, and I had not been able to bring myself to tell him that I knew the truth now. I still loved him and I didn't want to hurt him.

'Thanks, Da.' I went to kiss his cheek. 'And thank you for everything else.' I slipped the blue wool coat on and buttoned it to the neck, feeling glad of the cowl collar that reached almost to my chin: the wind was bitter outside and I would need it.

'Your grandad wanted you to have his watch and chain; it was all he had of any value and I was asked to see you got it. It's gold, Nellie, worth a few bob if ever you need it.'

'I shall never sell it.' The pain of not seeing Grandad before he died was still raw enough to bring tears to my eyes. 'Not that I need anything to remind me, I shan't forget him.'

'No, of course not.' There was a puzzled look on Sam's face and I knew he had sensed the change in me. 'I wish you had rung Miss Alice and asked her to fetch you. I don't like the idea of you going with strangers.'

'The Harringtons use this firm of carriers all the time so I'll be quite safe,' I said. 'Miss Alice was good enough to bring me. I didn't like to put her to the trouble of fetching me . . . ' I heard a knock at the back door. 'I expect that will be the van now. They said half-past eight.'

Sam reached out and drew me into his arms, giving me a hug. I hesitated, then hugged him back. He was still my da. Nothing could change that, even though things could never be quite the same.

'Take care of yourself, lass,' he said. 'You know where I am if you want me, don't you?'

'Yes, Da.'

'Have you said goodbye to your mother?'

'Oh, yes. We've said all we need to say.'

I had asked her who he was – the man who had raped her, the man who had saddled her with a child she had not wanted and could never love.

'No one you know,' she'd said, and looked away from me. 'I never knew him – he was a stranger. Don't ask me again, Nellie. I've never known who he was.'

I had wondered if she was lying but it was obvious that she would never tell me even if she knew.

'You'll come home again soon?' Sam was asking anxiously.

'When I can,' I promised, but I didn't look at him. ''Bye, Da – and take care of yourself.'

I walked to the door, glanced over my shoulder and went out.

My eyes were so blurred with tears that I hardly looked at the man who stood outside the kitchen door waiting for me with his cap in his hands. It wasn't until he offered to give me a lift up into his van that I really looked at him, and then I had to look twice to be certain.

'Tom?' I asked uncertainly. 'Tom Herries . . . is it you?'

''Course it's me.' He grinned at me. 'Ain't changed that much, have I? It's just me clothes and a lick of water behind the ears.'

'You do look smart.' I saw that his boots were nearly new and his trousers matched his jacket; they were good quality secondhand and the trousers were held up with braces. 'So you've found yourself a job then?'

'It's a start,' he replied, and gave me a shunt to help me up the high step into the passenger side of his delivery van. He shut the door then went round to climb into the driving seat. 'It ain't what I want to do, but it's the first rung on the ladder and I'm learnin' a lot. I'm going to have me own business one day – and then a whole chain of them.'

'How are you going to do that then?' I stared at him as he released the brake and the van started to move forward. 'Come into a fortune, have you? Or did you discover you were the long-lost heir to some lord or other?'

Tom laughed deep in his throat. 'You're a caution, you are, young Nell. No, I ain't come into no money, I'm planning on making some for meself.'

'Well, I wish you luck. At least you've found yourself honest work. When you first told me you wanted to be rich I thought you were planning on a life of crime.'

'You should know me better; that's a fool's game and I've got it up 'ere.' He tapped the side of his head, then his face became serious as he glanced sideways at me. 'I was very sorry to hear about Wilf, Nellie. I always liked him and I know you were fond of him.'

'He was me grandad,' I said croakily. 'I loved him. I loved him so much, Tom, and now – now he's gone. I shan't see him no more . . . ' The tears began to roll down my cheeks and I hunted for a handkerchief without success. Tom pulled a large red and white spotted one from his pocket. It was clean and had been ironed. 'Thanks, Tom. I can't find mine.'

'Keep it,' he said. 'Think about me when you use it.'

'Don't you want it?' I blew my nose as he shook his head. 'Thanks, it's very smart.'

'It's too fancy for a businessman like me. I shall have white linen ones in future – like the gentry.'

'You and your ideas!'

'Got to have ideas or you end up working for someone , else all your life.' He shot an inquisitive look at me. 'Are you still liking it up at the house then? I heard as how 'er ladyship was a bit of a tartar, and he . . . well, he weren't no better than he should have been when he were younger.'

'What do you mean?'

71

'Just watch out for him in dark corners,' Tom said and winked. 'Not that he'd be much trouble to you these days. Getting past it now, I shouldn't wonder.'

'Tom Herries! You wash your mouth out with carbolic.'

'Aw, come on, Nellie,' he said. 'Weren't nothing wrong with that, just a bit of friendly advice, that's all.'

I acknowledged that he hadn't really shocked me.

'I've never seen Sir Charles or her ladyship – except once from a distance. But Miss Alice and Mr Lucas, they're all right. Mr Lucas is painting my picture.'

'He never is! Well, fancy that.' Tom shot a startled glance at me. 'Not that you ain't as pretty as a picture, I've always thought that.'

'You're just saying that. Mr Lucas says I'm interesting – an innocent working girl.' I smirked a little then blushed.

'You ain't getting sweet on him, are you? Remember what I said about his father? Well, the same goes for him. You don't want to let him take liberties.'

'No, of course not! What do you think I am – daft in the head? No point in getting sweet on him, gentry don't marry girls like me.'

'As long as you know that.' Tom looked smug. 'Besides, you're my girl.'

'I am not!' I cried indignantly. 'I shall never marry you, Tom Herries – so don't you think it!'

'I ain't asked you yet, you're too young and I ain't ready.' A merry smile lurked in his dark eyes. 'But when I am, you'll be the first to know.'

'You just watch your lip!' I cried but his teasing had helped to ease the hurt inside me. With Tom I could relax and be myself.

He didn't speak for several minutes after that and when he did it was about other things. He told me about his job, about the people he delivered to and how every household was different.

'People are interesting,' he said, 'all as different from one another as chalk from cheese. I talk to them, get to know what they like and dislike, then I know what they want and make sure it's on the van. It's surprising how often they buy extra if you've got it there.'

I was beginning to realize that Tom wasn't making an idle boast when he said he'd got brains.

'Got it all worked out, have you?'

'You have to if you want to succeed in business, make a little extra like.'

I thought that maybe Tom would make something of himself after all and began to tell him about my life at the house, about how I'd started in the laundry room and hated it – at least while we talked I couldn't think about anything else. For this little time I was able to shut out my grief and the pain my mother had inflicted on me with her terrible revelations.

'Miss Alice spoke up for me,' I said. 'She's been ever so good to me, gave me a pretty scarf as well . . . almost the colour of my new coat.'

'That's a smart coat,' he said. 'The colour suits you.'

'Da bought it for me.' I caught back a sob as I remembered that Sam wasn't my da – that I was the child of an evil man who had raped and beaten my mother: the man who had made Rose Pearce the hard-hearted woman she was.

'It will get better in time,' Tom said. 'Grieving hurts, lass, but it don't last forever.'

'No, I suppose not.' I thought that the pain and shame of what my mother had told me would stay with me long after I'd ceased to cry for Grandad.

'Well, here we are then,' Tom said. 'I'll stop out here on the road – let you go in the back way.'

I waited as he went round to open the door and lift me down. He held me for a moment longer than necessary and I gazed up into his eyes then gasped as he bent his head and gave me a quick kiss on the mouth.

'What do you think you're doing? I'm not that sort of a girl, Tom Herries, and don't you think it!'

'What sort is that then, Nellie?' He smiled down at me. 'It were just a friendly peck, lass, to cheer you up.'

'All right – but just watch it in future!'

He turned back to the van then handed me a basket with a white cloth covering the contents.

'You give that to Mrs Jones,' he said. 'Tell her she can pay me the next time – and that I'll have the other things she wanted by then.'

I peeped beneath the cover and saw there were six jars of clear golden honey inside.

Tom nodded as I looked at him. 'You told me what was needed so I did a bit of business for myself.' He waved and opened the van door. 'I'll be seeing you, Nellie. Watch out for dark corners!'

I tossed my head and walked up the garden path, carrying the heavy basket. Tom Herries certainly wasn't lost for it! He had a cheek asking Cook if he could supply her honey.

I intended to apologize for him as soon as I saw her, but to my surprise she fell on the basket with glee.

'That young man's going a long way,' she told me with a twinkle in her eyes. 'Talk about the gift of the gab! His father must have been Irish – but this is the best honey I've tasted in a long time and I'll have a regular supply from now on.'

I gave her Tom's message then but she merely smiled mysteriously and went to stack her precious honey in the larder.

As I held my hands to the kitchen fire to warm them I discovered that I felt much better. It was almost like coming home.

'You should have let us know you were ready,' Alice said an hour or so later when she came to the kitchen to collect me. 'I would have driven over and fetched you myself.'

'It wasn't worth your trouble. I got a lift with the carriers – and I know the driver. He used to live in our village.'

'That's all right then,' she said, and there was a faraway look in her eyes. 'Lucas sent me to find out if you were back and I've had a word with Mrs Jermyns – you're to have the rest of the day off. Lucas wants to finish the picture . . . '

'The whole day?' I hadn't expected that, especially after being away for four days.

'Well, it will give you a chance to settle down again and Lucas is impatient to finish the portrait; he wants to exhibit it with some more of his work in London.'

'He's going to show my picture? You're pulling my leg, miss!' I didn't know whether to be upset or pleased.

'No, I'm not.' Alice looked amused and said, 'I'm decorating the Christmas tree this evening, Nellie. If Lucas has finished with you by then you might like to help me.'

'I'd love to do that. Are you sure it would be all right? I've missed a lot of work . . . '

'You needn't feel guilty about that – it hasn't been your fault.' Once again there was that odd, distracted expression in her eyes. 'I've something to tell you . . . ' She shook her head as I looked at her. 'Later – when we're doing the tree. But now you must be quick, Lucas is so impatient . . . '

I felt flustered as I hurried away, hardly believing that I was to have the whole day off just to be painted – and then help Miss Alice with the tree! Doris would be green with envy and Iris might not be too pleased about it either; she regarded Miss Alice as her property.

So much seemed to have happened in the past few days that I couldn't quite take everything in, but the ache inside me had begun to ease on the journey back with Tom Herries. It wouldn't go away, of course, but I might just be able to cope with it now – and I would be glad to get back to my regular work; I knew where I was in the kitchen with Cook.

I hesitated before knocking at the door of the studio, feeling suddenly shy. I'd never expected Mr Lucas to put my picture in a gallery and the thought had made me nervous. I waited for a moment, then the door was wrenched open and he stood there, his brows lowered in a frown of impatience.

'Come in then, what are you waiting for?'

'Miss Alice said you wanted me . . . '

Lucas reached out, his strong, paint-stained fingers encircling my wrist as he pulled me into the room and pushed the door shut. For what seemed ages he stood gazing intently down into my face.

'What have you done to yourself?' he asked at last, and the furious look in his eyes sent tremors down my spine. 'You've changed. It's gone – that look of innocence. It's completely disappeared!'

'W-what do you mean?' I was frightened by his anger. 'I haven't done anything.'

'It's gone!' Lucas cried. 'All that work for nothing! You're not the same. The picture is ruined. I can't paint you now – you're different.'

'I'm not . . . ' His attack on me was startling and unjust. 'I'm just the same as I was.'

Lucas took my chin in his hand and turned my face to the light. 'There's knowledge in those eyes – what have you been doing? I thought you went home for a funeral. Have you been with a man?'

His inference was shockingly plain. He thought I had been doing something wicked! I wrenched away from him, all the grief and pain of the past days welling up in me and pouring out in a torrent of resentful denial.

'How dare you?' I shouted. 'You have no right to say such things to me, sir. I haven't done anything like that; I'm not that sort of a girl and you ought not to accuse me of it.'

I tried to rush past him but he caught my arm, swinging me round so that I was flung against his chest. I struggled desperately and he held me close, imprisoning me so that I could not escape no matter how I fought him – and I did fight, with all my strength, kicking and punching him as the angry, shameful sobs burst out of me and the salty tears ran down my cheeks. I was letting out all the fury and resentment I had felt against my mother, venting it on him because he was so cruel and selfish.

'Stop it!' Lucas commanded and gave me a shake. 'I'm sorry. I didn't mean it. I know you're not a bad girl, Nellie. It's all right . . . hush then . . . I'm sorry . . . it's all right . . . '

I gazed up at him, feeling exhausted after my outburst. 'You ought not to have said it. I'm not a wicked girl. I'm not . . . ' I was still crying, tears and saliva mixing as he took out his clean white handkerchief and wiped my face. 'I'm not a bad girl . . . '

But how did I know what sort of a person I was? I'd been proud to be Sam Pearce's daughter – but what kind of a man would rape and beat a young woman? I felt sick with shame that I carried the blood of such an evil man in my veins, and it made me all the more determined to prove my innocence.

'I haven't done anything wrong. I haven't . . . '

'No, of course not.' Lucas stroked a wisp of brown hair from my eyes. 'Forgive me, Nellie. Please forgive me. I shouldn't have said it. I was disappointed because . . . well, I can finish the painting from my sketches and notes so all is not lost.'

I pulled away from him again and this time he let go. I glared up at him. All he could think about was his work; he didn't care that I'd been hurt, that my whole world had been turned upside down, leaving me feeling lost and alone.

'You're selfish, that's what you are. You don't care about anyone but yourself!'

For a moment his eyes flashed with temper, then a reluctant amusement came over him and he laughed. 'Yes, you have changed,' he said. 'You're right, of course. I am a selfish brute – but you wouldn't have said it four days ago.'

A hot colour swept up into my face as I realized how rude I'd been to the son of my employer. He could have me instantly dismissed.

'I shouldn't have said that.' I was certain that he was about to send me away in disgrace.

'No, no,' Lucas cried. 'Don't apologize, Nellie. I don't want that look any more.'

I glanced up and saw that he was sketching furiously. He sighed in exasperation.

'What can I do to make you angry again?'

'Why?'

'Because I've had a wonderful idea,' he said. 'I can finish the other portrait from my sketches; it was almost done anyway. If I paint another one – as you are now – it will be startling. Don't you see it? Innocence and Knowledge, that's what I'll call them – before and after.'

'Before and after what? You're not implying I've done anything wrong, are you?'

'Who cares what you've done – or haven't,' he muttered. 'It's brilliant . . . a stroke of luck.'

'You *are* selfish.' I glared at him. 'You don't care a bit about what made me change, do you?'

Lucas was lost in his work; he didn't look up as he said, 'Tell me about it, Nellie. I was sorry about your grandfather . . . ' He glanced up momentarily. 'Yes, that's just the expression I want . . . now try to look through me, as if I wasn't there . . . perfect.'

'I've a good mind not to sit for you. I thought you liked me but all you care about is . . . '

'Nellie, Nellie,' he chided, and came towards me. 'I think I should like you standing by the window with the light on your face.' He turned me so that I was looking outward. 'That's good. Now stare into the distance. I want that half angry, half wistful look . . . now go on, what were you saying?'

'I said, I thought you liked me?'

'Of course I like you, Nellie. I adore you . . . don't change your expression! I wouldn't have chosen to paint you if I didn't like you, silly girl.'

I scowled and Lucas smiled with satisfaction as my face settled into the expression he wanted. Of course he didn't care about me. Why should he?

'So you've finally decided to come back to us, have you?' Cook said as I went into the kitchen after I'd finished helping Alice with the tree that evening. 'There's a houseful of guests expected any day now and I shall need every pair of hands I can get.'

Alice had asked me to do the tree because she wanted to talk to me about Gerald and her plans to meet him over Christmas – and Lucas had kept me sitting for him most of the day. It wasn't fair that I should be blamed for doing as I was told but I accepted the reprimand without comment.

'I'm sorry, Mrs Jones. Mr Lucas wanted to start the new picture, and Miss Alice said it would be all right if I helped her with the Christmas tree.' I showed her a book Miss Alice had lent me. It was *A Christmas Carol* by Charles Dickens and the leather cover showed signs of wear as if it had been much read. 'Miss Alice said I should read this as we didn't have it at school. She thinks I ought to go on with my education through books in my spare time.'

'You can read it to me in the evenings,' Mrs Jones said. 'When we're having our nightcap. I like a good story.'

'I'd enjoy that,' I replied, and smiled at her. 'Wasn't it kind of Miss Alice to lend it to me?'

'I told you she'd soon be thinking she's one of them.'

Doris's spiteful words brought a frown from Cook. The

annoyance faded from her eyes as she pushed a cup of tea and a plate of fresh jam tarts in front of me.

'Well, well, I dare say you were only pleasing others,' she said. 'You look thinner, Nellie. It hasn't been a happy time for you these past few days.'

'No.' I blinked away my tears. 'I'm glad to be back with you and – and I'll make up the time I have off for Mr Lucas.'

'You can help me with the mince pies this evening,' Cook said. 'I shall be up late and it will be nice to have company while I work.'

Doris made a sound of disgust in her throat and went out into the scullery; we could hear her banging the pots and pans angrily as she started to wash up.

'Perhaps I should go and help her?'

'Sit there and finish your tea,' Cook said. 'She's took against you, lass, and there's no help for it. She's been here longer than you but she knows that you'll get on and she won't – Doris will never be more than what she is now. Hasn't the brains for being an upstairs maid and wouldn't feel comfortable if she was made up to it. She can't see that, though, and so she's jealous of you.'

'She doesn't hate Iris or Janet.'

'They were here first. You came after.' Cook shook her head. 'I shouldn't let it worry you, Nellie. You'll have to put up with her spite but she can't do you any real harm. Leave her be and she'll get over it in time.'

I knew that what Cook was saying made sense but I didn't like this atmosphere between me and the laundry maid. Doris couldn't do me any real harm, of course, but she would lose no chance to make things uncomfortable for me whenever she could.

That night I lay in bed thinking about all that had happened to me since I was called home. After my mother had told me I was not Sam Pearce's child I had felt as if nothing would ever be the same again, but now that I was back at Beaumont House I began to see that her revelations had made little real difference to me.

From the day she had sent me away my old life had been

over; I hadn't understood that then but now I realized it was true. I was no longer a child and I had lost someone I loved dearly, but for the time being my future was here, amongst the servants and family of Beaumont House. I was growing up – growing away from all that I had known.

I should grieve for Grandad for a long time but that was natural and right. The pain of my mother's rejection was very different, but I would learn to cope with that too.

I had to learn to live with the fact that Sam was not my real father. I had to accept Doris's dislike and not let it upset me. Already the discipline of life in the kitchen was becoming second nature to me; I enjoyed cooking and my work was a pleasure.

I was not sure how I felt about the time I spent in Mr Lucas's studio. He was selfish when he was working – but perhaps anyone who put so much of themselves into their work needed to be selfish. He was also moody and bad-tempered, but I knew he had good reason for his moods. Besides, once the paintings were finished I should probably see very little of him.

Being at Beaumont House was not so very terrible these days. Iris was my friend. I enjoyed being with Cook and she seemed to like me. Then there was Miss Alice: she was kind but her life was difficult and I wanted to help her all I could.

There was still a part of me that wept for all I had lost but I was determined not to let the pain overshadow my life. I would work hard and try to put the past behind me. I wasn't going to be a servant for ever. Alice and my old Headmistress had shown me the way. I would read and learn everything I could and one day I would make something of myself . . .

Chapter Six

Having made up my mind I was able to enjoy the atmosphere of Christmas in the big house, despite the ache in my heart that never quite went away.

Everyone was excited and there was a lot of laughter in the kitchen as the shelves in the large, cold pantry began to overflow with the results of Cook's hard work; there were two kinds of mince pies, one with an almond topping that melted on the tongue and was better than anything I'd ever tasted, cakes, sugared fruits, stuffed dates, fancy biscuits and homemade cream truffles rolled in pure cocoa powder – so delicious they made you want to eat the lot! – and then there were the meats: huge hams, joints of pork, beef and venison as well as the birds that would be cooked on Christmas Day. At home we always had roast goose for our special dinner and I was looking forward to my first taste of turkey.

'I'm more partial to a nice goose myself,' Cook told me. 'Turkey can be a bit dry if you're not extra careful in the cooking – but the master insists on his turkeys and Mrs Jermyns likes them, too, so we always have one in the servants' hall, besides the goose and a bit of beef. No reason why we shouldn't look after ourselves as much as them upstairs, is there?' She winked and took another sip of the sherry from the glass beside her.

Cook's herculean efforts required some extra special sustenance, and her partiality for a nice drop of dry sherry had brought a high colour to her cheeks. In no way could she have been accused of being intoxicated but she was certainly in a happy mood and this was reflected throughout the kitchen. Mr Sands was known to take the occasional nip of his employer's best port himself, and for the past three days there had been a jug of cider or beer on the table at mealtimes for those who fancied a glass. So it was not surprising that everyone was enjoying themselves.

That there was to be a big party in the drawing room on Christmas Eve was known throughout the house; we had talked of it for days in the kitchen and Iris went on and on about the decorations upstairs so much that Henry brought in masses of holly, mistletoe and greenery and hung it everywhere in the servants' hall; he even hung a bunch of mistletoe in the kitchen but when he insisted on kissing all the women every time he caught one of them under it, Mr Sands made him take it down again.

'Everything in its place, Henry,' he said, but in a jocular tone. 'You'll have plenty of time for kissing when we have our own celebrations in the hall.'

Henry had already been caught kissing Iris and then Janet in the passage outside the kitchens, and from the way he was giving me naughty looks I suspected him of planning the same for me.

The atmosphere was infectious, though, and I was beginning to feel a little better. I was still inclined to get moist eyes whenever I thought of Grandad, but refused to indulge in self-pity.

Mother wouldn't name the man who had raped her and after I'd thought it over I decided I didn't want to know. Sam Pearce was my da, the only one I would ever want or need. Things could never be quite the same but I was coming to terms with my grief.

Besides, Christmas was impossible to ignore. Everyone was happy and so I smiled and joined in the jokes and laughter even if I didn't always feel like it.

The first hint that anything was wrong upstairs came when Miss Parkinson knocked on the housekeeper's sitting-room door in tears and told her that she was leaving.

'Leaving?'

Mrs Jermyns hurried down to the kitchen to pass the news on to Cook.

'Well, you could have knocked me down with a feather,' she said. 'Mabel leaving – just like that!'

'Not right away!' Mrs Jones exclaimed. 'Not on Christmas Eve?'

'That's exactly what I do mean,' the housekeeper said. 'I asked her in and gave her a glass of sherry and she told me . . . ' She became aware of us all listening. 'Well, never mind that now – but she is certainly leaving this very day.'

'How will the mistress manage without her?'

'I was told they were thinking of leading a quieter life and wouldn't be entertaining much after this Christmas. But if you ask me it's him, Sir Charles . . . ' Mrs Jermyns recollected herself. 'Mabel knows but she wouldn't say any more.'

Mrs Jermyns obviously had her own thoughts on the matter but she was keeping them to herself – at least until she and Cook were alone.

'She's been with her ladyship for years,' Cook said, her chins wobbling in distress. 'This looks like the thin edge of the wedge to me, Mrs Jermyns. No doubt we shall be hearing more of this after Christmas!'

Mrs Jermyns nodded but would not be drawn further.

The news of Mabel's leaving cast a shadow over the house, both downstairs and up, as Iris reported when she came down with a load of dirty glasses that evening.

'If that's supposed to be a party . . . you could cut the atmosphere with a knife. They've all got long faces, the family that is – and everyone else looks as if they can't wait to escape!'

'What do you think is going on?' I asked. 'Do you reckon they'll tell us?'

'I've got an idea.' Iris glanced guiltily over her shoulder to make sure no one else was listening. 'I heard Mr Lucas say something about his father being in serious money trouble – but don't let on I told you, because I shouldn't have been listening.'

Things must be bad if Miss Parkinson had been let go. Did that mean some of the other servants would also be turned off? I would probably lose my job if that happened.

Doris was triumphant when we were washing up together in the scullery. 'You're sure to be let go after Christmas,' she said spitefully. 'You've spent half your time sitting around being painted.'

'That's not true – anyway, it wasn't my idea. I've worked hard when Cook asked me; it's not my fault if I had to have time off.'

Doris clearly thought my days at the house were numbered and was pleased about it. It would be upsetting if I had to leave because there was no way I was going home for good, not now.

It was past three in the morning when I finally got to bed. We had all been working non-stop from half-past six the previous day and were exhausted. Iris had come up a little while before me and was already asleep when I crawled into bed beside her. I wished I could talk to her but didn't want to waken her: it was going to be a busy day again very soon.

Christmas Day itself started at a more leisurely pace. The family had been to midnight mass the previous evening and breakfast was not required until past eleven; for once there was to be no lunch at midday and that allowed Cook to put all her efforts into the big dinner she was preparing for everyone.

I had been told I wouldn't be needed in Lucas's studio over the Christmas period so was surprised when halfway through the morning Alice came into the kitchen and asked for me.

Cook was stuffing the inside of a turkey with whole oranges and apples, the real stuffing of breadcrumbs, nuts and spices having been inserted beneath the top skin; the purpose of the fruit was to add moisture to the meat as it was cooking, and add a piquant flavour of its own.

'Will you be needing me?' I was reluctant to be taken away from the busy kitchen. 'I've done the vegetables but there's still the potatoes to finish.'

'How long will she be?' Cook asked. 'I can't spare her for more than an hour.'

'Oh, she shouldn't be that long,' Alice replied, a faint flush in her cheeks. 'It's just a little errand for me, that's all.'

'Go on then,' Cook said, wiping a white cloth over her brow to mop up the sweat. Her cheek was smeared with flour and she had a high colour. 'But don't be late. I need you here.'

I followed Alice from the kitchen and was surprised when she turned towards the passage leading out to the kitchen gardens and not to the stairs that led up into the main part of the house.

'I'm not sitting for Mr Lucas then?'

'No, he thought it best not to ask during Christmas,' Alice said. 'I want you to do something for me, Nellie – because I think I can trust you, can't I?'

'Yes, of course, miss. You know I would do anything for you.'

'I want you to take a letter to Gerald for me.' A faint rose colour stained her cheeks. 'I was to have met him today out near Weets Cross – do you know where that is?'

'Yes, miss.' I thought about it. 'It's beyond Gordale, there's a stony track but it's a fair walk, miss.'

'Yes, I know. Can you ride a bicycle with a crossbar, Nellie?'

'Yes, I think so. I've ridden my brother Bob's a few times.'

'Well, you'll find one in the bushes near the kitchen gate. Take it and ride out there as quickly as you can – you might meet Gerald on the way, because I should have been there an hour ago and he's probably on his way to see where I am. It's important he doesn't come here today. Give him my letter and tell him I'll ring him soon, but he mustn't come – not while Charles is in this mood!'

I tucked the letter into my apron pocket, then looked at Alice curiously as I helped myself to one of the coats hanging in the hall for casual use by anyone needing to pop outside on a cold day.

'Is something wrong, Miss Alice?'

'I can't tell you now,' she said, 'but you will all know soon enough. My brother intends to make an announcement to the staff tomorrow. You'll all be told at the same time, in the hall upstairs I expect.'

Iris had been right; there must be something seriously wrong if Sir Charles was going to make an announcement to the servants.

'Now you won't forget what I told you, will you?'

'No, I won't forget. I'll find him, miss, don't you worry.'

85

I went out, shivering in the cold wind and feeling it sharply after the heat of the kitchen. The bicycle was black and a bit rusty but it wheeled all right as I took it through the gate. I had some difficulty in getting my leg over the crossbar and had to hoist my skirts up above my knees to manage it, then as I started to peddle I wobbled and almost fell off. I set off, slowly at first, then with gathering confidence.

I had told Miss Alice I knew where Weets Cross was; it would have been more accurate if I'd said that I knew of it and vaguely whereabouts it stood, at the point where the townships of Malham, Bordley, Calton and Hanlith met. I did know that it was very old and probably built long ago by the monks, and had a good idea of which direction to take across the moors. Whether I would have found it very easily was something I was not destined to discover for I had not been cycling for more than a few minutes when a car swept by on the narrow road and I swerved, lost control of the bike and ended up in a heap in the shallow ditch.

'I'm so very sorry. Are you hurt?'

I looked up to see the man's anxious face bending over me and recognized him at once. He offered his hand; I accepted and was hauled out and brushed down with efficient concern.

'It was all my fault,' Gerald Simpson apologized again. 'I was in a bit of a mood and not looking where I was going – are you really all right?'

'Yes, sir.' I smiled at him forgivingly. 'You've saved me a journey. I was on my way to give you this letter from Miss Alice . . .'

'A letter from Alice!' He seized my arm. 'She's not ill, is she?'

'Please, sir,' I said, disengaging myself. 'You were hurting me.' I shook my head as he started to apologize. 'It doesn't matter. Miss Alice is all right but there's a bit of bother up at the house . . .'

'What sort of bother?' His eyes narrowed as he ripped the letter open, then a look of relief came into his face. 'For a moment I thought . . . but it's all right. It's just family business. She's going to meet me next week.'

'That's all right then.'

'You know what's going on, don't you?' He studied me in silence for a moment. 'Alice said you were to be trusted. Will you give her a message for me?'

'Yes, sir, of course.'

'Tell her I'll be here next week – but if she doesn't meet me then, I shall come and get her.'

Alice intercepted me on the way back to the kitchen. 'You were quick so you must have met him,' she murmured, more to herself than me. 'Thank goodness you stopped him. I daren't think what might have happened if he had arrived unannounced. Charles is in such a mood . . . '

'He was on his way. And in a hurry! We almost collided and I landed in a ditch.'

'Goodness!' Alice was concerned. 'Are you hurt?'

'Not a bit . . . well, I may have a bruise or two in the morning but nothing to bother about.'

'I'm terribly sorry, Nellie.'

'So was Mr Gerald but it's all right – don't you want to hear what he said?' Alice nodded. 'He read your letter and looked relieved, then he said he would meet you next week but if you weren't there he was coming to get you.'

A faint colour stained her cheeks. 'Yes, that's what I was afraid of today. He won't take no for an answer this time, not that I intend . . . ' She stopped and blushed, then met my frankly interested gaze. 'I'm going to marry him and nothing will stop me – why should it?'

'Good for you, miss! If I were you I'd marry him, too.'

Alice laughed, all embarrassment gone. 'He is nice, isn't he?'

'Yes, miss.'

'Well, I'd better let you get back to your work or Cook will be upset. I may pop into the servants' hall this evening just to say hello to everyone. I have a few small gifts for you all.'

I continued into the kitchens, feeling that it would be a shame if anything happened to stop Miss Alice marrying her sweetheart.

The pace increased as the day wore on and Cook was

working at furious speed, the sweat trickling down her face as she basted the birds and turned the spit-roasted meat, beat cream and egg whites to stiff peaks, then shaped fantastic puddings into works of art; but at last the family had been served, the tables set in the servants' hall and the food for our special meal cooked to perfection.

Mr Sands and Mrs Jermyns had joined the others for this rare occasion; the gardeners had come with their wives and children, helping to fill every space around the long table as the turkey, goose and roast beef were carried in triumph to the white-covered board and carved by Mr Sands with every bit as much ceremony as he had shown upstairs earlier in the evening and a good deal more enthusiasm.

I'd thought I would be too tired to eat this late in the evening, but my spirits suddenly revived as I smelt the delicious turkey with its special chestnut stuffing which was piled high on my plate together with crisply roasted potatoes, sprouts, buttered carrots and deliciously piquant red currant jelly. 'More tasty than cranberry,' Mrs Jones declared as she doled out yet another spoonful.

There was Yorkshire pudding with gravy on a side plate for those who could find room for it, and several other vegetables, but with the promise of the Christmas pudding and brandy butter to follow, I decided that I'd already been given more than enough. It was truly a feast and equal to anything that had been carried upstairs earlier.

We were eating and drinking for well over an hour before anyone thought of making a move. Henry suggested we have a bit of a sing song or a dance but his words were greeted with a chorus of moans and refusals: no one had the energy after such a feast. But when Mr Sands offered to tell us a story it was received with pleasure. He had a strong deep voice that could take on a chilling resonance when he chose, and his story, most suitably, was one that made the blood run cold, being of ghosts haunting the Dales on a Christmas Eve long ago.

'And there he lay, the finest of young men, cut down in the full bloom of his youth, his face as white and pure as the snow that was falling softly over the moors . . . Never again would he see the sunrise or the swallows skimming over the lake for he had dared to look on the face of the White Lady, and death was the price for his folly . . . '

You could have heard a pin drop in the kitchen as he finished his tale and the sound of a voice asking if she could come in made one of the children scream out in fear.

' 'Tis 'er! 'Tis the White Lady,' he cried, and everyone turned to stare at Alice in her floating white silk gown, their mouths dropping open in shock until they began to laugh at their own fear.

'Why, Mrs Jermyns,' Cook teased. 'You look as if you've seen a ghost!'

'Well, who wouldn't?' she said. 'After such a tale. You've frightened the life out of us, Mr Sands – but it was a good story.'

'Have I come at a bad moment?' Alice asked, looking puzzled. When she was told she had missed Mr Sands's story she laughed and said she would have come sooner if she had known.

She had brought a basket of gifts with her, and handed them out, forgetting no one. It was clearly her habit for no one seemed surprised, though Iris whispered to me that there would be no presents if it were left to the master and mistress.

'It's Miss Alice buys them herself and with her own money,' she whispered. 'We'll see a difference here next Christmas – that's if we're here at all.'

The presents were all very similar: handkerchiefs and scarfs for the men, sweet-smelling soaps, stockings and gloves for the ladies. I unwrapped my first pair of real silk stockings and exclaimed in delight.

'I've never had any silk stockings before. Thank you, Miss Alice, it's very good of you.'

Alice smiled and shook her head. 'They are just a small token of my gratitude to you – to all of you,' she said, then her voice dropped slightly as she leaned closer. 'Lucas has a gift for you but he says he will give it to you tomorrow – when you sit for him.'

I nodded but didn't say anything. When I turned round Doris was watching with an angry, suspicious stare. I glanced away, determined not to let her jealousy spoil what had been

89

a perfect evening, and then I saw that Alice had held up her hand for silence. An odd hush fell over the servants' hall as she began to speak.

'I wish that I did not have to say this at such a time . . . ' She paused as we all looked at her expectantly. 'But you must be aware that there have been changes – and that more changes are to come. Sir Charles will speak to you all in the morning at nine o'clock.'

'You can't tell us anything more?' Mr Sands asked. 'I'm sure you know we are all very anxious, Miss Alice.'

'Yes, of course. As far as I know no definite decisions have been made as yet, but I can't tell you more than that. My brother will speak to you in the morning.' And with that she was gone, leaving us to look at one another in apprehension.

Mrs Jones broke the silence at last. 'We'll carry the dishes into the scullery,' she said in a tone of authority, 'but there'll be no washing up tonight. It can wait for the morning. I don't know about the rest of you but I'm for my bed.'

Her words were the signal for the party to break up. Everyone drifted away, most helping to take a few of the dirty plates into the scullery before they departed.

Doris and I piled as many as we could into the sink to let them soak overnight. I was so tired I felt I would drop if I didn't soon get to bed, but Doris stood in my way, her eyes glittering with malice.

'You'll be the first to go,' she said viciously. 'You see if I'm not right.'

'At the moment I couldn't care less one way or the other,' I said. 'Good night, Doris – oh, and Happy Christmas . . . '

Doris's sharply indrawn breath was like the hissing of a snake but I was too tired to look round.

It was a very solemn group who gathered in the main hall the following morning. Everyone looked gloomy, obviously anticipating the worst when Sir Charles arrived several minutes later than expected.

I sought in vain for some resemblance between him and his son but saw no sign of Lucas's humour or sensitivity in the rather stout, pompous-looking man who appeared to glower down on us as if his difficulties were in some unexplained way our fault.

'You may be aware that certain changes are underway,' Sir Charles announced into the hushed silence. 'Because of Lady Amelia's delicate health we have decided to entertain less . . . this means a new direction in our lives. We shall close the London house for the time being and live here quietly.'

Mr Sands gave a discreet cough and drew a forbidding glance from his master. 'Will that mean more changes to the staff, sir?'

'Yes.' Sir Charles looked annoyed at the interruption. 'Nothing has been decided as yet, but if anyone has thought of leaving us for another position now would be a suitable moment. Otherwise . . . you will be informed of our decision within the next two weeks.' His dark eyes swept arrogantly over us. 'That will be all for the time being.'

He walked away, leaving us to stare at each other in dismay. A sign from Mr Sands prevented us from speaking until we were gathered in the kitchen once more.

'And what does that mean?' Iris was the first to voice what was in everyone's mind.

Mr Sands gave her a long, hard look, then gathered his dignity about him. 'It means that we've been given a chance to sort it out for ourselves,' he said. 'If some of us leave voluntarily the rest may be able to stay on – at least for a while.'

'But who should go?' Janet asked. 'It won't be that easy to find another job as good as this one, not around here anyway.'

It was so unusual for Janet to speak out that everyone stared at her, making her blush.

'It should be last in, first out,' Doris said and looked pointedly at me.

'I think we should all sit tight,' Iris announced, a spot of angry colour in her cheeks. 'Let them do their own dirty work – that way we're more likely to get some compensation. This is 1936, not the nineteenth century, and they owe us something for loyalty; there's better pay to be had elsewhere than we've ever had.'

'I agree with you,' Mr Sands said, surprising us all. 'We should wait for a few days, give ourselves a chance to think things over.'

'Very sensible.' Mrs Jermyns put in her pennyworth. 'I have no intention of leaving unless I'm asked – and I would advise you all to take time and reflect what this might mean for yourself and your future.'

I was looking at Cook, who seemed on the point of disagreeing but changed her mind, merely shaking her head and muttering to herself.

'Get on with your work, everyone,' Mrs Jermyns instructed. 'No point in standing around here.'

I went into the scullery to peel potatoes, my thoughts far from happy as I worked. Once I would have been only too glad of the chance to go home, but not now. It was awkward, though. Perhaps I ought to volunteer to be the first to leave? My mother might not exactly welcome me home but I knew Sam would say there was a place for me, at least until I could find more work. Yet I did not want to crawl back with my tail between my legs.

'You're wanted,' Doris said as she came into the scullery. 'Mrs Jones asked for you.'

I could feel her hostility, see the hatred burning in her eyes, and it made me uncomfortable. I wiped my hands and hurried into the kitchen.

Cook was sitting at the long pine table, a book of well-thumbed recipes open in front of her and a frown on her face. I took a deep breath. 'You sent for me?'

She looked up, her expression speculative. 'Have you made up your mind about wanting to be a cook then, Nellie?'

'It's what I should like to do, Mrs Jones, but I don't know if . . . I mean, the way things are . . . '

'I shall leave at the end of next month,' she announced in a tone of absolute conviction. 'It's going to be very different here and it won't suit me to stay. No, it won't suit me at all.'

'But they couldn't possibly manage without you!'

'Mrs Jermyns can cook after a fashion; they'll need her if I go. She's a year or so older than me and it wouldn't be as easy for her to find a new place.'

'But what will you do?' I was shaken. I had thought Cook's position unassailable.

'Join my sister in Bournemouth. When her husband died he left her a nice little sum and she invested it in a small hotel on the sea front. She has been after me for years, wants me to take on the cooking for her guests. I've threatened to leave this place often enough and now I shall. My mind is quite made up.'

It was obvious that there would be no swaying her this time but I could not imagine the kitchen without her. 'I shall be sorry to see you go – but perhaps I'll be gone first.'

'Don't let Doris drive you out, unless ... ' Her eyes were thoughtful as they rested on my face. 'I can't promise anything but there's a chance my sister might take you on.'

'Me – come with you? Do you mean it?'

'It's not a promise but I'll write and ask her – if you like the idea?'

'I should like it very much. Thank you, Mrs Jones.'

'Well, don't count on it but it's a chance. I'll see what I can do.' She closed the book and stood up decisively. 'Now get on with the vegetables. I want those finished before you go to sit for Mr Lucas.'

Doris had gone so I was not forced to endure more sullen stares when I returned to the scullery, and besides the promise of a new job was enough to lift my spirits. I didn't particularly want to leave Beaumont House, but if it was forced on me – as seemed almost certain – at least I wouldn't have to go home.

It was a little later that morning when Iris told me there was someone waiting at the back door to see me.

'To see me?' I echoed, staring at her in bewilderment. 'Who is it?'

'Just you go and find out for yourself.' She gave me a naughty look which sent me hurrying to investigate.

I was surprised when I saw Tom standing there. His hair was slicked back and he was wearing a smart suit that looked almost new.

'What is it?' I asked, my heart catching with fright. 'It's

93

not Sam or Bob, is it? You haven't come to fetch me home, have you?'

He shook his head and held out a bulky object wrapped in a soft cloth. 'This is for you – for Christmas. I couldn't get here before. Still, better late than never.'

'A present?' I gave him an old-fashioned look. 'What is it?'

'Open it and see.'

He thrust it into my hands. It felt hard and lumpy. I hesitated then unwrapped it, giving a gasp of surprise as I saw it was a silver spirit kettle and stand that shone so bright you could see your face in it.

'This looks expensive.'

The suspicion must have shown in my face. Tom laughed, his eyes dancing with a wicked delight.

'It's Sheffield Plate,' he said, 'and a good few years old I shouldn't wonder. Don't worry, Nellie, I didn't steal it. But I didn't pay a fortune for it either.'

'Where did it come from?'

'A farmer out Hanlith way bought a cottage after someone died. He wanted the contents cleared in a hurry and I paid him five pounds for the lot. This was in a cupboard under the stairs, as black as ink. I cleaned it up for you.'

'Maybe you could sell it,' I said doubtfully.

'I made a decent profit on the deal,' Tom said, a look of annoyance in his eyes now. 'I thought you might like it but if you think it's rubbish . . .'

'It's lovely,' I said quickly. 'I've never had anything this pretty, Tom – but you shouldn't have given it to me.'

'I wanted you to have it. It will look nice by the fire when you settle down to a place of your own.'

'Thank you. I'll keep it safe with my things for now.' I hesitated. 'I'd ask you in for a cup of tea and a mince pie but everyone's in a bit of a mood just now.'

'I've business in Hanlith,' he said. 'Tell Mrs Jones I'll be by to see her in the week.'

I watched as he walked off whistling, then rewrapped my kettle and took it back to the kitchen to show Mrs Jones.

'Stop fidgetting!' Lucas commanded, a note of irritation in his voice. 'You're restless today. I suppose it's because of what Father said this morning.' He glared at me. 'You should have more faith, Nellie. Neither Alice nor I would be prepared to see you go. Besides, what you earn wouldn't make the slightest difference.'

'What do you mean, sir? I should be the first to go. I was the last to come here.'

'That is irrelevant,' he said with his usual lordly arrogance. 'If Father really wants to cut his expenses he can get rid of some of the others. We shall hardly need a butler if we are not to entertain.'

'You'll never turn Mr Sands off!' I sounded so shocked that Lucas laughed out loud. 'It's not funny, sir!'

'Such outrage,' he mocked. 'You remind me of a particularly righteous do-gooder my mother sometimes invites to take tea with her in the parlour; they talk for hours about what needs to be done to help the poor – and do nothing.' A smile of pure malice played about his mouth. 'You needn't look at me as if I were a monster, Nellie Pearce. I wouldn't turn any of you off – but my father has other ideas. Please don't blame me for what he chooses to do.'

'I wasn't . . . only . . . only Mr Sands isn't a young man – and you don't understand how hard it is to find work.'

'Anyone who is sacked will be given six months' wages and a good reference. Alice will see to that.' Lucas brushed a strand of dark hair from his brow, transferring a blob of bright yellow paint to his forehead. 'What are you staring at?'

'You've got paint all over your face.'

'An occupational hazard.' He swiped at his forehead, making the smear spread. 'Stop laughing, Nellie! I want that wistful look. You are wasting my time and time is precious.'

'Yes, sir.' I stared out of the window. 'It is sad though, Miss Parkinson going – and her ladyship not well.'

'My mother is as well as she has ever been – and Mabel went because she and Father have disliked one another for years. Father has lost a small fortune on his investments, that's the truth of it. However, we are not quite ruined just yet. Your job is quite safe, Nellie – providing you stop fidgetting!'

'I might go anyway.'

'What did you say?' He was shocked into coming out from behind his easel. I resisted the temptation to laugh at the look of indignation in his eyes. 'I forbid you to think of leaving – at least until I've finished this portrait.'

I gazed out of the window once more. I didn't really want to leave despite the prospect of working for Cook's sister, which would be a step up for me – but perhaps it might be for the best: if I stayed here too long I might forget all the warnings I'd been given, because I liked Mr Lucas a lot in spite of his selfish ways.

'Don't look so sulky,' he said, startling me as he came towards me. He hesitated, then thrust a small parcel at me. 'This is for you – to say thank you.'

'For me?' I stared uncertainly. 'Why? Miss Alice gave me a present yesterday.'

'You've been patient,' he said with a rueful twist of his mouth. 'I'm a terrible tyrant when I'm working. Open it then, see if you like it.'

I undid a small velvet box. Inside on a bed of silk was an oval pendant suspended from a silver chain. It was made of ivory and mounted in a smooth band of silver; when I looked closer I saw that a miniature of me had been painted on the ivory with such tiny, painstaking strokes that my hair and eyelashes looked real and my eyes were emerald green.

'It's lovely,' I said in a hushed voice. 'You – you've made me look beautiful, sir.'

'I'm glad you approve,' he replied, a note of satisfaction in his voice. 'It's a pretty trinket if you like that sort of thing. Put it away and sit still. I want to get on.'

'It's too good. You hadn't ought to have done it, sir. I – I can't take it. It wouldn't be right.'

'Don't be ridiculous!' Lucas glared at me, the scar standing out vividly against his pale skin. 'Most of it was my own work. A friend of mine set it cheaply for me. Besides, most artists pay their models, and it's of no use to me. Take it and stop making so much fuss.'

Mrs Jones had been impressed by Tom's kettle, especially the way he'd made it shine so bright. What she would say about the pendant I didn't know. I wasn't sure that I dare show it to her.

I knew that such a gift between the master's son and a servant was to say the least unusual. It would normally mean that the giver was expecting something in return and its acceptance would convey compliance with those terms, but the situation was not normal – most masters did not paint their servants – and I was sure that Lucas had no hidden motives. When I risked a glance at him he was already back at his easel, lost in his work once more.

Chapter Seven

The following week was uneasy, with everyone going about their work in silence; the happy feeling that had prevailed in the kitchen before Christmas had vanished, leaving a strange emptiness. Cook was the same as always but the others looked at each other in a sullen resentment that made for an uncomfortable atmosphere. I tried talking to Iris about the future but was cut off abruptly every time I mentioned the subject. She was paler than usual and the delicate skin beneath her eyes was brushed with dark violet shadows.

'Do what you want,' she said when I asked what she thought about our situation, 'but I'm not leaving unless they turn me off. I want wages and a reference.'

I felt surprised and a little hurt at her attitude. Something was different about Iris; it wasn't just the prospect of losing her job either, she looked unwell.

'Are you all right?' I asked one morning when we were dressing in the icy cold of our little room. 'You aren't coming down with something, are you? Only you look proper poorly.'

'Mind your own business,' Iris said. 'When I want your opinion I'll ask for it.'

I was startled by the vehemence in her voice. It wasn't like Iris; she was always so cheerful, so ready to gossip or have a laugh.

'I was only asking.'

'Well, don't.' She turned away. 'Go on down if you're ready. I'll follow you in a few minutes.'

She obviously wanted to be alone. I had believed Iris was

98

my friend, but she seemed to have turned against me the way Doris had – or perhaps she was just worried sick.

I remembered Iris talking about how poor her mother was, and how difficult her life had been as a child, and thought I understood her moods. Iris helped to support her family: the prospect of losing her job must be frightening for her, though she had often said in the past that she would like to work in a shop if she ever left the Harringtons' service – but she was certainly upset over something. Perhaps I ought to have told her that I would probably be leaving with Cook at the end of the month. That might have put her mind at rest, since then no one would need to be dismissed. I would have done so except that Mrs Jones had told me to keep it to myself until it was certain.

I went into the kitchen for my breakfast, wanting to make an early start on my chores so that it wouldn't matter if I was kept longer in the studio. Mr Lucas had been working furiously the whole week and he seemed to forget all about the time.

The studio had no clocks but I could always tell when I had been sitting for nearly an hour; my neck began to get stiff and I felt restless.

This particular morning I had been sitting in one position for ages. I moved my legs slightly, taking care not to change my pose and wishing that Mr Lucas would say something; he had been silent throughout the session, seemingly lost in his own thoughts.

The sound of a man shouting, doors banging loudly and then more shouting, startled us both. The loud voices were followed by a scream of anguish and then a long wailing cry that echoed through the house and sent a shiver down my spine.

'What on earth was that?' Lucas dropped his brush as I jumped up; we looked at each other warily. 'That sounded like Mother.'

'It sounds as if someone is in pain . . . ' I broke off as we heard hurried footsteps and then the door was thrust open and Alice burst in, her face ashen.

'You had better come,' she said, looking directly at Lucas.

'I think Charles has had a stroke – and your mother is hysterical. I can't cope with them both.'

'Yes, of course.'

Lucas set off at a run, his palette abandoned on the floor. I hesitated, then started forward as Alice turned to follow him.

'Is there anything I can do, miss?'

'Yes.' Alice passed a hand over her face, obviously feeling flustered. 'Ask Henry to come up to Sir Charles's study at once. We shall need help getting my brother to bed – and someone must summon the doctor. Charles has suffered a stroke . . . ' Her voice caught with emotion. 'It's my fault. Gerald came and – and there was the most terrible row . . . '

'Oh, no, miss,' I cried, sensing that she needed to communicate, that she was barely holding back the tears. 'But that wasn't your fault. If they quarrelled . . . '

'Wasn't it?' Alice's face was pale and strained. 'I knew how Charles felt about Gerald but I deliberately went ahead and met him. I led him to believe I was going to marry him . . . '

'But you are – you love him!'

'Love?' Alice gave me a bleak look. 'How can love prevail against duty and guilt?' she asked. 'I must go now. Tell Henry to hurry.'

We went our separate ways. I met Henry on the stairs. He had heard from Iris that something was going on and guessed he might be needed; my urgent message sent him speeding past me. Iris was already in the kitchen, spreading the news of what had happened to Cook, Mr Sands and Mrs Jermyns.

'Miss Alice asked if you would telephone for the doctor.' I gasped out the words. 'Sir Charles has had a stroke and they want the doctor quickly.'

'Troubles never come singly,' Mrs Jermyns said in a tone of dire warning. 'We might have expected this.'

'What's been going on?' Iris demanded as soon as the housekeeper had departed to make the phone call. 'I know there was a row. I could hear them shouting and carrying on something awful in the study, then someone started screaming.'

100

'I think that was Lady Amelia,' I said. 'Miss Alice said she was having hysterics.'

'A dreadful thing,' Mr Sands said, and shook his head. 'Excuse me. I shall go and see if I can be of assistance to Miss Alice. Mark my words, it will all fall on her shoulders now. I wouldn't put it past him to have done it on purpose.'

'What did he mean by that?' I looked at Cook as he went out. 'No one can bring on a stroke on purpose, can they?'

'Of course not. He just meant that Sir Charles would do anything to prevent Miss Alice leaving with her sweetheart.'

'It's a rotten shame, that's what I think,' Iris said. 'She won't leave now. She'll think it her duty to stay here and look after things, you see if I'm not right.'

I had thought Miss Alice's secret was known only to me, but I might have guessed it was impossible to keep a thing like that dark in this house; they all seemed to know what was going on almost as soon as it happened.

'She won't really have to give him up, will she?'

'They've always put on her, the whole lot of them,' Cook said. 'I wouldn't blame her if she went off and left them to it – but she won't, of course. She'll stay and do her duty just as Iris said.'

'Poor Miss Alice.' I smelt something burning and turned round. 'Is that your tripe and onions boiling over, Mrs Jones?'

Cook gave a cry of alarm and dived at the stove. I watched until a small moan made me turn to look at Iris who had gone green, gulped, and placed a hand over her mouth. She made a dash for the scullery where she was violently and loudly sick. She emerged a few minutes later, looking a little ashamed.

'I think I must have eaten something that disagreed with me,' she said, and her eyes slid away from Cook's. 'I've cleared up, Nellie. I think I'll go out for a breath of air – it was the smell of the tripe that set me off.'

'You do that,' Cook called after her. 'Don't come back until you're feeling better.'

'She hasn't seemed well for a day or so. I asked her if she was coming down with something but she didn't want to talk about it this morning,' I said as Iris went out.

101

'I'm not surprised. Get on with your work, Nellie – though whether they'll be wanting anything much to eat upstairs this evening is another question. Mrs Jermyns is right, troubles never come singly. We shall have more before long, you see if I'm not right.'

I fetched a bucket of hot soapy water to scrub out the pantry; I did the scullery, too, thinking I could still smell the slightly acrid odour of Iris's vomit. I felt sorry for her being sick like that. It must be all the worry over whether or not she was going to lose her job.

The tension increased as the day wore on. No one knew quite what was going on, though Alice sent Henry down to say they would need only a light supper of sandwiches and soup.

'How is the master?' Cook asked when he came into the kitchen. 'What did the doctor say – was it a stroke?'

'Yes, he thinks so,' Henry said, 'though a mild one by the sound of it. Sir Charles seems to have a weakness down his right side . . . can't move that arm or leg at the moment . . . but it hasn't affected his senses. He knew what he was saying before they gave him a sedative all right.' Henry pulled a face. 'He didn't want it but the doctor insisted that he had to rest.'

'Is he sleeping now?'

'Thankfully,' Henry said, and looked odd. 'He won't be best pleased if he's to be confined to a wheelchair.'

'Will it come to that?' Cook asked. 'These things get better sometimes, don't they?'

'The doctor told Miss Alice it would be a long job; he'll need looking after – someone to haul him about, wash and dress him . . .'

'She can't do that, poor lass,' Cook objected. 'He's much too heavy for her.'

'I can manage him,' Henry said, a self-conscious note in his voice. 'Miss Alice spoke to me, said she hoped I wasn't thinking of leaving.'

'No, they'll need you now more than ever,' Cook agreed and shook her head. 'Looks as if your job is safe at any rate.'

Henry's neck reddened. 'Well, it's a good place for me.

I've been thinking I ought to offer to go but . . . well, now it looks as if the choice has been made for me.'

'Yes, it does. I suppose that means Mr Sands will be leaving then. They won't be entertaining much for a while, that's certain now. Poor Miss Alice, she'll have it all to do. Lady Amelia won't cope without her, I'd bet my bottom dollar on that.' The Americanism slipped from her lips unconsciously, making Henry grin to himself. We all knew of Cook's passion for gangster films. 'It just isn't fair on her!'

Cook turned away to beat the eggs she was whisking for an omelette with sudden ferocity and a hushed silence fell over the kitchen. Miss Alice was everyone's favourite and we all thought much as Cook did.

As the days passed it was clear to everyone that Alice had accepted the burden pressed upon her shoulders. Sir Charles was confined to bed and Henry told worrying tales of his irascible moods, of his impatience and frustration at being an invalid.

'Like a bear with a sore head, he is,' Henry declared. 'Not that he's too bad with me – it's Miss Alice he takes his spite out on. He's on to her from the minute she comes into his room until the second she leaves – but she never says a word back to him, just takes it all and smiles as nice as you like. Apologizes for him, says we have to be patient with him. If I were her, I'd be off like a shot – but what can she do?'

It was the considered opinion of us all below stairs that Miss Alice was being put upon shamefully.

Lady Amelia had retired to her own bed, declaring that she was too ill to be disturbed, which meant that Alice was left to cope with her brother's temper, her sister-in-law's vapours, and the running of the house. Her ladyship seemed to have taken a liking to Janet who had assumed many of the jobs that had formerly been Miss Parkinson's, leaving Iris to do the heavier chores in the rest of the house – which didn't improve her temper.

I caught glimpses of Alice as I passed her on my way to the studio now and then; I noticed the dark shadows beneath her eyes and felt sympathetic towards her but was afraid to say anything. An air of oppression hung over the house as everyone wondered what was going to happen next.

Alice asked to talk to Cook a few days after Sir Charles's stroke. Mrs Jones went up to the parlour, where she was invited to sit down – and to change her mind about leaving.

'She told me there was no need for me to leave and that she would personally guarantee my wages,' Cook told us over a plate of macaroons and a pot of best Indian tea. 'But I've given my word to my sister now and I shan't go back on it.'

One by one all the servants were invited to a meeting with Alice. Mr Sands was given a year's wages and told very regretfully that his services were no longer required; he would, however, be given an excellent reference and Miss Alice would do all she could to help him find another position.

'She's a lady, that's what she is,' he declared to Mrs Jones later that same afternoon when we were gathered for our tea in the kitchen. 'I'm not sorry to be leaving after the way things have turned out – but I feel sorry for her, having all this to put up with.'

'It's a proper shame,' Cook said, looking upset and crumbling a sticky coconut twirl between her fingers. 'She'll never get another chance to escape, and it's not right. It's not right, Mr Sands.'

I didn't say anything but I thought it was unfair. Why should Alice have to give up her chance of happiness for someone who had never been kind to her?

The rest of us were summoned in turn and told we were assured of a place if we wished to continue our service. One of the gardeners had already found himself a better job with the large Fountains estate which owned so much of the land in the area, and he departed with his family an hour or so after his interview.

I was invited to Miss Alice's small sitting room last of all. I stood outside the door tucking my hair beneath my cap and trying to quell the butterflies in my stomach. Everyone else had been asked to stay on, but I was still nervous about my own position.

'Ah, Nellie, come in, please.' Alice was standing by the window, a sad, wistful expression in her eyes as she turned to greet me. 'You must be wondering what is happening . . . '

I advanced towards her, shocked by how pale she was, by the new hollows in her cheeks and the dark violet shadows beneath her eyes: she looked as if she hadn't slept for days.

'How is your brother, miss?'

'A little better, thank you.' Alice smiled and motioned me to sit down. 'I left you to the last, Nellie, because I wanted to be sure how things were. It seems that almost everyone has decided to stay with us . . . '

'Except Cook and Mr Sands.'

Alice nodded and sighed. 'I'm afraid I was forced to let Mr Sands go,' she said. 'He would be wasted in this house now. I am prepared to pay for the services of the people I need but not to keep up a state we shall not require. And Mrs Jones has made her own choice. I can't compel her to stay on if she doesn't want to, Nellie.'

'No, of course not. I shouldn't have criticized you, miss – not you, when you've been so good to everyone.'

Alice made a negative movement with her hand. 'It was selfish of me not to have done something earlier,' she said. 'But I thought I should not be living here for very much longer.'

'Have you made up your mind to stay then?' I asked, and when she was silent, 'It's a crying shame, miss, that's what it is.'

'Yes.' For a moment Alice's mouth trembled, but she lifted her head, fighting tears. 'I don't have much choice, I'm afraid. The doctor tells me that another stroke could kill my brother.'

'But that isn't your fault! Surely you have a right to be happy, the same as everyone else?'

'I should have taken my chance years ago,' she said. 'Now there is too much in the way. I couldn't be happy if I deserted my family when they need me. Amelia is lost without Charles. She will become an invalid and stay in bed for the rest of her life if I let her. And Charles . . . ' A flicker of pain passed across Alice's face. 'I blame myself for what happened. He was already under a terrible strain and I allowed Gerald to tell him I was leaving.'

'So you were going with him then? And then they

quarrelled and it happened . . . that was what the shouting was about?'

'Yes. Lucas said you heard some of it.'

'Not the words, miss,' I reassured her. 'Only the banging and the noise of her ladyship carrying on.'

'Yes.' She sighed, her shoulders seeming to droop for a moment, then she straightened up and looked at me. 'Mrs Jones tells me that there's a chance you might be offered work with her. Shall you like that?'

I thought I caught a note of disappointment in Alice's voice and hesitated: I ought to go, make the break now while there was still time, but I couldn't bear to see the sadness in her face or to think that I might be contributing to the burden she must carry.

'I'd rather stay with you, miss,' I said, 'if you'll have me, that is?'

'Oh, Nellie, I'm so pleased.' The shadows seemed to lighten and Alice's smile was almost back to normal. 'I'm going to need someone to help me get through all this – and we've become friends, haven't we? I feel that we have, don't you?'

'Oh, yes, miss! You know I'll do anything for you. Anything . . . '

'From time to time I might want you to take a message for me.' Alice's pale face was suddenly flushed with colour. 'I've heard from Gerald, you see. He – he refuses to give up and I – I should like to meet him occasionally if I can.'

'You know I'll do whatever you ask, miss.'

'It won't be very often.' Alice had begun to look guilty again. 'I can't leave while Charles is in a wheelchair and Amelia is ill but . . . just to see him now and then, that isn't so very wrong of me, is it?'

'No, miss, it isn't wrong at all. I'll take a message for you whenever you like.'

There was a companionable silence between us for a moment, then Alice seemed to come to herself.

'And now to something much nicer,' she said. 'Lucas wants you to sit for him for the rest of the day. He says he will finish the portrait by then – isn't that exciting?'

I looked at her doubtfully. 'When is he going to let us see it – see both of them?'

'When they are finished,' she replied. 'Perhaps this evening or tomorrow. He wants to finish today because he is leaving for London in the morning and the paintings must go with him.'

'Mr Lucas is going to London?' My heart felt as if it had suddenly been squeezed tight, making me breathless. 'Will he be gone long, miss?'

'I shouldn't think so,' she replied. 'I can hardly believe that he has agreed to a show at all; only a few months ago he was still refusing even to speak to his friends.' Her eyes seemed to linger on me for a moment. 'But I suppose it depends on how successful the show is. He used to spend most of his time in London, before the accident . . . '

'It would be best for him if he stayed there with his friends and became successful, wouldn't it, miss?'

'Yes, I believe so,' Alice agreed, 'though of course we should miss him.'

'Yes, miss. You would be lonely without him, wouldn't you?'

'Lucas must live his own life. All I want is for him to be happy.' Alice ran her fingers over the polished surface of the table in front of her. 'I'm glad you have decided to stop with us. Run along now, Nellie. You mustn't keep Lucas waiting.'

Alice was once more staring out of the window as I left and made my way to the studio, which was south-facing and in the main body of the house. I hadn't realized that Lucas was going away so soon and it made me feel as wistful as Miss Alice had looked a few minutes earlier. I was going to miss the times I had spent with him, even though it was uncomfortable to sit for so long and I was sometimes ignored for most of the session. Of course once the paintings were finished it was bound to end anyway, and perhaps that was for the best.

I should be very foolish to let myself like Mr Lucas too much.

I woke shivering in the night as I heard a muffled cry from the girl beside me. Sensing that something was terribly wrong I put out a hand to touch Iris and encountered a patch of something warm and sticky.

107

'Iris – have you been sick again?' I reached for the lamp beside me but her hand clasped my wrist. 'Iris, what's wrong?'

'Don't put the light on just yet, Nellie.'

'Why?'

'I haven't been sick – it's blood. I've had a – a miscarriage.'

For a moment I was so shocked that I wasn't sure I'd heard her right. Iris had had a miscarriage! I hadn't even guessed that she was pregnant – but I should have when she was sick like that. No wonder she had been so touchy recently.

I lit the lamp beside the bed; its light threw a pale sheen over Iris's white face. I pushed back the blankets and saw the dark crimson stain on the sheets; the blood had soaked them, Iris's nightdress and my own.

'Oh, Iris,' I whispered, feeling sick and shaken. 'What made it happen?'

'I took hot gin and sat in a hot bath.' She looked at me with fear in her eyes. 'Someone told me what to do. I know it was wicked of me but when Miss Alice said we could stay on I had to do something. I was praying they would turn me off and give me six months' wages. I could have gone away then and no one the wiser.'

'What are we going to do about this?' I threw back the blankets. 'If Mrs Jermyns finds out . . . '

'She'll send me packing and there'll be no wages.'

'Miss Alice wouldn't let her.'

'Wouldn't she?' Iris sounded bitter. 'You don't seem to realize what I've done. I've broken all the rules, Nellie. Even Miss Alice would turn against me now . . . ' A sob broke from her and she covered her face with her hands in shame.

I stared at her, then climbed out of bed and began to pull on my clothes. 'We've got to get rid of these sheets – and wash our nightgowns.'

'You're not involved,' Iris said. 'Why should you risk your job to help me?'

'Because you're my friend. You would do the same for me, wouldn't you?'

Iris was silent for a moment. 'Perhaps. I don't know . . . '

She caught a sobbing breath. 'I never thought I should be such a fool! I don't know what to do.'

'Let's make a bundle of these. I know where the key to the laundry room is kept; I'll put all these things in the copper in the old soapy water. With any luck most of the blood will soak out. In any case Doris is usually so sleepy first thing that she may not notice – and if she does, what can she prove?'

'But what about our sheets?'

'I'll bring clean ones back and we'll make up the bed. We'll have to wash our nighties in the bowl and dry them up here somehow.' She was so wan and pale that I felt protective of her. Perhaps she had been silly but she was my friend and I didn't want her to get into trouble. 'Don't worry, Iris. We can cover this up and no one need ever know.'

'You're a good friend, Nellie.' Iris blinked away a tear. 'You haven't even asked me who – who it was.' She swallowed hard and looked ashamed.

'That isn't my business. Don't tell me, not unless you want to?' Iris shook her head. 'No, best not. What I don't know I can't be forced to tell.'

'It's better for you if you don't know.' Iris groped for the black iron rail at the bottom of the bed; her face had gone even whiter and she was trembling. 'I feel a bit groggy.'

'Stay here and clean yourself up,' I said. 'I'll bring you a tot of brandy back if I can manage it.'

'Don't get yourself in more trouble,' Iris protested weakly. 'I'll be all right in a few minutes.'

She didn't look as if she would be all right; she looked as if she might collapse at any moment. It was a horrible, frightening experience and neither of us knew what to do.

I gathered the soiled sheets and went to the door, listening for a moment before I opened it and peeped out. It was still very early; there was no one about, nor likely to be for another hour or so.

I ran the full length of the hall, holding my breath lest one of the doors should fly open and someone come out to investigate. I had no idea what I would say if they did or how I would explain the blood-stained bundle I was carrying; my only thought was that I must not let Iris down.

My heart thumped painfully as I walked softly down the stairs; it was darker here but I could just manage to pick my way along a short landing, down more stairs, past Mrs Jermyns's room – oh, lord, don't let her wake up! – down the final staircase and along to the side door. It creaked a bit as I opened it and I paused, my nerves jumping, before I emerged into the icy chill of the yard. My face tingled with the bitter cold as I sprinted the last few feet to the laundry room, found the key on the ledge above the door, fumbled with the lock and then went in, my throat catching as I smelt the damp and the odour of stale soapy water.

The first hint of dawn was beginning to break through as I lifted the lid from one of the big, old-fashioned coppers and discovered that it was still full of soapy water from the day before, a thin film of scum floating on the surface. Doris usually emptied the coppers first thing in the mornings before refilling them with clean water for the new wash. With any luck she would drain the water from the small tap at the bottom without looking inside, then, when she discovered the sheets she might think she had overlooked them the previous day and simply pile others in on top. Even if she was suspicious and found the blood stains she would not know where they had come from.

After pushing the soiled linen well down into the stale, sudsy water, I went to the big airing cupboard behind the boiler and took out two fresh sheets, then relocked the door and ran back to the house, remembering to lock the side door after me. I had done it: we were in the clear! It was only when I reached our room that I remembered the brandy. I went in and thrust the clean linen at Iris, who had managed to dress but still looked ill.

'You did it then?'

'Take these! I'll be back in a minute.' Before Iris could argue I was out again and running for the stairs.

It was when I was on my way back for the second time that I met Doris coming along the upper landing. She was yawning and scratching her neck but a suspicious look came over her face as she saw me, and instinctively I slid one hand behind my back. It was the worst thing I could have done!

'You're up early, Doris.'

'So are you.' She stared at me. 'What have you got there?'

'Nothing – just a glass of water.'

'Liar!' Doris caught my arm, then gave a cry of triumph as she saw what I was hiding. 'You've been stealing brandy. You wait until Mrs Jermyns hears about this!'

'It's for my cold.' I coughed. 'It's only the cooking brandy. Mrs Jones won't mind.'

'We'll see about that,' she replied with a malicious smile. 'You've no right to take that without permission. Stealing's stealing. You'll likely be turned off for this – and a good thing too!'

'Be a tell-tale then,' I muttered. 'The cat will get your tongue, Doris.'

I walked past with as much dignity as I could manage. It was sheer bad luck bumping into her this early. If I'd only remembered the brandy the first time it wouldn't have happened. I could only hope that she wouldn't discover the sheets before the blood had had a chance to soak out.

Lucas had promised to show me the paintings that morning, before he left for London. As I walked into the studio I saw that Alice was already there. She greeted me with a welcoming smile.

'Isn't this exciting?'

'Yes, miss.' I glanced at the pictures, which were covered with large white sheets. 'I can't wait to see them.'

'Well, now you shall.' Lucas took the corners of each sheet in his hands, removing them both with a flourish. 'Innocence and Knowledge – what do you think?'

'Lucas . . . ' Alice breathed. 'I'm impressed, I really am. I've seen your work before and admired it – but it was nothing like these. They have such depth and feeling – and the way you've used colour . . . this is something new, Lucas. You've never painted quite this way before.' She moved to kiss his cheek. 'Congratulations, dearest. I'm sure they will be a success.' She turned to me at last. 'What do you think of them?'

I was staring fixedly at the painting entitled 'Knowledge' and my eyes were bright with tears. How could he? Oh, how could he do this to me? I rounded on Lucas with a spurt of indignant rage.

'You've made me look wicked,' I cried. 'That's not me. I don't look like that.'

'Sometimes you do,' he replied, his brows raised as if surprised by my reaction. 'You can't see yourself as I do – but that look is in your eyes when your thoughts are most private.'

'You didn't ought to have made me look like that . . . sort of wild and wanton,' I said stubbornly. I hated the painting; it was too revealing, too much of an intrusion into my private thoughts – thoughts I had believed I'd kept hidden. 'I look bad . . . like a bad girl, and I'm not. You know I'm not, sir!'

'You look sensual,' Lucas replied, a hint of obstinacy in his face. 'There is a hidden sensuality about you, Nellie.' He sighed and thrust long, sensitive fingers through his hair. 'You may not believe me now but one day . . . '

'Tell him he can't show it!' I appealed to Alice tearfully. 'It isn't me, miss. It isn't me!'

'I think it is you,' she said carefully. 'As Lucas sees you.' She glanced at him as if trying to read his mind, then back at me. 'You don't look wicked, Nellie – just hauntingly beautiful. You can't expect Lucas not to show it, not after all his hard work. Besides, I think it is a compliment. I should like someone to think I looked like that.'

'Someone does,' Lucas remarked softly, his eyes full of warmth and affection as he looked at her. 'You are a fool not to go to him, Alice. Generous, sweet and wonderful, but a fool just the same. You shouldn't let my father win.'

'It isn't just Charles. Please don't say any more,' she begged, her eyes moist with tears. 'We've been through this so many times. I couldn't leave while Amelia needs me and Charles might have another stroke.'

'Alice . . . '

They had forgotten me. It was as if I wasn't even there. I remembered Cook's warning and felt angry – angry and hurt. They both used me when they wanted me but neither of them cared that I had been hurt.

Chapter Eight

I was scrubbing the back stairs with a bar of strong-smelling yellow soap when Doris came to tell me that Mrs Jermyns wanted to see me in her sitting room. The look in Doris's eyes was so triumphant that my heart plummeted all the way down to my black, lace-up shoes. I was in trouble now: she must have told about the brandy I'd taken.

'You'll catch it,' she hissed as I got up off my knees. 'Putting on airs as if you were better than the rest of us – see where it gets you now, Nellie Pearce!'

I ignored her taunts, but my heart was beating faster than normal as I took my bucket to the kitchen, emptied it and then made my way up to the housekeeper's room. Her wireless was playing loud orchestral music. I hesitated outside, licking my lips nervously before knocking. I had to knock twice before the wireless was switched off and a voice told me to come in.

Mrs Jermyns gave me an old-fashioned look as I entered. She was wearing a dull brown dress that made her look more than usually colourless and her hair was dragged back into a severe knot at the back.

'Ah, Nellie – this is a serious matter, you know. Very serious indeed.'

The room was larger than Miss Alice's but furnished with heavy dark wood pieces and the fabrics were faded into indistinguishable, sludgy colours. On the sideboard I saw a collection of photographs in cheap frames and there was a large, fairly new wireless on a table near the fireplace, but little else to give it any comfort or cheer.

'I'm waiting for an explanation.'

I swallowed hard, then raised my eyes to meet her icy stare. 'I'm sorry, Mrs Jermyns,' I said, 'but it was only the cooking brandy and I thought I had a cold coming on.'

'Oh, the brandy ... ' Mrs Jermyns nodded. 'That was wrong of you, to take it without asking – but this other matter is much, much worse. I'm disappointed in you. Very disappointed. I thought you were coming along well and now you've let us down.'

'I – I don't know what you mean ... ' I replied but my voice sounded guilty even to my own ears and my heart had begun to pound. Doris must have found the sheets and put two and two together!

'I think you do,' Mrs Jermyns said, becoming even more stern. 'Doris saw you coming upstairs very early this morning and then she found a pair of blood-stained sheets in the copper. She also discovered that two sheets had been taken from the airing cupboard and naturally she thought it her duty to inform me of these discoveries ... ' There was an ominous silence during which I seemed to hear the beating of my own heart. 'What can you tell me about any of this, Nellie?'

'Nothing.' I looked her in the eyes but knew that my cheeks were bright red. I had never been able to tell lies and now I wanted to sink through the floor. 'I just went down for the brandy, that's when I met Doris on the way back.'

'If you felt like telling me the truth I would try to help you. But lying will not save you, Nellie. I have no patience with liars, none at all.'

I was silent. There was nothing I could say without betraying Iris's secret and I was determined not to do that. It was my fault Doris had found the sheets. If she hadn't met me coming back with the brandy she wouldn't have been suspicious.

'I am not lying,' I said in a whisper. 'There's nothing I can tell you, Mrs Jermyns.'

'I shall give you one more chance to tell me the truth, Nellie.'

I hung my head and said nothing. I was very uncomfortable and a little frightened but I couldn't have spoken if my life depended on it.

'Very well, you leave me no alternative.' Mrs Jermyns went to her cupboard and took something out, bringing it back to thrust it accusingly under my nose. 'I believe this belongs to you?'

I glanced at my own nightgown; the pale blue winceyette was marked with dark brown stains that were obviously blood. Suddenly, I realized what Mrs Jermyns must be thinking and I went cold all over. She couldn't think that of me! She couldn't – but the expression on her face told me that she could and did.

'Yes, it is mine – but it isn't what you imagine.'

'And what do you think I am imagining? I have seen those sheets, Nellie. Bloodstains like that are not from a normal period. I am not a fool and I know that someone has suffered a miscarriage. Was it you?'

So there was still some doubt in her mind. She was a harsh woman but not without a sense of justice: all she wanted was the truth.

I looked at the floor, wishing it would open and swallow me up. This was awful but I could not betray Iris now; it had been my idea to put the sheets in the laundry and it was my fault that Doris had become suspicious. If I hadn't gone back for the brandy we might just have got away with it – now we should probably both be dismissed.

A clock was ticking loudly on the mantelpiece and a log hissed and crackled on the fire. My mouth was dry as I tried to find something to say and failed.

'I'm waiting for your answer, Nellie.' I remained silent and the housekeeper made a sound of distress deep in her throat. 'So you refuse to answer me? Very well, I shall speak to Miss Alice about this . . . '

'I haven't done anything wrong!' The words were torn out of me at last.

'I think you may have been used,' Mrs Jermyns said. 'But we shall see what Miss Alice has to say. In the meantime you may go back to your work.'

My eyes were stinging as I walked from the room. I felt resentful and angry. It was so unfair of Mrs Jermyns to

115

accuse me of having had a miscarriage! She was a suspicious, mean-minded woman . . . and yet she had given me a chance to speak out in my own defence, but I couldn't. I wasn't sure whether it was loyalty or stubbornness that had held me silent, perhaps a bit of both. She ought not to have needed to ask!

I wasn't a bad girl, why did they all seem to think I was? After the picture Mr Lucas had painted they would all think I'd been doing something I ought not to and the blood stains on my nightgown seemed to prove their suspicions. Of course I could have saved myself if I'd told the truth but that would have meant instant dismissal for Iris. Besides, they should all have known that I wouldn't do anything like that . . . the unfairness of it pricked at me like a thorn and I set my mouth stubbornly. Let them send me away in disgrace if they liked, I wasn't going to beg or plead for my job. If they couldn't trust me then I didn't care, I would leave rather than betray my friend.

I was so angry that when I got to the kitchen I walked straight past and out of the house, not bothering with a coat. It was freezing outside, the ground white with frost, but I didn't notice and wouldn't have cared if I had. I was burning with indignation.

I walked and walked, not bothering where I was going. A bitter wind was blowing over the moors, which seemed to stretch endlessly in all directions, and had never looked more bleak, but I was too miserable to be interested in my surroundings. No one cared about me so I might as well be dead.

How long I walked I have no idea. My thoughts were as bitter as the inclement weather. I was the unwanted child of a rapist, my mother hated me – and Mr Lucas had painted that terrible picture. How he must have laughed! The expression on my face was that of a wistful young girl in love – and who else could I be in love with but the man who had painted me?

If Miss Alice had cared about my feelings she would have told him he couldn't show the picture – and Mrs Jermyns had such a low opinion of me that she thought I had suffered a miscarriage.

It was almost dusk when I sat down in the shelter of some rocks; I brought my knees up to my chest, leant my arms on them and bowed my head, then, all at once, I started to sob. Heartbroken, wracking sobs that shook my whole body.

I cried for a long time, until I was exhausted, then I curled up on the ground like an unborn child in its mother's womb, huddling into myself and my misery – and slept.

It was dark when I woke. My body ached from the cold and I was shivering, my teeth chattering. The anger and self-pity that had driven me out on to the moors had gone and now I was frightened.

I stood up and looked about me, trying to peer through the gloom which was broken only by a sprinkling of stars: my fear intensified as I realized I was lost. I had no idea which way to go or how far I had wandered from the house.

Gradually my eyes became accustomed to the dark and I could see shapes and patches that were lighter than others. Which way should I go? I had come towards the rocks so I should walk away from them – but to the left or the right?

From somewhere nearby I heard the call of a nightbird; it was strange and scary in the loneliness of the moors and I screamed in terror as a grey shape rose from the ground in front of me, the broad wings of an owl beating in slow rhythmic motion as it rose into the sky.

I started to run, blindly, wildly, in a panic. I was lost . . . lost in a wilderness and no one would find me. I should die alone on these moors in such bitter weather and suddenly I wanted to live. I wanted to live! I wasn't going to let them beat me. I would go away and become a famous cook and show them all! I would show them all – and especially Lucas . . . He had laughed at me but he wouldn't laugh when I was rich and famous!

Anger returned and with it my courage. I stopped running and told myself to calm down. I would just keep on walking and in time I would come to a farmhouse or . . .

'Nellie . . . Nellie . . . '

What was that? I had heard a cry so faint that I couldn't be sure. It had sounded like someone calling my name – but it couldn't be. No one knew I was out here . . . no one cared . . . but yes, there it was again . . . I spun round towards the source of the sound and saw something . . . a flickering light. It was a lantern . . . they were looking for me . . . someone had organized a search party.

'Nellie . . . Nellie . . . ' the same voice called over and over again, impatient, demanding . . . desperate? 'Nellie . . . where the hell are you? Nellie . . . '

'Over here! I'm over here!'

I walked quickly towards that flickering light, my heart lifting. Mrs Jones must have reported me missing. I had forgotten her . . . she would have been concerned when I didn't return . . . she liked me . . . yes, *she* would have wondered where I was.

'Nellie!'

I was close enough now to see that the lantern was being held by a tall man. It must be Henry . . . and yet I knew it was not. How could it be Mr Lucas? He had gone to London . . . and yet it *was* him. I knew instinctively that it was him.

'I'm here.'

He came towards me, nearer and nearer, his strides long and hurried, covering the ground between us more swiftly than I would have thought possible – and then I could see his face in the yellow glow of the lantern. He was furious! My knees began to knock and I was frightened again but for a very different reason from the one that had made me panic earlier.

'What on earth do you think you're doing?' he demanded. 'You stupid little fool! Wandering out here on a night like this, and with no coat – don't you know you could have died in this weather?'

I felt very foolish and blinked in the light of his lantern. 'I . . . I'm sorry,' I whispered. 'I was upset and I didn't think.'

He grabbed my arm, holding me as he looked down at my face. 'You've been crying – not about that painting? You're not such a fool. I won't show it if you hate it that much.'

'No . . . ' I swallowed hard. 'It wasn't just about that.'

'All this nonsense over the sheets then.' He glared down at me and his fingers bit into my flesh as he held on to me. 'Do you know I've missed my train to London because of you? And I had appointments! Jack had arranged for me to meet

118

some important clients in the morning and I've had to cancel.'

'Who – who is Jack?' My teeth were still chattering but not from the cold.

'Jack Henderson. He's my agent and a good friend, and worked hard to set up those meetings. Now he'll have to do it all over again – and that's your fault.'

'I'm sorry, sir.'

I was ashamed now and close to tears again.

'And so I should think.' He shook me hard, then wrapped a thick blanket around my shoulders. 'You deserve a good spanking, Nellie, do you know that?'

'Yes, sir.'

'It's lucky for you that I'm the one who found you,' he said. 'Mrs Jermyns has been having hysterics and the rest of the household is in uproar.'

'I – I didn't mean to upset anyone.'

'Didn't you?' His eyes narrowed. 'I think that's just what you did mean – to teach us all a lesson. To teach me a lesson – wasn't that what you wanted, Nellie?'

'Perhaps . . . I'm not sure.'

He nodded, his expression relaxing. 'That's what I thought. Well, you have – so you can come home now and get yourself warm.'

His stride lengthened and I struggled to keep up with him. What did he mean? Had it really upset him because I had been lost on the moors for a few hours?

As we approached the edge of the moors I saw a small group of men gathered together with lanterns and torches. A buzz went through them as they saw us and one man moved towards us: it was Tom Herries and his expression seemed to me to be a mixture of relief and anger.

'Are you all right?' he asked harshly. 'You've given us all a scare. What made you do it?'

To hear almost the same words from his lips as those Lucas had hurled at me was too much. 'It's none of your business,' I replied in a sharper tone than I ought. 'I don't know why you're here, Tom Herries.'

Lucas glanced at me with a frown. 'It was your friend who insisted on the search when he realized you'd been gone

119

several hours,' he said. 'If he hadn't caught me I should have been on my way to London. You should thank him, Nellie.'

My cheeks were flaming. I'd been embarrassed enough when I'd seen all those curious eyes staring at me and now I wished I could crawl away under a stone. Lucas had found me but it was Tom who had made him organize the search party.

'I'm sorry,' I said, hardly daring to glance at him. 'I'm a bit upset.'

'Aye, I can see that.' Tom nodded to Lucas. 'Thank you, sir. I'm obliged for your help.'

He walked away, his shoulders stiff and square. I longed to call after him but Lucas had hold of my arm as he hurried me towards the house.

'Alice will never forgive me if you catch cold,' he said. 'Though it might teach you a lesson if you did.'

Of course it hadn't upset Lucas that I'd been lost. He was simply annoyed at missing his train.

I was ill the next morning, not desperately ill but coughing and sneezing, my eyes running from the chill I had taken.

'You should have told Mrs Jermyns the truth,' Alice said when I was summoned to her sitting room after breakfast. 'It was so silly of you to run away like that, Nellie.'

'Yes, I know. Mr Lucas was very angry with me.' I sneezed into my handkerchief.

'He missed his train because of you,' she said. 'You wouldn't expect him to be pleased.'

'No, miss.' I blew my nose. 'Did he get off this morning?'

'Yes, I drove him to the station myself.'

'Oh . . . good.'

She shook her head at me. 'This business with the sheets – it was bound to come out in the end. You couldn't really have thought you could cover it up?'

'It was my idea to put the sheets in the laundry,' I replied awkwardly. 'I couldn't betray her, miss.'

'No, I don't suppose you could,' Alice replied in a soft voice. 'It was foolish though. Why didn't you come to me and explain? Surely you could have trusted me?'

'Iris thought you would turn her off with no wages.'

120

'She ought to have known better. You should have known better, Nellie. I shall have to let her go, of course. Lady Amelia would be outraged if she learned of this – but Iris has been given money to help her until she finds a new job.'

Iris was no longer sleeping in the same room as me. I had not seen her since the previous morning but I knew she was not leaving until later, when the carrier would come to take her to the station.

'But will she find work – without a proper reference?'

'I have given her a reference, just to say that she worked for us for several years. I could not do more, Nellie.'

Alice gave me what was for her a stern look and I knew I was wrong to have questioned her; she was always fair but she could not go against her principles. Iris had broken the rules and she was lucky to have been given more than her wages; most employers would simply have turned her off.

'No . . . you've done all you could. I know it's her own fault. She ought to have had more sense – but I still feel sorry for her.'

'Yes, so do I,' Alice said sadly. 'She wouldn't tell me who the father was – someone from the village was all she would say. It is wrong that she should suffer while he . . . but that is the way of the world. Perhaps Iris will have learnt from this; it may help her to make a new start somewhere else. She says she'll go to London and work in a shop or a restaurant.'

'That's what she's always wanted.' I fiddled with my apron. 'I never thanked Mr Lucas for coming to look for me.'

'He insisted on joining the search party, even though it meant cancelling his appointments. Not that it matters, he was able to arrange new ones for this afternoon.'

He hadn't told me that. But he had wanted to punish me.

'Will he be gone long do you think, miss?'

'Yes, I think he may. If the show is a success he may go abroad to work for a while. He says that he needs to broaden his horizons, experience more of the world, if he wants to become a really good painter. If it had not been for his accident I believe he would have gone long ago.'

'I see . . . ' I wasn't sure why that news should upset me – or why it hurt because he had gone without saying goodbye. 'I'd better get back to the kitchen then. Cook will be wanting me. Unless there was something else?'

'No, nothing else,' Alice said. 'But I'm going to ask Cook to release you sometimes in the afternoons so that you can help me. I have so much more to do these days, with my brother and Amelia both unwell. Would you like to spend some time with me, Nellie?'

'Yes, please.' She was being so kind and I felt awful for the trouble I had caused. I had behaved childishly and I was ashamed of myself. 'I'm sorry about the way I went off. It won't happen again.'

'You were upset. Lucas upset you with that painting – but it is really very good, Nellie.'

'Yes, miss, I know. I told him he could show it if he wants.'

'Well, we'll say no more of what happened. It's over now.'

'Thank you, miss. You know I would do anything for you.'

She nodded. 'I'll talk to Cook and Mrs Jermyns about your new duties. And then we'll see . . . '

I saw Tom when he came to the house with a parcel for Mrs Jones that afternoon. He nodded to me but didn't say much until I went out with him to the back door.

'I never thanked you for what you did, Tom. Not properly. I'm sorry. I – I felt such a fool when I realized the trouble I'd caused . . . all those men out searching on a night like that.'

His frown disappeared. 'From what I heard it wasn't all your fault, lass. They should've known you hadn't been up to any monkey business . . . and if you had, someone else would have been most to blame. You're a bonny lass but too young for such things.'

'I'm glad someone believes in me,' I said. 'It wasn't just the sheets, though. I was upset about something else.'

'Because he was leaving?' Tom's gaze narrowed. 'Don't let him turn your head, Nellie. He's not for you.'

'It wasn't that. You don't understand.'

'Don't I?'

Tom looked at me in a hard, straight way that wasn't like him and made me uncomfortable. I knew he thought I was

122

being silly over my employer's son, and perhaps in a way he was right, but it was more than that. I was tempted to tell him how my mother had hurt me with her revelations but I didn't. It wasn't my secret.

'No, you don't, and I can't tell you,' I said. 'Anyway, I've got work to do.'

'So have I. There's a house to be cleared and a delivery round to finish. Be seeing you, Nellie.'

He walked off without a smile.

Now that Iris was going the little attic room suddenly seemed too large for me. I missed the warmth of her body beside me in bed, and the friendship we had shared.

'I'll write sometimes,' she promised before she left. 'That's if you want me to, if you're not ashamed to know me?'

'Of course I'm not!' I hugged her. 'I wish you didn't have to leave.'

I felt that it was my fault, that I had somehow let her down and told her so, but she shook her head.

'It's best I go,' Iris said. 'I couldn't stay here now. Miss Alice was very good about it but I wouldn't feel right. It's best I make a fresh start somewhere else.'

So she left and for a while everything went on much as it had before, except that I could barely bring myself to speak to Doris. We passed each other in silence, the dislike and distrust mutual now. I would never forgive her for what she had tried to do, and I knew Doris would do anything she could to harm me. Mrs Jermyns, too, was a little stiff with me, though she had apologized for misjudging me.

'I should have known it was Iris,' she told me a few days later. 'But you were very wrong to try and cover up for her. I hope you have learned your lesson and will be more honest in future.'

'She was my friend,' I replied. 'I was only trying to help her.'

'A misguided action in my opinion – but we'll say no more about it.'

Her expression was sour as she walked away, leaving me smarting with suppressed indignation. If it hadn't been for

123

Miss Alice I would have changed my mind and left with Cook at the end of the month!

I was still helping her in the mornings, but in the afternoons I polished and dusted the rooms Miss Alice used, helping her with the flowers for the whole house and running messages to the gardeners and the housekeeper: on two occasions I took a letter to Gerald Simpson when Alice was unable to get away to meet him.

'Why don't you meet him here?' I asked, when she said she simply didn't have the time to keep their appointment in the village.

'I daren't risk it,' she admitted. 'If Charles were to hear of it . . . '

'Not at the house,' I agreed. 'But there's a little summer-house in the wild garden. No one goes there and the kitchen gate is usually locked. If Mr Gerald had a key . . . '

'The summerhouse?' Alice was thoughtful. 'No one has been near it for years. Lucas used to walk in the gardens but I don't think even he ventured inside much. It will be in a terrible mess . . . '

'If you gave me a key to the gate I could clean it up. It would give you somewhere to be alone with Mr Gerald – and no one need know anything other than that you were taking a walk in the gardens.'

'No one but us. It would make it so much easier for me to meet him . . . I'll think about it and let you know when I've decided.'

After a few days she gave me the keys, asking me to do what I could with the summerhouse.

'It may be beyond your powers to make it usable,' she said, 'but do your best and let me know.'

I slipped away that same afternoon, smuggling the brushes and cloths I needed out of the house on pretext of cleaning the back yard and the scullery windows.

It was exciting to unlock the gate and walk into the secret garden, though at this time of year it looked forlorn and bleak, the trees shorn of their summer finery. Yet there was still an odd charm about the place and the sound of a thrush trilling from a holly bush made my heart lift. I smiled as I imagined Alice meeting her sweetheart here; it was a place for lovers, a secret, magical world that appealed to something deep inside me, something that was separate from the sensible side of my nature – the part of me that still sighed for the times I had spent in Mr Lucas's studio even though I knew it was better this way, that I must try very hard to put him out of my mind.

I'd seen Tom a couple of times when he'd called at the house and he'd been his normal cheerful self. He was proving himself a good friend and even Mrs Jermyns had started to buy from him.

'You've only to mention you want something and he has it on the van next time,' Mrs Jones said more than once. 'And he doesn't overcharge either.'

I knew she liked Tom and I was beginning to lose my suspicion of him. Just because my mother looked down on his family there was no reason why I should follow her example. Miss Alice had placed her trust in me and I had a mind of my own now.

The summerhouse was dusty from long years of neglect, but in surprisingly good condition. I cleaned and polished the inside but left the windows dirty; we didn't want anyone to suspect that it was being used as a meeting place and from the outside it looked just the same. After I had finished I swept the kitchen yard and washed the scullery windows so that no one questioned what I had been doing.

'You've been a long time,' Cook said when I returned. 'I wanted to have a little talk to you, Nellie.'

'It was nice to be out in the air for a while,' I replied, turning away so that she shouldn't see my blush. 'The sun was quite warm out of the wind.'

'Yes, it has been a nice day,' Mrs Jones agreed. 'The snowdrops are out in the yard and the other bulbs are beginning to come up, makes you think that spring will soon be here . . . ' She motioned to me to sit down for my tea. 'I thought you might like to have these.' She slid a pile of stained and worn exercise books in front of me. 'They are all my own recipes but I know them by heart; I thought they might come in useful for you – you can have a go at making some of them when you have time.'

'For me?' I felt a thrill of pleasure as I flicked through the

125

books and saw the pages of neat handwriting. 'I should love to have them but are you sure you won't need them?'

'Quite sure.' Cook nodded to herself. 'I understand why you've decided to stay on here, Nellie, but don't give up your dreams. If cooking is what you want to do, you should one day. You won't want to stay here all your life.'

'It's not that I'm not grateful for your sister's offer but . . . I can't leave Miss Alice in the lurch.'

'You being you, of course you can't,' Mrs Jones said. 'You're a good lass, Nellie. Do what you have to do – but one day you might want to move on. If I can be of help to you, you have only to ask.'

'Thank you.' I blinked hard. 'I'm going to miss you when you go.'

'You can write to me now and then if you like.' She stood up and went to move the kettle on to the hob. 'If you've finished your tea, Miss Alice said she had some blouses needing ironing. You had best go and see if you can help her. She's more than enough to do, poor lass.'

I was thoughtful as I left the kitchen. There had been genuine emotion in Cook's voice, as if she too regretted that we must part. Sometimes I thought it might have been better if I had gone with her to her sister's hotel in Bournemouth, right away from this house and all its reminders of Mr Lucas.

When the letter came from my mother, thanking me for the cards and money I had sent for Christmas, I was due another two days off. I hesitated before asking Mrs Jermyns if I could take both of them together but she granted my request without argument.

'I suppose it is a long way to go,' she said, sniffing to show her disapproval. 'If Miss Alice has no objection you can stay overnight – but be back before supper on Sunday!'

I promised I would and it was arranged that Henry would take me in Miss Alice's car and the carriers would bring me back. I doubt if I should have gone at all if it had not been for my mother's letter.

'I bought socks and wool to knit a pullover for Bob and your da just as you asked,' she had written. 'And flowers for

126

Wilf's grave – though that's a waste I don't approve of, but it was your money. There was nothing I wanted for myself and the rest of what you sent is in the sideboard drawer if you need it. Bob has been asking for you – he's made something for you in school and it's too heavy to send by post – and Sam wondered when you were coming. I know we had words but you can come if you want . . . '

I decided that I would go, if only to show her that I wasn't bitter. I had cried away my pain out on the moors that terrible afternoon and in some strange way it had made me feel much better about myself. I had not asked to be born the way I was, and I was no longer ashamed. It was Ma's tragedy that she could not conquer her shame, but I was not going to let the fact of my birth ruin my life.

I had a new life now and I was beginning to put down roots, to feel that I belonged somewhere.

My homecoming was not marked in any special way, though Sam and my brother were pleased to see me. Da had given me that coat before Christmas but he had a new pair of leather court shoes waiting for me and Bob had made me a wooden trinket box.

'It's for sewing things and bits and pieces,' he said proudly. 'I made it myself in woodwork class.'

I thanked him and told him it was lovely, then I took him down to the village shop and bought him some sweets. On the way back we passed a horse-drawn caravan and I saw Tinker Herries sitting on the driving box. A lad of about Bob's age was perched beside him, and as he saw us, he called out a cheeky greeting and waved to us.

Bob waved back, then looked at me guiltily. 'Don't tell Ma I waved to him, will you, Nellie? She takes on something awful if I talk to the tinkers – but Jerry's all right. His father is a cantankerous old devil, but he can't help that, can he?'

'No, he can't,' I agreed. 'But you would be better staying away from the family, Bob, and not just because Ma disapproves. You don't want to get in trouble, do you?'

He agreed that he didn't and the subject was dropped.

When Tom Herries came to meet me the next day with the carrier's van I remembered the advice I had given to my brother, but Tom was different. Tinker Herries was a drunkard and it was better that Bob should keep well away from him and his brood – but Tom had left all that behind him. He was a hard worker and so respectable that Ma didn't even recognize him when he came to the door – something that was not lost on Tom.

He winked at me as I got into the van and I shook my head at him. What Ma didn't know wouldn't hurt her – but I wasn't going to make fun of her behind her back.

'You just watch it,' I said. 'And we'll have less of your lip this time, Tom Herries!'

He touched his cap as if saluting but he was grinning to himself. It wasn't long before he was back to his old ways, teasing me and telling me about his ambitions. I didn't mind; it passed the time – and besides, I liked Tom.

When I took a tray of tea up to Miss Alice's room after supper that evening she told me that she had heard from Lucas.

'He telephoned me this morning,' she said. 'Just to let me know that he was leaving for Paris tomorrow. From there he will probably go on to Rome and Athens . . . '

'He'll be away for some time then,' I said and dropped my gaze so that she could not see how her news had affected me.

'For at least a year, perhaps two,' she said and sighed. 'I shall miss him – but it's what he wants . . . '

'Yes, miss.'

She glanced at me then. 'He told me to tell you that your paintings were much admired. He could have sold them several times over but he has decided to keep them for the time being.'

'Oh . . . '

I was glad that he wasn't going to sell them, but I wondered why.

'Did you enjoy your visit?'

'Yes . . . it was all right,' I said. 'But I don't think I shall go over for a while.'

'If you don't want to go home you could come into town with me next time you're due a day off and do some shopping,' she said. 'I could leave you to get what we both want and meet Gerald.'

128

'Yes, miss – that would be a good idea.'

She was using me as an alibi for meeting him but I didn't mind. I wanted to help her and in our way we were friends, though we were both careful not to step over the line that divided our two worlds.

'I thought you might like to read this?' Alice handed me a book of poems. 'You know you are welcome to borrow any of my books whenever you want, Nellie.'

Her smile seemed to ask for understanding and I accepted her unspoken apology. Alice *was* making use of me, she needed me, but in return she was helping me to educate myself. It was a fair exchange.

I was thoughtful as I left her and went back to the kitchen. It was foolish of me to feel upset because Mr Lucas had gone away. If there was a divide between Alice and me there was an even bigger one between me and my master's only son.

Chapter Nine

'Well, here we are then, safe and sound.' Tom Herries stopped the van: it was his own now and paid for. He had done very well for himself over the past two years with his rounds as a tallyman but said this was only a start, a stepping stone to the future he had planned. He turned to look at me, a slight frown wrinkling his brow. 'Why won't you let me take you to the dance next Saturday? It's only a village affair. I'll have you back before eleven. Surely they'll let you out for one night?'

I didn't answer at once. I wasn't sure why I kept turning Tom down every time he offered to take me to the pictures or a dance. I liked him and we had become friends over the years. He had just fetched me from my home – the first time I'd visited in months – and hadn't charged me a penny. I knew he called more often than he needed with his deliveries to Beaumont House, and that it was for my sake, for the chance of seeing me and being invited into the kitchen for a cup of tea and a cake.

'You make the best rock cakes I've ever tasted,' he'd told me more than once. 'Eh, lass, but you'll make someone a bonny wife one of these days.'

I was well aware that Tom thought of himself as the man I was destined to marry. His hints had grown stronger over the months, more so since my sixteenth birthday.

At sixteen years and a few weeks I had left childhood long behind. My mirror told me that I had a woman's body with slightly heavy, well-formed breasts, a satisfyingly slender waist and hips made for childbearing. I sometimes wished I could be as slender as Miss Alice but we were from different stock – and Tom was fond of telling me that I was a real woman.

'Not one of your wilting lilies but a proper armful,' was the way he had described me once. I hadn't spoken to him for a week afterwards. Tom was inclined to be cheeky but I could always keep him in check because he was genuinely fond of me.

He smiled at me persuasively as he lifted me down from the van, his hands lingering about my waist until I pulled away from him.

'Go on, say yes,' he urged. 'It's just a little dance – not a Roman orgy.'

'You daft thing!' I laughed at the look in his eyes: Tom Herries was a bold one, but sometimes he seemed like a soft puppy dog, begging for a pat and a kind word. 'All right then, I'll come – providing Miss Alice doesn't mind.'

'It's me lucky day!' Tom said and kissed me swiftly on the lips, receiving a swifter smack of the ear for his pains. 'Aw, Nellie! It was just a peck.'

'And that was just a tap. To remind you to keep your hands to yourself. You behave, Tom Herries, or I'll change my mind.'

'You never would!' Tom looked downcast.

'Come for your tea on Friday and I'll give you my answer then.'

I turned and walked up the sloping path to the house, well aware that he was watching me all the way. At the top of the steps I stopped and turned to wave at him. He waved back, then began to whistle cheerfully as he got into his van and drove off.

Henry was chopping wood in the yard. He paused as he saw me, wiping his blue and white striped shirt sleeve across his face to mop up the sweat.

'It's warm today, Nellie.'

'Yes, it is,' I replied, my tone slightly cool. Henry had recently developed a way of staring at me that I didn't much like.

'Been to visit your folks then?'

'Yes.' He stood in my way. 'Did you want something, Henry?'

131

'Maybe.' His eyes went over me suggestively. 'Fancy coming down the pub for a drink one night?'

'No, thank you.'

'Suit yourself then.'

He shrugged and stood aside, but I could feel his eyes following me, burning into the hollow between my shoulder blades. He seemed to have become arrogant of late, too sure of himself, as if he thought his position unassailable. It wouldn't be easy to replace him, of course. Sir Charles had had another small stroke six months earlier and needed constant attention. Not many young men would want Henry's job; most of them preferred to be off to the city where there was a bit of life; they wouldn't want to be buried in the country playing nursemaid to a bad-tempered invalid. Alice worried about what we would do if Henry decided to leave.

The bond between Alice and me was becoming ever stronger. Quite often we spent most of the afternoon talking about the books we had read and enjoyed together. We had begun with the classics and poetry but now Alice had introduced me to the delights of modernism; I was reading Yeats, Lawrence and most recently had graduated to Virginia Woolf's novels, though her essay about modern fiction was still a little beyond me.

It was a strange education I had won for myself and it had lots of gaps in it, but there was no doubt that I was no longer the naive, ignorant girl who had first come to work in the kitchens. Alice had told me many times that she was proud of the way I had come on.

'It was Lucas who first suggested I should give you books to read,' she said to me once. 'He recognized the thirst for knowledge in you, even when you may not have been aware of it yourself. He said it was your eagerness and defiance that inspired him to paint you – you are kindred spirits in a way, Nellie. He has always been a rebel and saw that same streak in you.'

It had surprised me that Lucas had been interested enough to ask Alice to help me. Sometimes he seemed so utterly selfish but then he could do something wonderful . . . as when he had spent so much time painting the miniature for

132

me when it wasn't really the kind of work he liked. Of course it would be foolish to read too much into Alice's words but it gave me a warm glow inside and made me wonder when Lucas would come home.

It was cooler in the kitchen, with its newly white-washed walls, its heavy oak dressers, stacked with blue and white pottery, and the stone floor which had worn smooth with use. Mrs Jermyns had just made a cup of tea. She looked up as I entered but didn't smile; we tolerated each other these days but were not friends – not the way Cook and I had been, were still through our letters.

I had heard once or twice from Iris, too, but not for a while now – not since she had got married and settled down. I thought that she wanted to close the door on the past and I didn't blame her. I hoped she wouldn't let the fact, that the first child she had conceived – and then miscarried – had not been her husband's, overshadow her life.

'How was your father then?' Mrs Jermyns asked.

'Better. Ma said it must have been a summer chill – but she was worried about him or she wouldn't have written me.'

'You should go home more. You're entitled to your day off.'

'Yes, I know. Perhaps I will.'

Sam was always pleased to see me, I knew that, but I didn't often visit. The relationship between me and my mother was still fragile. It wasn't resentment on my side so much as a withdrawal on hers; she wanted to keep a barrier between us and so I stayed away. I'd gone this time only because she had written to say Sam had a bad chest and a cough that kept him awake nights.

'He won't ask you to come,' the letter said. 'But he wants to see you.'

It was a big concession from my mother to admit that and I had acknowleged it, not in words but in my manner. We were still not friends but we tried to act as if things were normal whenever Sam was around.

He was so proud of the way I had begun to better myself. He couldn't have looked more pleased if he'd been my blood kin when I talked to him about the things I'd learnt.

His cough had cleared up by the time I managed to get

over, but I had been shocked by the change in him since my last visit.

'You've lost weight, Da,' I said as I saw the way his clothes hung on him. I kissed his cheek, looking at him anxiously. 'You're not really ill, are you?'

'Nay, lass.' He smiled cheerily. 'If I've lost a few pounds it's not before time. It will all go on again over Christmas.'

'Well, as long as you're all right.'

'All the better for seeing you.'

'I know it has been a while, but there's always so much to do.'

'You're the one who looks thin,' Sam said with a frown. 'They work you too hard, Nellie.'

I shook my head. 'I'm doing what I want, Da. Cooking and looking after Miss Alice. I do hardly any scrubbing these days – honest, it's like being on holiday.'

It wasn't strictly true, of course. I worked very long hours, cooking, cleaning, and looking after Miss Alice's clothes, but it was our time together in the afternoons that made it all worthwhile: it was those times, when I felt that we were more like friends than mistress and servant, times when Alice opened her heart to me, sometimes weeping, sometimes laughing, that meant so much to me.

'Drink your tea then,' Mrs Jermyns said, pushing the cup in front of me. 'I haven't baked. I thought you would do it when you got back.'

I nodded, drawing the thick blue and white cup towards me and sipping my tea. It was as I liked it, strong and sweet with just a drop of milk. Mrs Jermyns could make a cup of tea and cook a plain dinner, but she had a heavy hand with cakes and pastry and by mutual agreement she left the fancy stuff to me.

Mrs Jones's parting gift had been a godsend and I was becoming proficient at making the various recipes; I was even beginning to vary them slightly and to invent new ones of my own, like the almond buns Miss Alice was so fond of for her tea. Cooking was a gift, or a calling as Mrs Jones had said when I first mentioned my interest. One day I was going to have to make up my mind whether I wanted marriage or something different, but not for a while.

134

Besides, there was yet another interest in my life now. Sometimes on a Saturday afternoon I went down to the vicarage to help Mrs Roberts with the new classes she had started to teach the gipsy women who came to work on the land with their menfolk to cook and sew. It was very satisfying to watch a woman make a tray of buns for the first time and I thought that I might have enjoyed teaching if I'd been given the chance, but that was not something I dwelt on. Cooking was an art and in a way I had the best of both worlds. Besides, I was happy and I had no desire to leave Beaumont House just yet.

I finished my tea, shaking my head as Mrs Jermyns offered another. 'No, thank you. I think I'll just pop upstairs and see if Miss Alice wants anything.'

'She went for a walk earlier,' Mrs Jermyns said, 'but she may be back by now.'

I was well aware that Alice had arranged to meet Gerald that afternoon; it was almost three months since he had last managed to get down and Alice was afraid that he was becoming tired of travelling from York for a stolen hour, tired of hiding like criminals as if what they were doing was wrong.

Nothing very terrible ever went on in the summerhouse. Sometimes they kissed, but mostly they simply talked. Alice had too strong a sense of decency ever to go beyond a kiss, and Gerald cared for her too much to ask for something she was not willing to give.

'He must have the patience of a saint,' she confided tearfully once after a meeting fraught with tension and pain for them both. 'I don't know how long I can expect him to go on like this, Nellie.'

'Why don't you find a nurse for Sir Charles?' I suggested. 'Surely you've done your duty, miss?'

'Who would stay?' Alice asked with a sorrowful shake of her head. 'My brother's temper doesn't improve.'

'But you can't give up your whole life for his sake. If anyone has a duty towards him, it must be Lady Amelia.'

It was the truth but we both knew that Sir Gerald's wife had no intention of taking up the burden she had so swiftly laid on Alice's shoulders. She lost no opportunity to blame

135

Alice for what had happened to her husband or to complain that her own health was frail. No one could have prevented Alice from leaving if she had simply walked out, but she was held fast, caught by the invisible bonds of her own strong sense of duty – and of guilt.

She was standing looking out at the garden when I knocked and then entered the small sitting room, its silk-covered walls rosy in the soft evening sun which flooded in through the long sash window. I was struck by the sweetness and sadness of her face, and felt anger against the people who used her so shamefully: they had no right to take advantage of her goodness and generosity.

Alice turned, the sadness leaving her face, in its place affection and a deep concern for me.

'You're back so soon,' she said. 'Did you find your father better than you expected? I thought you might decide to stay over for a day or so.'

'Mother wouldn't be too happy with that. No, I've seen my Da and he seems better – though he's lost too much weight.'

'Has he consulted a doctor?'

'Only our local man. I asked him if he ought to go to hospital but he says he'll be all right in a day or two.'

'Perhaps he will,' Alice said, 'but you should visit again soon, Nellie – keep an eye on him yourself. If you want to go home you don't have to wait for your day off, just let me know when you're going.'

'We'll see, miss. Did Mr Gerald come then?'

'Yes, he came . . . ' Alice sighed. 'I don't know whether it's harder when I see him or when I don't.'

'I could help Henry with Sir Charles,' I offered. 'If you wanted to go away for a few days . . . have a bit of a holiday like.'

'I'm not sure that my brother . . . ' Alice broke off as the telephone rang. She reached for it, her face breaking into a smile of delighted surprise as she heard the voice on the other end. 'Lucas! My dear – how nice to hear from you. Where are you? London . . . goodness! I had no idea you were in the country. You are coming down – when? Next Saturday . . . that's wonderful. I shall look forward to it. It was good of you to let me know – goodbye for now.'

She replaced the receiver and looked at me, her eyes shining. 'You heard, of course. Lucas is coming to visit – he will be here on Saturday.'

'That will be nice for you, miss.'

How could I sound so calm when my insides were churning?

Lucas was coming home! In the past two years he had sent the occasional postcard from wherever he happened to be: Paris, Rome, Greece – and for the last year or so New York. Now – just like that – he was coming back to the Dales.

'Yes, yes, it will,' Alice agreed and looked thoughtful. 'Of course there's no question of my going away while Lucas is here, but perhaps afterwards I might think about it.'

'You should do it.' I hesitated, then, wanting to change the subject, 'Tom Herries asked me to the local dance this Saturday. Would you mind if I went?'

'Of course not.' Alice's smile was warm and generous. 'I'm grateful for all you do, Nellie. As I've already told you – you are welcome to take time off when you like. I'm well aware that you work far more hours than we pay you for. Sometimes I wonder why you stay here.' Almost at once she shook her head. 'No, of course I don't. I know it's for my sake.' An anxious look came into her eyes. 'But I don't expect you to stay for ever, Nellie. One day you'll want to get married and when you do . . . '

'We'll face that when we come to it. I'm not ready just yet so you needn't start worrying.'

Alice smiled. 'Isn't it good news about Lucas? I know his show in New York went well, and now he will be having another one in London. I can't wait to see him again.'

I was silent as Alice went on and on about Lucas, his work, his successes, his travels, and the arrangements we needed to make for his homecoming. My heart had missed a beat at the mention of his name, my mouth felt dry and I had a tingling sensation at the nape of my neck.

'I've some baking to do,' I said as Alice stopped talking at last. 'I'd better get on with it.'

'And I should pop in and see if Charles wants me to read to him for a while,' she replied. 'I shall tell him and Amelia

137

that Lucas is coming home. Amelia will be pleased even if Charles isn't particularly.'

I was thoughtful as I walked downstairs. It had made me feel very odd just now to know that Mr Lucas was coming home, but that was silly; it could make no difference to me. The best thing I could do was to stay out of his way as much as possible and hope that it was a short visit.

My dress was a shiny blue cotton with a tiny white polka dot; it had full skirts that brushed my ankles as I moved, a cinched-in waist, puffed short sleeves, and a sweetheart neckline. My hair had been freshly washed and waved with curling tongs heated over the kitchen fire, and around my neck I wore the silver chain Lucas had given me but not the pendant: that was safely tucked away in my handkerchief sachet, far too precious to be worn.

'You look pretty tonight,' Tom said as he came to the kitchen door to fetch me. He looked dapper in his smart pin-stripe suit with sharply cut revers and a silk waistcoat. His manner was oddly shy and unlike himself as he thrust a spray of white roses at me, saying, 'You could pin these on your dress if you want.'

I thanked him and, discovering a little gold safety pin, fastened it to the sash at my waist; then I picked up a lacey shawl Alice had lent me for the evening and draped it over my arm.

'Shall we go?' I asked. 'I don't want to be out much after eleven. Mrs Jermyns likes to lock up by a quarter past at the latest.'

'We'll be back by then, I promise.' He held out his hand and after a moment's hesitation I took it. 'It's going to be fun tonight, Nellie. I reckon we'll have a real good time.'

As we left the kitchen Doris came along the passage towards us, her eyes sullen as she noticed the roses and the shawl.

'Going somewhere?'

'To the dance in the church hall,' I replied. 'Miss Alice knows about it.'

'All right for some!' Doris glared at us and continued down the hall.

138

Tom pulled a comic face behind her back and I laughed, causing Doris to glance back over her shoulder at us, her eyes dark with hatred.

'Come on.' I pulled at Tom's arm. 'Let's get out of here. I don't want to waste a moment.'

It was a warm evening, the air soft with the scent of roses, honeysuckle and night stocks. Laughing, we hurried through the kitchen gardens, down the sloping path which, through various cracks in the paving, had been invaded with thrusting herbs that released their own pungent scents as they were crushed beneath hurrying feet, to Tom's van parked outside in the lane. He opened the door and gave me a hand up the high step, then went round to get in beside me, glancing my way as he said, 'Did Mr Lucas arrive then? You said Miss Alice was expecting him this afternoon, didn't you?'

'She was but he hasn't come yet.' I smoothed the skirts of my dress so that the material wouldn't crease too much. 'He's driving himself down so he could turn up at any time. I hope he isn't going to let her down.'

Tom nodded but made no comment. 'I want to show you something before we go to the dance,' he said. 'It won't take five minutes and you don't have to get out of the van.'

He was excited about something but it was obviously a secret because he wasn't going to tell me any more just yet. I had an idea what it might be – Tom's ambitious plans for the future were well known to me now – but I would let him tell me himself when he was ready.

'The rooms up top are small,' Tom said as he stopped outside an empty shop in the High Street, 'but there's three of them so I could put in a bath – and there's a kitchen behind the shop. It will be mine by Christmas and it will take me three months to get it right, because I'll have to work nights and Sundays – but it could be ready for spring . . . ' He paused and looked at me significantly. 'What do you think then, Nellie?'

'It will be nice for you to have a shop, Tom. I know that's what you've always wanted.'

'The first of several I hope,' he said, 'but that's not what I meant – and you know it. I'm asking if you'll marry me and move into them rooms? Mebbe you could look after the shop while I'm out on my rounds, just for a while. Once I've built it up a bit I'll have a lass from the village in and you'll be free to look after the house – and the babies. And one day not too far down the road we'll have a real posh house with fancy carpets on the floor and everything you've ever wanted.'

He looked so eager. I didn't want to hurt Tom; he was a decent, likeable man and there was a soft spot in my heart for him, but – and it was a big but – I wasn't certain I wanted to be his wife and settle in the village with a house and children to look after.

'I'm not sure . . . ' I stopped as I saw his face fall. 'You know I'm . . . I'm fond of you, Tom. I do care for you, more than you might think, but I'm not ready to marry, not yet.'

'I should have waited until it was all done,' he said ruefully. 'You're only sixteen . . . '

'You're not much more than twenty yourself, Tom.' I touched his hand, wanting to make up for any hurt I might have inflicted. 'Let's wait another year or so, shall we? You don't want a wife and children too soon; you've your business to think about – and there's Miss Alice. In another year she might be wed to her Mr Gerald and I'll be more settled in my own mind.'

Tom's eyes searched my face. 'You've not set it against marrying me then?'

'No.' I smiled at him. 'I just want more time.'

'Then we'll say no more about it. I've always been ahead of meself. I knew it was too soon but I had to ask.' He started the van again. 'Let's get to that dance.'

Another man might have sulked after proposing and being turned down, but Tom hadn't given any sign of his disappointment. Instead, he'd gone out of his way to make the evening pleasant for me.

It was a good evening. I enjoyed the music and dancing with Tom was fun; he taught me how to do the foxtrot and the quickstep and I was surprised at how light he was on his feet.

After it was over I waited in the hall porch while he went to fetch the van round. I was humming a Gershwin tune

when he hopped out and opened the door for me. He'd got
good manners, I'd noticed that particularly this evening.
Some of the other young men at the dance had seemed
uncouth and ignorant beside Tom. I'd had to change partners
occasionally to be sociable but I'd been glad to get back to
my own.

'I've had a lovely time,' I said and kissed his cheek. 'Thank
you for taking me tonight and – and ask me again next
summer . . . about . . . you know.'

'You needn't worry about that, Nellie lass.' Tom was as
cheerful as ever. 'I don't give up that easy. One of these days
you're going to say yes. Blokes like me don't grow on trees,
you know.'

'You've got a good opinion of yourself, Tom Herries,' I
said, but it wasn't so very far from the truth. Most girls in
my position would have jumped at what he was offering; I
wasn't sure why I hadn't, but something – some inner voice –
was telling me to wait.

'If you don't value yourself, no one else will,' Tom replied.
'I'd better get you home – it's a quarter to eleven.'

I closed my eyes as the van bumped along the narrow
country lanes. My head was still full of the music and I felt
relaxed, my fingers drumming in time with the tunes I had
danced to in Tom's arms.

'It was fun this evening.' I opened my eyes to glance at
him in the half-light. 'Can we go again?'

'I reckon we might,' Tom replied and began to whistle.

I was oddly reluctant to get out when the van stopped in
the lane outside the kitchen gardens, but Tom was mindful
of the time and insisted on walking me up to the back door. I
tried the handle and was relieved to find it wasn't locked; I
had wondered if Doris might have turned the key just to
spite me.

'Well, I'd best get in then . . . '

'I'll be by in the week,' he said, half-turned, then swung
back to take me in his arms. 'You know I love you, Nellie?'

I nodded, making no attempt to pull away as his mouth
sought mine. His kiss was warm, sweet and tender. I was a
little breathless as he let me go.

'Good night, Tom – and thank you again.'

'Good night, lass. It was my pleasure.'

I opened the door and went in. As I paused to lock up behind me I fancied for a moment that I could smell cigarette smoke.

'Is anyone there?'

There was no answer; it must be my imagination. Tom didn't smoke – he thought it a waste of good money. Henry smoked cheap ones now and then, but mostly outside because Mrs Jermyns didn't approve of smoking in the kitchens; this, however, was a different smell, strangely exotic, almost scented, like some of those expensive brands they sold through the pages of the magazines Sir Charles still had sent through the post – but Sir Charles didn't smoke any more, nor would he have dreamt of ever coming this far below stairs.

I must be imagining things, I decided, as I ran up to my own room. Or perhaps it was on my clothes. Several men had been smoking at the dance. Yes, that must be it. I would have to wash Miss Alice's shawl before returning it, to make sure that it didn't smell . . .

For some reason I couldn't sleep. I had thought I would go out like a light the moment my head touched the pillow as I usually did, but though I dozed off for a while I was awake half the night and ready to get up by the time the birds had begun their dawn chorus. It was no hardship to leave the comfort of my bed and wash in the cold water from the washstand, not when it was already warm and the promise of another lovely day was calling me outside.

Once dressed I saw no point in remaining in the house. It was Sunday and apart from cooking the dinner, perhaps some baking and any little jobs Miss Alice might need doing, I could please myself: the routine had become much more relaxed over the past year or so and the rough work could be left until Monday.

Perhaps I would just dust and tidy the summerhouse, though. It was a good opportunity to sneak the things I needed out of the house without prying eyes following my every movement; besides, I needed no excuse to slip away to the wild garden: it was still my favourite place, a place to

142

spend a little time alone and dream – and I had plenty to occupy my thoughts, for I had not been able to dismiss Tom's proposal from my mind as easily as I'd imagined.

A decent woman really had only two choices: to marry and have a family or live alone and support herself. I believed I would have little or no difficulty in finding work as a cook, either in a private house or a small hotel. Mrs Jones still regretted that I'd chosen to remain at Beaumont House and often said that she would like to see me again.

'Come for a holiday if nothing else,' she had written in her last letter. 'You ought to see a bit of the world before you settle down, Nellie.'

Was that why I had asked Tom to wait, because I felt I owed it to myself to grow a little as a person, to see what was going on outside the solitude of the Dales? As a child I had been to York a few times with my father but I'd never been as far as London. I couldn't really imagine what it must be like with all those cars and the people rushing everywhere. I'd once seen the bustle of the city in a film at the cinema, and of course Miss Alice passed her magazines on to me when she was done with them, so I knew there was a big world out there to see and explore, but as yet I'd felt no desire to flee the safety of Beaumont House, though there was a part of me that wanted more.

Unlocking the summerhouse I began to plump up the cushions on the old cane settee and dust the table; Miss Alice had gradually brought things from the house and now it had a cosy, almost lived-in look with magazines and books. There was even a bottle of sherry with two glasses on a tray. I saw they had been used and left; I must remind Miss Alice to take them back to the house and replace them with clean ones.

'And what are you doing here?' I stood absolutely still as I heard the voice behind me. For a moment I was frozen, unable to move or think. 'It is Nellie Pearce, isn't it?'

I turned slowly towards him, my hands clutching nervously at the duster. My eyes went to his, to his face, moving over every well-remembered feature. I saw changes . . . something had been done to the skin at the corner of his eye, releasing the puckering so that he no longer looked as if he were

143

squinting. The scar was still there of course but there was a vast improvement in his looks.

'Your eye . . . '

'I had an operation in New York. Jack found the surgeon for me – it's an improvement, isn't it?'

'Yes,' I said quietly, then after a pause, 'Yes, it's me, Mr Lucas – and I'm afraid you've caught me trespassing in your special place again.'

'What's this?' Lucas stared at me disbelievingly. 'So modest – so submissive? Can this be the same Nellie Pearce I knew?'

I retained my pose, hands clasped, head demurely bent; my heart was racing so madly that I was afraid of betraying myself if I looked up, afraid that he would be able to read my mind.

'I don't know what you mean, sir.'

'Look at me, Nellie.'

There was such a tone of command in his voice that my head came up and my eyes looked straight into his, recognizing the streak of malicious humour I remembered so well.

'That's better,' Lucas said. 'I see you were trying to deceive me – why?' His eyes swept round the summerhouse and came to rest on the used sherry glasses. 'Ah, now I begin to understand – you have been using this place as your love nest, that's it, isn't it?'

I met his mocking gaze defiantly. 'You always did like teasing me, sir. You shouldn't do that.'

'But the evidence is there,' he protested. 'How can you ask me to ignore what I see?'

'The glasses were left from a little picnic Miss Alice and I had a few days ago.' I dared him to contradict me and my expression brought a shout of triumphant laughter.

'That's very much better,' he said. 'That's the Nellie I knew and loved – you would lie until you were blue in the face for Alice, wouldn't you?'

'I don't know . . . '

'Oh, don't you? You're such a bad liar, too.' His strong, slightly sunburned fingers reached out to encircle my right wrist. 'Nellie, Nellie, what am I going to do with you?' His

144

forefinger moved caressingly over the back of my hand. 'You don't need to protect Alice from me. Don't you know how much I care for her? She has told me about her meetings with Gerald: we never have secrets from one another.'

I laughed nervously. 'Well, I couldn't be sure – and we've tried to keep it a secret from everyone. It would cause so much trouble if . . . '

'If my parents found out?' Lucas nodded. 'They both treat her abominably. She is a fool to stand for it. I've told her over and over again that she should get a nurse in for Father and leave.'

'So have I – I want her to take a little holiday. She could meet up with Mr Gerald and have some fun for once. I've offered to help Henry with Sir Charles.'

'Have you indeed?' Lucas raised his brows. 'Is there no end to your generosity, Nellie?'

'You're making fun of me, sir.'

'But I'm not. I have noticed before how loyal you are to those you care for.'

I shook my head but didn't say anything; the look in his eyes made my knees go weak and I felt as if I'd been running very fast.

'I should go now,' I said. 'I've finished here and it will soon be time to start on the breakfasts.'

'Not for hours yet, surely?' Lucas was still holding my wrist and showed no sign of wanting to let go. 'Need you run away so soon? Couldn't we walk for a while? There's something different about you – something intriguing. I can't decide what but I know you've changed.'

'You've been away a long time.'

'Yes, I know, but it's more than that. You were an amusing child, a rebel after my own heart – but now there's much more to you. I want to talk to you for a while, discover the new Nellie. Please stay. You could tell me how things have been since I've been away . . . how Alice is really coping. She insists that everything is fine but I'm not sure. Stay for her sake if not for mine.'

His pleading made me weaken. This was the attractive, charming side of Lucas, the side I had seen so seldom in the past but which had enchanted me.

'We could walk in the wild garden for half an hour or so, I suppose.' I tucked the duster into my apron pocket and together we left the summerhouse, locking the door behind us. 'Perhaps you can persuade Miss Alice to think of herself more. She ought to get out and meet people instead of staying home all the time; she's even given up most of her committees and her charity work these past six months or so.'

'We can't have that,' Lucas said. 'I shall have a serious talk with her. Even if she won't marry Gerald she ought to have some sort of a social life.'

'Yes, sir, that's what I tell her. She says she's quite happy with her books and her music – but it's not right, sir.'

'No, it isn't.' Lucas glanced at me. 'Do you think you could manage to call me something other than sir? My name is Lucas, you know.'

'Of course, Mr Lucas, if you prefer it.'

'I suppose it would be too much to ask you to drop the Mr – at least when we are alone like this?'

'It wouldn't be proper.'

'No, but it would be far easier and more companionable,' he replied, his eyes challenging. 'You're not afraid of me, are you?'

'Afraid of you – why should I be?'

'Why indeed?' The wickedness was back in his eyes. 'The world is changing, Nellie. I think all this sir and Mr is a bit formal between friends, don't you? And you think of Alice as your friend, I know.' He smiled his satisfaction as I nodded. 'Don't you think we could also be friends?'

'I don't know, s— Mr Lucas.'

'You don't quite trust me, do you?'

'Yes, of course I do.' I looked away, trying to hide the fire in my cheeks. 'Listen to that thrush? Isn't that a rare treat? She's over there – in the holly bush.'

'If you trusted me you would know that I would never do anything to hurt you, Nellie. I am your friend whether you realize it or not.'

'Are you?' I caught my breath as I saw the expression in his eyes. 'Miss Alice tells me your show in New York was very successful.'

146

'All my shows have done well since I painted those portraits of you . . . ' He stopped walking and looked down at me. 'Would you consider sitting for me again, Nellie?'

My heart stood still; I took a deep breath. 'I don't think it would be very wise, do you, Lucas?'

My use of his name stunned him and he was rendered speechless for long enough to enable me to gather my defences.

'Excuse me,' I said quietly. 'I really do have a great deal of work to do.' And then I walked away.

I took care not to visit the wild garden for the next two days. It would be wiser to avoid being caught there again by Lucas, especially now that he had begun to break down the barriers between us; those barriers had served as a protection, drawing an invisible line over which neither of us could step. I had felt safe on my own side, for I knew Lucas was not the kind of man who would use his position to force me into anything; he had his own brand of honour, which would prevent him from taking an unfair advantage – but I'd sensed a subtle change in our relationship and Lucas was not above seducing a girl he had invited to be his friend. Especially a girl who was now more able to meet and challenge him on his own ground.

His time away had changed things; I was no longer a child and he had become a stranger, a visitor rather than the master's son. It would not matter if his wicked eyes did not send such shivers of delight down my spine. How foolish I had been to fall in love with him!

Even when I was fourteen I had been very aware of the attraction between us, but I'd been too young and innocent fully to appreciate the danger of a relationship that was not quite what it seemed. The sickening reality of Iris's miscarriage and subsequent dismissal had opened my eyes, but Lucas had gone away at that very moment and it had not been necessary for me to think about my own position – until now.

I must do nothing that might lead both Lucas and me into temptation! I had ceased to think of him as 'Mr Lucas'. He had asked me to use his name and now I could think of him in no other way; the damage had been done; barriers were crumbling in my mind, making me more vulnerable.

'Nellie Pearce, you're a fool!'

I spoke the words aloud whilst in the middle of beating a basinful of cake mixture, then glanced round the empty kitchen and was thankful that no one had heard.

There was a nagging ache in my heart – was it only three days ago that I'd thought I might be happy married to Tom? Now I could not imagine ever being happy again.

Chapter Ten

'Is something wrong?' Alice asked the next afternoon as we worked together in the rose garden, snipping off the dead heads and picking the best buds for the house. 'You seem very quiet. You're not ill, are you?'

'No, I'm not ill.' I knelt down on the edge of the lawn to gather fallen petals keeping my face averted so that Alice should not suspect anything. 'It's the weather – don't you feel it?'

It had been muggy all day, as if the heat had brought on the threat of a storm; the air seemed thick with thunder flies, tiny black midges that got in your hair and eyes, making your skin crawl.

'Yes, I do,' she admitted. 'Lucas went off for a swim earlier. I almost wish I had gone with him.'

'You should have that holiday, miss.'

'Yes, perhaps I should. Lucas has offered to stay on for a week or two.' Alice's voice held a tremor. 'I ... Mrs Jones has invited me to visit her at her sister's hotel in Bournemouth ... it would be an excuse ... ' Her cheeks were pink as she looked at me. 'If you wouldn't mind helping with Charles while I'm away?'

'Of course I wouldn't. When are you thinking of leaving?'

'The day after tomorrow.' Alice looked both nervous and excited. 'I shall only be gone a week.'

'You don't have to hurry back for my sake.'

'It will be so good to get away – just for a while. I shan't feel so guilty if Lucas is here. He has promised to spend time

149

with his mother and to read the newspaper to his father –
which is really all I do for Charles.'

'It's only right that he should do his bit.'

'He agrees with you. I think he feels guilty because he can
escape whenever he likes .. but it's always that way for us,
isn't it? Women have a duty to love and serve their families,
don't you agree?'

'I suppose so,' I said, 'but don't we have rights, too?
Aren't we entitled to happiness for ourselves?'

'Happiness, yes, I think we all hope for it – but as a right?'
Alice's eyes clouded. 'Can we really find happiness at the
expense of others?'

I thought about it, then sighed and shook my head. 'No, I
don't expect so, but it's a bit unfair, isn't it? I mean, why is it
always women who have to sacrifice their own desires for the
sake of the family?'

'Because it has always been that way. Men sacrifice themselves in war: the destiny of many women is to love and serve
all their days.'

'All their days ... ' My skin prickled. 'That sounds like
poetry. But I still say it isn't fair.'

'You're quite right.' Alice smiled. 'However, it is going to
take a social revolution to change things and I'm not sure it
would necessarily be for the better. Goodness knows what
will happen if the ordinary, decent women of this country
ever decide to put themselves first.'

'Society will crumble, I shouldn't wonder,' I said, and
giggled. 'The whole world will fall apart.'

'Oh, Nellie, Nellie!' Alice's delighted laughter trilled out.
'Sometimes you say the funniest things!'

'Can anyone join in or is it a private joke?'

We swung round at the sound of Lucas's voice. His dark
hair was still wet from swimming; he looked refreshed and
cool, making us very aware of how hot and sticky we felt.

'Oh, yes, very private,' Alice said. 'You wouldn't understand it.'

'Try me?' His brows rose and he transferred his questing
gaze to me. 'What have you been saying to make Alice laugh
like that? I'm sure it was wicked.'

'It was not,' she contradicted. 'If you must know we were

150

talking of duty – and that's all I shall tell you. Don't you dare to plague us further, Lucas. You look disgustingly cool and I'm cross with you for it; it's not fair when we're both sticky and uncomfortable. I think I shall go and take a cool bath, these midges are driving me mad.'

Lucas looked amused. It wasn't often that Alice admitted to being cross and it showed that she was probably tired, and very much in need of a holiday. His eyes followed her as she walked across the lawns for a moment, then came back to me.

'Don't run away,' he said as I bent to pick up my trug. 'Unless you're cross with me, too?'

'Why should I be?' I was unwise enough to meet his eyes and my heart missed a beat as I saw the warmth and passion in them.

'I thought you might have been avoiding me?'

I was silent.

'Yes, I rather imagined it was so. You've felt it, too – haven't you?' Still I was silent. 'You don't have to be afraid, Nellie. I would never hurt you – never force you to do anything you didn't want. You do know that, don't you?'

My mouth was dry and my voice seemed to have deserted me, but I managed to say yes.

'Good.' He smiled down at me, his eyes soft and warm. 'I've persuaded Alice to go away for a few days.'

'She told me.'

My heart was beating so rapidly that I felt as if I had walked up the side of a mountain very fast. The best thing I could do would be to make an excuse and leave at once, but my feet felt as if they were stuck to the ground and I was reluctant to tear myself away.

'It's cooler up by the Tarn,' Lucas said. 'Why don't you take some time off for yourself and go for a walk on the fells?'

'I do occasionally – but now I think I should follow Miss Alice's example and wash before I get tea ready.'

'If that's what you want.' He shrugged, then caught my arm as I turned away. 'You haven't changed your mind about sitting for me? I keep trying to sketch your face from memory but I can't . . . I need to see you . . . '

There was such longing, such appeal in his eyes that my

151

heart contracted with a sudden sharp pain. My brain told me that I should continue to keep a distance between us but my heart and body were singing another tune, a sweet, plaintive melody that I could not deny.

'Perhaps on Sunday afternoon for an hour or two . . . if I have time.'

'I won't ask for more than you can give,' Lucas promised, and I knew that he was speaking of more than time.

'On Sunday then. But you must let me go now, I have things to do.'

'Yes, I know.' He released me.

At the archway that led round to the back of the house, and eventually the kitchen gardens, I paused and looked back. He was still standing on the same spot, watching me. The smell of musk roses stirred my senses and for the first time in my life I was aware of sensual desire, a desire so strong and sweet that it made me feel weak with an over-whelming longing to be in his arms.

'You're a fool, Nellie Pearce,' I told myself as I continued reluctantly on my way. 'And if you're not very careful you're going to get yourself into trouble.'

Alice went away on the Friday morning, though not with-out a few doubts and a gentle push from both Lucas and me.

'Supposing something happens while I'm away?'

'We shall cope,' Lucas said and sent me an agonized glance. 'What are we to do with her?'

'We know where to contact you if necessary,' I said, then on impulse reached up and kissed her cheek. 'Go on with you, you daft woman. We shan't need you – just relax and have a good time.'

'You will telephone?' Alice gave me a hug, then looked rueful. 'I'm being silly, I know. You are both perfectly capable of managing without me.'

She was finally persuaded into her car. I waved until it disappeared down the drive, then turned back to find Lucas watching me.

'You haven't changed your mind about Sunday?'

'No.' I ran the tip of my tongue over lips that were

unaccountably dry. 'I'll come to the studio at about three – if that's all right?'

'I thought I might work in the summerhouse as it's such lovely weather. Could we meet there?'

'If you would prefer it. Excuse me, I have rather a lot to do.'

Lucas did not try to detain me and I hurried away to the kitchen. With Alice absent there would be extra work for me to fit into my busy routine. She usually kept her brother's room neat and tidy because he hated the intrusion of servants, but for the next few days he was just going to have to put up with it.

Mrs Jermyns was in the kitchen when I collected the polishing cloths.

'I thought I might as well do Sir Charles's room first – get it out of the way.'

'Yes.' The housekeeper nodded. 'He'll want fresh flowers and so will Lady Amelia. Janet will do hers while Miss Alice is away, if you see to the master's.'

I collected the vase of flowers I'd arranged earlier, then went up to the upper landing where the main bedrooms were situated. I'd helped Janet to clean them since Iris left, although I'd seldom been inside that of my employer, except to spring clean when he was safely downstairs and would not be disturbed. Of late, though, he had taken to his bed more and more, refusing to let Henry carry him down to his study. I hesitated outside, then knocked once.

Henry came to open the door.

'Is it all right to clean now?'

'I've just finished shaving him,' Henry replied. 'Wait a minute and I'll ask.'

I heard their conversation through the open door.

'It's Nellie,' Henry said. 'Is it all right for her to come in and dust?'

'Where's Alice?' Sir Charles demanded irritably. 'She knows I don't like maids fussing about.'

'She's gone away, sir.'

'Sheer selfishness,' Sir Charles complained. 'Never thinks of my comfort, always does as she pleases . . . '

'Shall I tell Nellie to come in, sir?'

153

'I suppose so. If you must.'

Henry came back and admitted me into the room. The light was restricted because the windows were shaded and closed, making it feel stuffy and smell stale.

'I shan't be long, sir.' I smiled and nodded at the man in the bed. 'May I open the window for you?'

'No, you may not.' He glared at me from sunken eyes. 'And don't speak to me unless you're spoken to. Just get on with your work and go.'

'Yes, sir.'

I set the vase of fresh flowers on the large mahogany desk near the window, then polished the top and rubbed it until it shone, before turning my attention to the chest of drawers, the wardrobe and the bedside table, plumping up the cushions on the sofa at the bottom of the bed; finally I picked up the vase with the previous day's flowers and went out, closing the door behind me.

Once outside I allowed myself a backwards glance of disgust. He was the one to talk of selfishness! If I were Alice I would never come back to be used and verbally abused day in and day out by that man. It was a wonder Henry put up with it, though he seemed to thrive on his position as the old man's nurse, perhaps because he did much as he pleased. I knew he helped himself to Sir Charles's cellar and did very little other than attend to his master, leaving most of the jobs that were properly his to Doris and me.

'What sort of a mood is he in?'

I hadn't noticed Lucas coming towards me until he spoke. He was carrying the newspapers and obviously preparing to visit his father.

'I've just cleaned the room,' I said, 'so he wasn't very happy – but I'm sure he will be pleased to see you.'

'I'm not.' Lucas pulled a wry face. 'We never have exactly seen eye to eye. But I promised Alice I would do my duty and I shall.'

I nodded and we passed one another; at the end of the hall I glanced back to see Lucas disappear into his father's room. He had not bothered to knock and I wondered what kind of a reception he would receive, but that wasn't my affair.

I spent the first half of the morning preparing and cooking

the dinner, but in the middle of making a delicate sauce I was summoned upstairs by Henry to help him change Sir Charles's bed linen, which had been soiled and needed to be taken down to the laundry where it was received by a disgruntled Doris.

'That's the third time this week he's done that,' she grumbled. 'It makes more work for me but no one ever thinks about that. It would serve them right if I just went off without a word!'

'Why don't you – if you're not happy?'

Doris glared at me. 'That's what you'd like, isn't it, Miss Hoighty Toighty? You'd have it all your own way then, wouldn't you?'

'I've no idea what you mean.' I sighed. 'Isn't all this a bit silly, Doris? There's no need for us to be bad friends.'

Doris turned her back on me, her face sour as she dumped the sheets in a tin bath to soak for a while before washing them. I went back to the kitchen; my sauce was ruined and I had to start all over again. I was thoughtful as I settled into my routine; I hadn't known that Sir Charles was sometimes incontinent, Alice never complained of it, though it must be her who usually had the task of helping Henry with the bed. How many more tasks was she expected to perform during the day?

When I carried Sir Charles's lunch up to his room I met Lucas coming out again. He pulled a face at me, then showed me the leather letter case he was holding.

'I had no idea how much Alice did for him,' he said. 'He's had me writing letters for the past hour or more – and I spent an hour and a half reading the papers earlier . . . '

'Alice usually does all this.' I glanced down at the tray I was carrying. 'I don't think anyone really appreciates how much she does do for both Sir Charles and Lady Amelia.'

'I've promised to take my mother out this afternoon,' said Lucas. 'Excuse me, I mustn't keep her waiting for lunch.'

He looked so harassed that my mouth twitched at the corners. It was barely four hours since Alice had left and Lucas was already longing to escape!

'All right, I know,' he said and gave a self-deprecating

smile. 'I'm not the stuff martyrs are made of and I can only thank God for Alice.'

'She always says that a nurse-companion would never stay five minutes. I suppose that's why she feels it her duty to do what she can.'

'But it isn't, is it?' Lucas frowned. 'It is properly my mother's. I shall speak to her about it, this cannot be allowed to go on.'

I thought privately that if Lucas wasn't careful he would only store up more trouble for Alice when she returned.

When I took the lunch tray in I discovered that a jug of water had been spilt over the bedside chest I'd polished earlier, and though Henry had done his best it was still damp. I used the white cloth I'd covered the tray with to dry it a little, which brought a glare but no comment from Sir Charles.

As I went downstairs again I wondered how Alice stood her life here; it was so much worse than I'd ever imagined.

Sir Charles took a nap in the afternoon, which gave everyone some relief. On Sunday I finished my chores then slipped away to the wild garden, taking care to lock the kitchen gate after me. My heart was beating very fast and I had an odd feeling of guilt mixed with excitement, rather like a little girl doing something she knew she ought not but was determined on anyway.

Lucas was waiting for me, the door of the summerhouse open and his easel set up on the steps. I hesitated, then he looked up and smiled, beckoning me nearer.

'I've got a surprise for you,' he said, and when I reached the door he pointed to a table just inside. It was set with glasses, champagne cooling in an ice bucket, a silver dish with small marzipan comfits and chocolates, and a basket of delicious soft fruits. 'I thought it would be nice for you to have something you hadn't prepared yourself for once.'

'Champagne . . . I've never tasted it.'

'Then there's not a moment to waste.' Lucas took the bottle out of the bucket, wrapped a cloth around it and pulled the cork, which came out with a bang and sent a group of chattering finches winging up into the trees in a flurry of green and yellow. 'Try dipping the strawberries in it,' he suggested as he handed me a glass. 'I think you might like it.'

He had spread a blanket on the verandah and I sat down, my legs curled to the side. I took a cautious sip, laughing as the bubbles went up my nose.

'It's nice,' I said, 'but I want to sneeze.'

Lucas offered me the basket of strawberries and I took a large, very ripe red one, dipping its sweetness into the champagne, then biting into the soft flesh of the fruit; the juice ran down my chin and I went to wipe it off but Lucas bent forward and licked it away with his tongue. I stared up into his eyes in surprise, then gasped as he reached out to tangle his fingers in my hair, holding me while his mouth sought mine.

It was as if something had exploded inside me, making me tingle and burn all over. Lucas smiled and drew back, watching as I struggled with the emotions warring inside me.

'I shouldn't have done that,' he said, 'but I couldn't resist it. Drink your champagne and eat some of these strawberries.'

He sat with his back against a wooden post, watching as I took him at his word, then reached for his drawing pad and pencils, beginning to sketch with rapid, confident strokes.

'I must look awful. You don't want to draw me like this. I didn't even have time to change my clothes.'

'It isn't your clothes I'm interested in.' Lucas's eyes swept over me. 'If I had my way I would paint you in your true glory, without a single piece of cloth in the way . . . '

My cheeks flooded with hot colour. 'You never mean it – not with my clothes off?'

Lucas shook his head and laughed. 'Don't look so terrified, Nellie. I know better than to ask. Not that it would be so very terrible. All the great artists have painted the women they love in the nude. Perhaps one day I shall paint you that way, but not yet.'

I wiped my mouth and put down the empty glass. I was trembling inside and could not bear to look at him. Was he saying that he loved me? It wasn't possible. He might want me, men often wanted to make love to pretty girls, but that

157

didn't mean they loved them, not in the way I wanted to be loved.

Lucas lent over to me, tipping my chin so that I was forced to look into his eyes. 'Is it so impossible' he asked in a soft voice, 'that I should love you? I have – for a long time I think, though I wasn't always aware of it.'

His lips caressed mine in a gentle, undemanding kiss that made me sway towards him, wanting more. Lucas laughed but drew back, his eyes speculative as he looked at me.

'It must be the champagne,' he said. 'You're not used to it. I mustn't take advantage.'

'It isn't the champagne.' I felt as if I were melting, my limbs were weightless and I was floating. 'It's you – it has always been you.'

'My sweet, lovely Nellie ... ' He shook his head. 'I promised no harm should come to you from this – and I can keep my word, you know. I'm often selfish and thoughtless, we both know that, but I won't hurt you.'

The tears stung my eyes. 'But you have,' I whispered, 'you already have ... '

'What do you mean?'

'I – I love you,' I said and scrambled to my feet. 'And – and it's wrong.'

I tried to leave but Lucas was too fast for me; he caught my arm, swinging me back and into his arms, encircling me, holding me tight as he whispered against my hair.

'No, no, don't run away, my darling. There's no need ... I promise you, there's no need.' He touched my cheek with his fingertips. 'Why is it wrong that we should love one another?'

'You know why.'

'No, I don't.' He kissed my nose then my brow and the corners of my eyes. 'You are so lovely, so special. I want to kiss every part of you, to love you and have you for my very own.'

'Please don't,' I begged. 'You don't know what you are doing to me. I can't bear it ... '

'Have you so little faith in me?'

'What do you mean?'

'Do you think I haven't considered what this means?' he

asked. 'I promised I wouldn't hurt you and I won't – I won't seduce you, Nellie. I want you to be my wife.'

'You can't mean that!' I was shocked. 'It's impossible, you must know that?'

'Why?'

'Because we come from different worlds. You know we can't marry. Everyone would be against it, our families, our friends – everyone!'

'If we don't care, why should they?' Lucas frowned down at me. 'I didn't think you were a snob, Nellie.'

'I'm not!'

'What you're saying is snobbery – of another kind to the sort my mother practises, I'll grant you that, but it's the same thing.'

'No, it isn't. I'm thinking of you – your friends would laugh at you behind your back; they would think you had let your class down.'

'That's ridiculous!' Lucas glared at me. 'Alice has been telling me you're reading Virginia Woolf and Lawrence; she says you can discuss the books intelligently with her – so why should my friends despise you?'

I looked at him helplessly. 'Don't you understand how wide the gap is between us? It's true I've read books I would never have known existed if it weren't for Alice – but that doesn't change who and what I am.'

'You're Nellie, and beautiful.' He stroked my hair, his fingers firm and strong as they sent shivers down my spine. 'You don't have to worry about what other people think. I spent part of the past two years working alone on a Greek island. It was almost paradise but it had one thing missing – if you were with me I should be content there for the rest of my life.'

A swift surge of anger rushed through me and I pulled away from him. 'Is that your idea of love? You want to hide me away from everyone because you're ashamed. What happens when you begin to regret all you've given up? Will you hate me then – or will you come back to visit your friends and leave me on the island, safely out of sight?'

Lucas moved away from me. 'That's a disgusting thing to

159

say.' His eyes were colder than I had ever seen them. 'Just what sort of a person do you think I am?'

'I don't know. I don't know . . . '

I ran away from him before the tears could fall.

There was going to be a storm; it had been stiflingly hot all day and I'd been baking for hours. Now I felt that I must go outside in the air for a few minutes or I would die.

'I'm going for a walk,' I said to Mrs Jermyns. 'I need a breath of air.'

'You have looked a bit peaky for a couple of days,' she replied. 'I hope you aren't sickening for anything.'

I shook my head. I knew exactly what was wrong. It was two days since I'd run away from Lucas and since then my heart had felt as if it were breaking. We had met once or twice as he came from his father's room but he'd passed me without speaking, averting his eyes as if he could hardly bear to look at me.

But perhaps it was best that way. Lucas couldn't have been thinking clearly when he'd asked me to marry him. He was a rebel and spent his life so wrapped up in his work that perhaps the differences between our worlds meant little to him. In his lordly arrogance he might even believe that he could step over the divide and carry me back with him, but in my heart I knew better.

It was much cooler outside than in the stuffy kitchen. I stood breathing in the sweet night air, then decided I would go for a walk to ease the tension which had been building inside me for the past two days.

I had the key to the wild garden in my pocket. My fingers reached for it, rubbing the smooth metal. Why shouldn't I go there? It was my favourite place, somewhere I could be alone. I unlocked the gate, leaving it on the latch after I'd gone through; there was no point in locking it at this time of night, the gardeners had finished hours ago and no one else was likely to be about.

As always the peace of the old garden relaxed me. It was my fault that Lucas was angry with me. I'd been too quick to accuse him of dishonesty, but his suggestion that we should

160

marry had aroused a sharp longing and hope: a hope that was dashed by the chill of reality all too soon.

Lucas had spoken on impulse. We were both very aware of the strong physical pull between us, but he knew that I would resist all attempts at seduction. His declaration had been a desperate measure and one he must already have come to regret.

I had been thinking of him when I'd said everyone would be against a marriage between us, but my family also would find it difficult to accept. Even Alice – who was my friend – would be shocked.

I had been walking for some minutes when the smell of cigarette smoke suddenly alerted me to the fact that I was not alone. It was that odd smell I'd noticed in the kitchen after I came back from the dance with Tom: an exotic, scented smell. Lucas sometimes smoked Egyptian cigarettes – could it be him? Was he here, waiting for me to come to him?

'Lucas?' I heard a twig snap. 'Is that you?'

A man came towards me through the twilight. I drew my breath in sharply: it was Henry!

'What are you doing here?'

'I might ask the same of you.' He leered at me. I saw that he was smoking one of Lucas's cigarettes and now that he was closer I could smell the whisky on his breath. 'Or do I need to ask? Can I guess why you're here?'

His expression was unpleasant, gloating, and it made me uneasy.

'I came for a walk,' I said. 'It was hot – but I'm cooler now so I shall go back.'

'For a walk?' He lurched closer. 'Or was it to meet your lover? Perhaps I should say one of your lovers . . . '

'Wash your mouth out with carbolic!' I cried. 'I'll have none of that filthy talk, thank you.'

'Such an innocent,' Henry slurred. 'You had me fooled for a while but not any more. I saw you kissing Tom Herries a week ago Saturday night, and I know you come here to meet the other one.' His manner was suddenly threatening. 'It seems to me that I might as well help myself to a little of what you're giving the others . . . '

161

I ought to have seen this coming; it had been apparent for a while, all those sly looks he had been giving me, the innuendo in his voice when he'd asked me to go for a drink one evening.

'Don't you dare touch me!' I took a step back. 'I don't have any lovers – and I'm not doing what you think I am. I'm warning you, Henry, if you try to touch me I shall scream.'

'I'm going to do more than touch you . . . ' He sprang at me, grabbing my arm and trying to pull me against him. I struggled and broke away, dodging past him and running as fast as I could. 'Come back, you little bitch!'

I fled towards the summerhouse. If I could only reach it before him, I could lock myself inside and wait until he sobered up. But Henry had no intention of letting me get away that easily. He pounded behind me, crashing through the shubberies and swearing as the rose thorns tore at his clothes and skin. He was catching me, plunging through while I weaved in and out of the bushes. Suddenly he was in front of me, planting himself in my way, laughing at me as I tried to swerve. I screamed as he threw himself at me; the weight of his body knocked me down and I found myself lying on the ground with him on top of me.

'I've got you now,' he muttered, his hands clawing at my breasts while his wet, slobbering mouth covered mine. 'I'll bet you love it, don't you? Can't get enough of it. I'll show you what a real man can do . . . '

I screamed again, struggling beneath him as he began to pull up my skirts, one hand moving down to thrust between my legs and tear at my underclothes. Preoccupied with his attempt at rape he released one of my wrists; in that instant I stuck my fingers out like two prongs and jabbed at his eyes. Henry gave a cry of pain and jerked back; I brought my knee up with all the force I could muster, making him yell in agony, then I was wrenching away from him and on my feet. He growled like a wounded animal and reached out for my ankle, tugging at it and trying to bring me down again. I had temporarily blinded him; he was cursing as he tried to unbalance me but his impaired vision hampered him and he couldn't see my foot as I kicked out at him and struck him hard on the temple. He gave a groan and jerked a couple of times, then his fingers went limp and slipped from my ankle.

He was dead! I was filled with a sudden panic. I had killed him! I backed away in fear. All of a sudden I was running, wildly, blindly . . . straight into the solid wall of a human body. The smell of oils mixed with that special muskiness I knew so well made me look up as Lucas held me, steadying me.

'What's wrong?' he asked. 'I thought I heard a scream.'

'It was Henry . . . he had been drinking . . . he tried to . . . '

Lucas's fingers bit deeply into the soft flesh of my upper arms. 'To rape you?' His eyes were like molten steel in the moonlight. 'I'll kill him!'

'No . . . ' I was recovering now. 'It's all right. I fought him . . . I think I may have killed him . . . '

'That's plenty good enough for him,' Lucas muttered furiously. 'I've thought he was getting above himself – but that he should attack you . . . '

'He thought I had come to meet you.'

'Go back to the house and say nothing. Leave this to me.'

'But if I've killed him . . . '

'I doubt if you have – but whatever has happened, I'll see to it.' He gazed down at me. 'Trust me, Nellie?'

'Yes.' I blinked hard. 'You know I do.'

'Good.' He gave me a little push. 'Go on now. I'll deal with Henry, whether he's dead or alive.'

Thunder rolled threateningly across the sky, then there was a terrific crack and lightning lit up the small attic room, making me jump. I wasn't usually frightened of storms but that had come very close. I was on edge as I went over to my window and looked out; it had begun to pour with rain, a sheet of water lashing down with an evil ferocity.

Lucas had been so long! Was he still out there? Perhaps he was burying Henry's body under a bush . . . A shiver of revulsion went through me. It was all so horrible.

'Nellie – may I come in?'

The sound of Lucas's voice made me spin round. He was standing hesitantly in the doorway and I ran to him, pulling him inside and closing the door.

'You were so long. I couldn't bear to wait downstairs.'

'It's all right. You're not a murderess. Henry has a headache and feels very sorry for himself, but is otherwise unharmed.'

'Thank goodness!' My knees felt shaky and I retreated to sit on the edge of the bed. 'I was afraid I had killed him.'

'It isn't that easy to kill a man. You might have done it if you'd used an iron bar but as it is he has been unfortunate enough to survive – I say unfortunate because that's how he feels now I've finished with him.'

'You haven't done anything foolish.' I looked at him anxiously. 'He was drunk. He won't do it again.'

'He won't get the chance! I've dismissed him, thrown him out with all his baggage. I'll thrash him if he ever comes back – and I've refused to give him a reference.'

'Why did you do that?' I cried. 'Who is going to look after your father now?'

'I'll get a nurse in. Someone properly trained; it's about time he had the right kind of care.'

'A nurse won't stay,' I protested. 'Then Alice will have to do Henry's job.'

'No, she won't. I'll find someone reliable.' Lucas set his jaw stubbornly. 'Just trust me, Nellie. Believe me, it can be done – it will be done.'

'If you say so.' I refrained from asking what we were going to do until the nurse could be found.

'Why won't you ever trust me?' A note of irritation had crept into his voice.

'I do trust you.' I got up and moved towards him. 'Don't be angry with me, Lucas. I didn't mean to insult you the other day. It was just so – so impossible.'

'Nellie . . . ' His voice softened, becoming tender. 'Don't cry, my darling. We'll find a way, I promise you. I can't let you go. I need you, want you so much . . . '

Afterwards I was never quite sure how it happened, but suddenly I was in his arms and he was kissing me, whispering feverish words of love that swept all caution before them. I could no longer find the will to resist when every nerve in my body was throbbing with the need to be close to him. Lucas

164

gazed down into my eyes and I understood what he was asking without words.

'Yes,' I said. 'I love you. I want this as much as you.'

'Are you sure? Quite sure you know what this means?'

'It means I am committed to you – for always if you want me.'

'Never doubt it,' he murmured, and then his lips were on mine. 'Nellie, my little love, I want you so much . . . '

I stood shyly as he unfastened the buttons at the neck of my gown but my gaze never wavered as I looked up at him, nor did I flinch as his gentle, eager hands stripped away the layers of clothing until I was completely naked. Lucas's eyes dwelt for a moment on my full breasts, flat stomach and rounded hips, whispering hoarsely, 'You're even lovelier than I imagined.' Then he knelt before me, his hands on my hips, his face pressed against my flesh. For a moment or two he stayed there, simply holding me, as if worshipping at the shrine of his own personal goddess, then he rose, bent to gather me in his arms and lifted me on to the bed.

I watched with unashamed interest as he began to undress, discarding first his shirt, then his shoes, socks, flannels and finally his silk underpants. I'd seen my brother in the bath at home and was aware of differences between male and female, but this was my first experience of a naked, sexually aroused man. My eyes opened wide at the sight of his swollen penis and, as he knelt on the bed beside me, I put out a tentative finger to touch it. I was surprised at the heat of his flesh and at the way it quivered and leapt beneath my touch, and I laughed.

'Will it hurt?' I asked, curiosity banishing any nervousness I might have felt. Suddenly I wanted only to please him, to do whatever he demanded of me. 'I don't know what you want me to do. You will think me an ignorant girl.'

'I think you are quite, quite perfect,' he said, but there was laughter in his eyes. 'Oh, Nellie, my precious innocent, I don't want you to be anything other than you are. I want to teach you what loving is all about.'

'Teach me to please you.'

'We'll learn to please each other – and I'll try not to hurt you, though it may just at first.'

165

He lay down beside me, his hand caressing my hair and cheek. I moved towards him, feeling the burn of his heated flesh against mine; his mouth covered mine in a sweet, tender kiss and suddenly it was all so simple and right. Lingering doubts and fears fled as his hands stroked my back with long, firm fingers, arousing sensations I'd never dreamed of and releasing a hot surging tide that started somewhere deep inside me and spread through my veins until I was awash with desire.

'That feels nice,' I murmured against his chest. I blew at the crisp dark curls. 'Your hair is tickling my nose, Lucas.'

'Say it again,' he murmured as he rolled me on to my back, his mouth sucking at the rosy tips of my breasts. 'You taste like honey.' He looked up at me. 'Say my name again.'

'Lucas ... Lucas ... Lucas ... ' My voice rose as his tongue and lips trailed down my navel to the soft hair that covered the mound of my femininity, then his hand parted my thighs and his tongue probed at the moist centre of my secret being, flicking and darting with a delicate sensitivity until my back arched and I cried his name once more, 'LUCAS ... '

His body slid over mine. I could feel the pulsating heat of him nudging at me, then he was thrusting at me, gently at first then harder as he penetrated deep inside me. I was conscious of some pain but felt it a small price to pay for the pleasure of being with him this way. I loved and was loved, nothing else mattered; it was what I'd longed for and in my heart had always known would happen one day. This was my destiny, to love and surrender myself for that love – for good or evil, for pain or sorrow, better or worse.

When it was over I lay quietly in his arms, my head nestled in the hollow of his shoulder. I could taste the salt of his sweat on my lips and his scent was imprinted into my senses; I felt that I would never forget this night, never regret it, no matter what happened in the future, but I did not speak my thoughts aloud. He would think that I did not trust him and be angry.

He was very still as he lay beside me.

166

'Lucas . . . '

He opened his eyes and smiled. 'I was almost asleep – what's wrong?'

'Nothing. I just wanted to tell you that I love you.'

He pulled me down to him, stroking my hair, then his eyes travelled round the room, 'I never realized what these rooms were like. You can't stay here. Tomorrow you must move into the best guest room.'

I lay back on the pillow. 'No, Lucas, not yet. We should wait for a while – at least until Alice comes back. Once everyone knows . . . ' I faltered as he tensed beside me. 'I can't stay here as your . . . '

'My future wife,' he supplied. 'Why not?'

'It would cause so much trouble. Please, Lucas . . . please let's keep this a secret, just until we're ready to go away together.'

'You won't change your mind?'

'How could I? You know I love you. I belong to you now – don't I?'

It was all a dream. Even as I lay in his arms, his hands gently caressing me, a part of my mind was warning me that I was letting Lucas blind me to the truth. This was foolish and wrong, but I wasn't strong enough to fight it.

'Yes, you belong to me now.' He sounded like a cat purring with satisfaction. 'I have no intention of letting you go again, Nellie Pearce.'

I was silent for a moment, then, 'My parents may not like the idea of us marrying any more than yours.'

'Will you come away with me if they refuse?'

'My – my father won't refuse us, even if he doesn't like it. It's my mother . . . she might be difficult.'

I closed my mind to the doubts that crowded in on me. Perhaps Lucas was strong enough to make it happen. He wanted me to trust him and despite my natural caution the barriers were crumbling and I was swept away on a rushing tide of love and hope. It would all come right because we loved each other.

'You haven't answered my question.'

'You shouldn't need to ask it.'

'Oh, Nellie,' he whispered. 'Do you know why I love you

so much?' I shook my head. 'It's because you make me laugh inside all the time.'

I withdrew from him. 'You shouldn't laugh at me – it isn't respectful.'

'I'm not laughing at you, only because of you – don't you see the difference?' He reached out, drawing me back to him. 'Because you make me happy, you make me feel whole. Before you came here I had forgotten how to laugh.'

I ran the tip of my forefinger down the length of his scar; it was smooth and shiny, not rough as I'd always imagined.

'Because of this?'

'And other things . . . '

'What do you mean?' I was suddenly uneasy and he sensed it.

'Forgive me, darling. I shouldn't let the dark moods touch you . . . they come and go but I won't let them hurt us. You are special to me, Nellie. The day you met me in the wild garden I was in the deepest despair . . . close to taking my own life. Then I saw you staring at me with a mixture of fear and defiance in your eyes and something happened to me. I wanted to paint again. I wanted to paint you. You are my talisman. You bring me luck.'

'Is that all I am to you – a lucky charm?'

He laughed and kissed me. 'Surely you don't need to ask that after what happened just now? I love you . . . more than I've ever loved a woman. As much as I'm capable of loving anyone. I know I'm selfish and arrogant – but I do need you. Please believe me.'

There was something in his eyes that made me wonder just how important any woman could ever be to Lucas.

'It is going to be all right, isn't it?'

'Yes, my darling, of course it is.'

Lucas was stroking my back. He was becoming aroused again and I clung to him, trying to shut out the creeping fear that was worming its way into my mind. I mustn't let myself doubt; we loved each other and nothing could change that.

'I love you,' he whispered. 'I shall always love you, never forget that, Nellie.'

I offered myself up to him, letting the surging desire sweep back the insidious fear. Only this feeling, this urgent need to be one with him, mattered to me now. It was too late for doubts, too late for anything but this.

Lucas made a series of phone calls the next day and succeeded in finding a trained nurse who was willing to live at Beaumont House, but the earliest she could be expected was at the weekend, which meant that until then we should have to cope on our own.

'I can manage to shave him, but you'll have to help me with everything else,' Lucas said. 'That's if he'll let me near him with the razor . . . '

It was to be expected that Sir Charles would complain at the change in his situation. Lucas informed him of it in a stormy interview. I never knew exactly what had been said, though the whole household was aware that there had been raised voices in the master's room: they were not slow to voice their own opinions over the midday meal.

'What a commotion!' Mrs Jermyns declared. 'I wish I knew what made Mr Lucas send Henry off like that . . . I can't think what Miss Alice will say about all this.'

'Her ladyship is most upset,' Janet put in. 'She feels quite unwell. It really was thoughtless of Mr Lucas, turning the house upside down. I hope no one expects me to help with Sir Charles, I've enough to do as it is.'

'It's all right,' I said. 'Mr Lucas and I will manage until the nurse comes.'

'Quite cosy for the two of you,' Doris muttered in a low voice. 'Makes things easier for you with Henry gone, don't it?'

'What did you say?' Mrs Jermyns demanded. 'Don't mutter, Doris. Speak up if you have something to say. I can't stand muttering.' Recently her hearing had become less than perfect but she would never admit it.

'I only said I had work to do,' Doris replied, and, with a malicious glance at me, she went out.

'We all have work to do,' Mr Jermyns grumbled. 'This means longer hours for all of us. A nurse won't do all Henry's work, you can rely on that if nothing else. She'll expect to be waited on herself, I daresay – as if we didn't

169

have enough to do as it is. This would never have happened if Miss Alice had been here . . . '

Later, when we met outside his father's room, I told Lucas that he was not popular with the rest of the household.

'Perhaps I should have let Henry work the week out,' he admitted, 'but I couldn't bear the thought of him in the house after what he did to you.'

'They're all wondering why you threw him out.'

'Don't say anything,' Lucas warned, 'or you'll be blamed instead of me. You were right, Nellie. It is best to keep our relationship a secret for now.'

I thought that perhaps Doris had begun to suspect something, but didn't bother to tell him. It was only for a few days. After that Alice would be home and then everyone would know. Even I was beginning to believe it would really happen.

'We had better go in,' I said. 'The bed will need changing and Sir Charles doesn't like to be kept waiting.'

I wondered if perhaps he would flatly refuse to be washed or helped by a servant he had always chosen to ignore, but, although sullen and unhelpful, he allowed me to do what was necessary and an hour later I left him looking clean and refreshed. He was sitting up against a pile of pillows waiting expectantly for Lucas to begin reading the papers to him when I took the soiled linen down to the laundry room.

'More work,' Doris grumbled. 'Put them down there; I'll see to them when I can.'

I deposited the sheets, hesitating as I considered asking what she had meant by her remarks earlier.

'Want something?'

'No, nothing,' I replied and went out. I wasn't going to give Doris the satisfaction of knowing she had touched me on the raw.

I didn't regret what had happened; I loved Lucas and the memory of our passionate loving was warm and sweet inside me, but I knew what everyone else would think. They would believe that I had forgotten my place, that I had allowed Lucas to seduce me: something that was fine and beautiful would be tainted by their scorn and disbelief. I didn't want that to happen, I wanted to keep this feeling of shining happiness safe from prying eyes for a while longer.

Alice telephoned later that afternoon to say she had decided to delay her return for a few days.

'I didn't mention Henry – it would have spoiled it all for her,' Lucas told me afterwards. 'She would have come rushing back and I want the nurse safely installed before she does.'

'Yes,' I agreed fervently. 'Otherwise Sir Charles will insist that Alice can take over herself.'

I had been up and down stairs half a dozen times that morning, summoned by his impatient ring for the most trivial things, and twice while I was making the invalid comfortable he had pinched my arm, giving me a malevolent glare afterwards as if daring me to complain. Of course I had said nothing, either to him or to Lucas. Sir Charles wanted me to make a fuss but I was determined not to let him win, even though I suspected he had deliberately spilt a cup of tea over the bed just so that I had to change it again.

'Somehow I don't think Alice will let him use her quite as much as in the past . . . '

'What do you mean?'

'It's just a feeling I have,' Lucas said with a tantalizing shake of his head. 'Of course I could be wrong . . . '

Later that night, when I lay in his arms, I asked again what he had meant; this time he nibbled at my earlobe and sighed, then lay back, his hand idly stroking my thigh.

'It's just that having had a few days of freedom, she's going to find it difficult to slip back into the old ways – at least, I hope she is. Father's finances have recovered a little since he's been forced to leave them to his brokers; he can afford a couple of nurses and a companion for Mother if need be. I don't see why Alice shouldn't marry Gerald now. If she leaves it much longer she will probably lose the chance. No man is going to wait for ever. The poor devil has been remarkably patient already.'

'I know. I would so like her to be happy. I shall hate to think of her alone after we've gone.'

171

'Then I'll do my best to persuade her to stop playing the martyr and think of herself.'

'That's not fair – she does it out of goodness and kindness. You make her sound awful, as if she did it so that everyone would say how wonderful she was.'

'I didn't mean it like that.' Lucas gave a sigh of exasperation. 'You mustn't take everything I say literally. You know what a wicked tongue I have – but I'm very fond of Alice.'

'Yes, I know.'

Lucas had begun to fondle my breasts. I realized he wanted me again and tried to relax, to let my mind empty of everything but the man beside me. It was difficult. Despite all my efforts to make myself worthy of him there was still a yawning gulf between us – it was a fundamental difference in attitude, culture and class that would not disappear simply because I had read a few books.

Was it after all too wide to bridge?

Lucas gazed down at me. 'What's wrong? Have I upset you – or are you just tired?'

'Neither.' I could not put the tiny, nagging doubts into words.'I was just thinking about Alice – but it's all right now. Kiss me, Lucas.'

I put my arms around his neck, bringing his head down so that our lips met. His arms encircled me and I felt desire quicken. It didn't matter that he thought so differently on so many things; it couldn't be allowed to matter that the gap between us was far wider than either of us had realized, that I did not always understand his reasoning – only this mattered, this surging, glorious feeling of wanting to lose ourselves in each other's flesh.

The nurse arrived at exactly the time she had given Lucas. She was a tall, strongly-built woman in her middle years with big arms, straight, dark brown hair, grey eyes that seemed to penetrate right into your mind, and a no-nonsense manner that made short work of Sir Charles's tantrums. From the moment she entered his room it was obvious that she was in charge and that she meant to have full control of the sick room.

'You'll be very much better sitting up in a chair, sir,' she

172

said. 'Lying there all day will give you bed sores; we don't want that, do we? And we shall all be the better for a little fresh air –' she gave Sir Charles a bright, meaningless smile and threw open the window '– there, that's very much more comfortable.'

'I thought Father would throw a fit,' Lucas said as he unfastened the buttons of my dress that night, 'but he was like a lamb. I think Margaret Wimbush has taken his measure. She obviously knows how to handle men like my father – he needs someone to sharpen his wits on. I can see them having wonderful battles once he's got his second wind. Mother and Alice were always too easy for him. This could do him the world of good.'

'Do you really think so?' I looked at him doubtfully. 'Alice has always been afraid that he might have another stroke if he became overexcited or upset.'

'That's why he always wins.' Lucas pulled a face. 'Can't you see that he uses his illness to exploit others? My father is a selfish, inconsiderate bully, Nellie. He needs someone like Miss Wimbush to keep him in order.' He slipped my petticoat down over my hips. 'I'm selfish, too – and I don't want to think about Father, not just now.'

I was tired but didn't resist as he swept me up and carried me to the bed. Lucas was right; he was selfish and thoughtless sometimes, but I loved him and I would never have dreamt of refusing his love-making, even if I did have a throbbing headache . . .

Chapter Eleven

'These are the best yet,' Tom Herries said as he bit into a
freshly baked coconut pyramid. 'The top is crunchy but I
like the soft, sticky centres. I've said it before and I'll say it
again, you're a champion cook, Nellie.'

I concentrated on the groceries he had delivered, checking
them off the list without looking his way. It was incredibly
hard to behave naturally with him; I hadn't realized how
difficult this was going to be and couldn't bring myself to
meet his eyes. Tom was expecting me to marry him one day
and I hadn't stopped him building on his hopes – I'd even
encouraged him the last time we'd met – and now I didn't
know how I was going to let him down gently.

'They're showing a Clark Gable film this weekend,' he
said. 'We could take a run into town in the van if you liked.
If we went to the early house you could be back well before
eleven . . . '

'Is it the one that got best picture three or four years
back?' I asked, my interest aroused. 'The one with Claudette
Colbert?' I hesitated as he nodded, then realized it was out of
the question. 'Mrs Jones told me about it – it was good, she
said.'

'It Happened One Night, that's the title,' Tom said, and
lifted his cap to scratch beneath it. 'What do you reckon then
– shall we go?'

'I can't. Miss Alice has only just got back and I've a lot of
work to catch up on.'

Tom shrugged; I had turned him down so many times he
was used to it. 'Well, I'll be off then. See you next week.'

'Yes, next week.'

I couldn't look at him as he went out. I ought to have come straight out with it and told him I wouldn't be seeing him again, but he was bound to demand explanations and there were none I could give him ... at least none that wouldn't hurt him. I felt so guilty: I didn't even know if I would still be here next week. Besides, my mind was upstairs with Alice and Lucas.

What were they saying to each other? Had Lucas told her about me yet?

After Tom had gone I became restless. I hadn't spoken to Alice yet, because Tom had arrived almost at the same moment and I'd decided to wait until the flurry died down. Mrs Jermyns had taken a tea-tray up to the sitting room but they would have finished with it by now. I would fetch it down and perhaps have a word with Alice.

As I passed Mrs Jermyns's room I heard the sound of her wireless; it was very loud and the newscaster was saying something about Mr Chamberlain in Munich. Mrs Jermyns was having more and more problems with her hearing. Someone really ought to persuade her to see a doctor, I thought, the news of Mr Chamberlain's triumphant return from Germany brushing over me like so many leaves in the wind. At the moment I was concerned only with what was going on inside this house.

Miss Alice had been good to me but I wasn't sure how she would feel about my becoming Lucas's wife. She would be surprised, of course, perhaps a little dubious about the wisdom of a hasty marriage – but would she be angry?

The door to Alice's sitting room had not been properly closed. Feeling nervous, I paused outside to wipe the palms of my hands on my apron before knocking, and the sound of Alice's slightly agitated voice made me hold back.

'I don't think you've given this much consideration, Lucas. Have you any idea what it will mean, marrying a girl like Nellie?'

'I've told you, I'm in love with her. P̶ ̶ some of the best work I've ever done were those portraits. She's my talisman.'

'That's hardly a reason for marriage.'

175

'Don't look like that! Of course it isn't my only reason. Nellie is very beautiful.'

'Yes, I agree – but think ahead, Lucas. Think about how you might feel in a few years' time.'

'I didn't expect you to be like this, Alice – the parents, yes, but not you.'

'Is that why you're doing it? To pay Charles back? I know you don't get on but . . . '

'I must admit it gives me a certain pleasure to know I shall have fulfilled all his darkest expectations, but it isn't the reason I'm doing this.' He swore softly. 'Nellie is fresh and young and lovely. Look at me, Alice. I'm not exactly a catch for any woman, am I?'

'Oh, Lucas . . . ' Alice's voice had softened. 'I'm not being a snob, really I'm not. You know I want you to be happy and I'm fond of Nellie but . . . '

'But?' There was an ominous note in his voice.

'She has the strict morality of her class. Don't turn away, Lucas! I just think you might find that irked you after a while. Besides, you're in such a hurry. She's still so young and naive in many ways . . . '

I backed away, my cheeks on fire. I couldn't go in now to save my life! Alice was only saying aloud what I'd known in my own mind, but I was humiliated by what I'd heard. I'd thought we were friends, that she would understand about loving someone despite all the barriers other people might try to erect. At the very least I'd expected her to try and understand.

I walked away; my eyes were stinging and I felt mortified. I ought to have waited for Miss Alice to send for me instead of just going up myself, then I wouldn't have heard them arguing over me.

'It's your own fault, Nellie Pearce,' I told myself fiercely. 'You were warned not to forget your place. It's your own silly fault.' It was, of course, but that didn't stop it hurting, didn't stop the sense of disappointment and embarrassment.

I had been forcibly reminded that I was a servant – that the gulf between Lucas and me was perhaps too great to be breached even by love.

*

'You're wanted in the master's room,' Mrs Jermyns said, coming into the kitchen as I was taking a tray of cinnamon biscuits from the oven. 'They smell good . . . Miss Wimbush says the bed wants changing again.'

'I'll go now. Will you turn the biscuits out for me when they've cooled?'

'Yes, of course.' Mrs Jermyns eyed me sharply. 'You look a bit peaky – anything wrong?'

'No, I'm all right.'

I avoided looking at her as I left the kitchen and walked slowly upstairs. I didn't feel like talking, besides, there was nothing to say. If even Miss Alice was against us marrying . . . the sound of a harsh, cruel voice came to me as I reached Sir Charles's room and I paused to listen to what it was saying.

'You're a dirty old man! You deserved to be punished. If I had my way you would lie in your own filth all day.'

'I-I'll have y-you dis-m-missed!' The words were slurred but defiant and I smiled – but my smile faded as I heard the nurse's reply.

'Just try it!' There was a loud crack that was unmistakably a slap. 'Tell tales and I'll have you confined in a lunatic asylum, you crazy . . . '

I pushed open the bedroom door and stared in stunned disbelief as Margaret Wimbush moved away from the bed. There was a red mark on Sir Charles's face and, as I watched, a single tear escaped from the corner of his eye and rolled down his cheek.

'Oh, there you are,' Margaret Wimbush said with a false smile. 'I'm afraid we've been naughty again, the bed needs changing.'

I ignored her. 'Are you all right, sir?' I asked. 'Shall I call Miss Alice?'

His eyes flew to the nurse and there was fear in them, the kind of fear known only to the vulnerable, the elderly and infirm.

'There's no need for that,' Miss Wimbush answered for him. 'Whatever you think you heard . . . '

'I know exactly what I heard,' I said, suddenly angry, 'and Miss Alice is going to hear about it, too.'

177

'You interfering little . . . '

'Try it!' I dared her. 'I'm not a sick old man who can't fight back. You'll feel the palm of my hand – and I'm pretty strong.'

'He pinched me,' the nurse retaliated in the way of all bullies faced by someone with the courage to stand up to them. 'You don't understand. With some of these old people the only way is to establish domination, make them see you won't put up with their tantrums or . . . '

'A pinch doesn't give you the right to hit him or to say the kind of things I heard.' I looked at her in disgust. 'You're not fit to have the care of a sick person – and you won't, not when Miss Alice . . . '

'How dare you!' She advanced on me threateningly, her hand raised.

'What's going on here?' We both looked round as Alice came into the room. 'Why are you arguing?'

For a moment there was absolute silence, then the nurse spoke. 'I demand you dismiss this girl at once. She is interfering in my work and Mr Harrington said I was to have complete control. I won't stay here unless you dismiss her.' A smile of triumph played over her mouth. 'You won't find me easy to replace – not in this godforsaken place.'

Alice studied her in silence, a cool, proud expression in her eyes, then turned to me. 'Will you tell me what has been happening here, please?'

'She hit Sir Charles for making a mess in the bed,' I said, giving the nurse a defiant look. 'She called him a dirty old man and said he should lie in his own filth – and then she threatened to have him shut up in a loony bin if he told you she had hit him.'

'She's lying,' Miss Wimbush said, but the colour had drained from her cheeks and she looked frightened. 'You can't believe her. You can't take the word of a servant over mine. I'm a qualified nurse with years of experience . . . dedicated to looking after the sick . . . ' Her voice trailed away as she realized neither of us believed her.

'You will please leave immediately,' Alice said in a tone of quiet authority. 'Nellie wouldn't lie about something like this.'

'I was employed by Mr Harrington. You have no right . . . '

'I have every right,' Alice said. 'Mr Harrington will see you are reimbursed for any inconvenience. Good day.'

For a moment their eyes clashed, then the nurse went out, slamming the door behind her. I turned to the invalid.

'We'd best have you out of all this, sir. If you'll put your arms around my neck I can lift you out while I change the sheets and Miss Alice will get you some clean pyjamas.'

'S-sorry f-for . . . '

The stuttered apology made me smile. 'Why bless you, sir, it's nothing to me. A few minutes' work and you'll be comfortable again.'

'Th-thank you, Nellie.'

It was the first time he had ever used my name.

Between us we changed the sheets, washed, wiped and dressed our patient, then tucked him back into a clean dry bed.

'I'll take these down,' I said, gathering the sheets. 'If you want me I shall be in the kitchen.'

'Thank you,' Alice replied with a smile. 'We'll talk later.' She turned to her brother. 'Now, Charles, perhaps you would like me to read to you for a while . . . '

I closed the door softly behind me.

'She actually had the nerve to ask Lucas for a reference,' Alice said later that evening as we shared a cup of tea in her sitting room.

'I hope he didn't give her one!'

'Naturally he refused – though he paid her until the end of the month.' Alice pulled a wry face. 'I'm afraid he's feeling guilty over all this.'

'It wasn't his fault. She seemed very efficient when she came.'

'Efficiency isn't everything.' Alice sighed. 'For all his failings Henry looked after Charles; they got on well, too.'

'It's all my fault. If I hadn't told Lucas . . . '

'Nonsense!' Alice was firm and decisive. 'Henry deserved to be dismissed, though I would have given him a reference for his years of good work here.'

'Lucas was angry for my sake.' I blushed. 'He – he's told you . . . '

179

'Yes, my dear.' Alice got up and bent to kiss my cheek. 'I know he loves you and I'm very happy for you both.'

'Are you? I thought you might think it wasn't right . . . that Lucas should marry someone from his own class . . . '

Alice was silent. 'Did you hear that? I'm so sorry, Nellie. I didn't mean it the way it sounded. I was concerned for you, because . . . because it won't be easy for you.' She looked steadily into my eyes. 'Do you understand what I mean? I'm not trying to patronize you, please believe me – but some people will . . . '

'Yes, I know. I know what folk will say. I don't care about them – as long as you don't mind?'

'Of course I don't. I love both you and Lucas dearly. You must know that?'

'I – I thought we might be friends . . . ' I was still uncertain. 'If you don't think I'm presuming too much . . . '

'We are friends, we have been for a long time,' Alice said. 'And I haven't thanked you for standing up for Charles the way you did earlier.'

'I can't abide to see folk mistreated, especially when they can't hit back.'

'Charles isn't exactly helpless, or sweet-tempered,' Alice said with a faint smile. 'Don't think he's suddenly going to reform – this morning was reaction, nothing more. I believe he was really frightened of that woman, but he won't be of us and I dare say the complaints will start very soon.'

'Maybe we'd feel like complaining if we had to live the way he does,' I said, and laughed. 'Her face when you told her to go! You were wonderful, miss – like an avenging angel, burning sword in hand.'

'Please drop the "miss",' she begged. 'You were doing very well when I arrived – but it was as well I did. We are rid of her now.'

'Shall you employ another nurse? I could stay on for a while . . . '

'I wouldn't dream of it, nor would Lucas allow it. Yes, I think another nurse would be a big help, but this time I shall interview her myself.'

'I'll stay until she comes,' I said. 'There's no need for us to rush off.'

180

'Well, if you could . . . ' Alice looked grateful. 'We'll see what Lucas . . . ' She broke off as the door was suddenly flung open and he appeared on the threshold. At the sight of his stricken face she rose to her feet. 'What is it? What's wrong?' she cried, her voice rising. 'Something has happened . . . '

'It's Father,' Lucas said in a strangled tone. 'I – I think he may be dying. He asked for you . . . '

'Oh, no!' Alice cried and rushed from the room.

I glanced at Lucas and then followed her.

There was nothing anyone could do for Sir Charles; this time it was his heart, and after a short period of severe pain, during which he clung to Alice's hand with an intensity that spoke more surely than any words, he lapsed into an unconscious state from which he was never to recover.

Lady Amelia paid a brief visit to her husband's room shortly before the end came that evening. She wept bitterly and clung to Alice.

'Whatever shall I do?' she cried, her gaunt face shocked and pale. 'Oh, Alice, I can't manage alone. You won't desert me? Promise you won't leave me! I couldn't bear to be alone . . . I just couldn't . . . '

'Call me if anything happens.' Alice threw an agonized look at me as she led her weeping sister-in-law away. 'I shall be back soon.'

I resumed my place at the dying man's side. I did not doubt that Lady Amelia's distress was genuine, though perhaps it would not be too uncharitable to think that most of it was for herself. My sympathy was for Alice, since it was obvious that Lady Amelia meant to cling on to her for all she was worth.

Sir Charles's breathing was very shallow. I thought the end could not be long now and wondered whether his death had been hastened by the events of the past few days. No one would ever know for sure, but I was aware of a vague feeling of guilt, as though I ought to have done something. Perhaps if I'd never taken that walk in the wild garden . . .

Was Lucas wracked with guilt, blaming himself for his father's death? Was that why he hadn't come near all the afternoon? I wished he would come.

Then, as if in answer to my thoughts, the door opened and he entered. He looked tired, his eyes heavy and dull as if he had just woken from a deep sleep.

'How is he?' he whispered.

'Peaceful. It can't be long now.'

'Perhaps it's a merciful release – it wasn't much of a life for him, and it will be a relief for Alice. She'll be free at last.'

'Lucas!' Alice walked in as he spoke, her expression shocked. 'How can you say such a thing at a time like this?'

'It's the truth.'

'However much I have sometimes wished to be free, I have never wished Charles dead.'

'I didn't say that.' Lucas was frustrated and angry. 'Don't twist my words. You know I didn't mean it like that, but it must be a relief all round – for him as much as anyone.'

'Your mother is prostrate on her bed,' Alice replied. 'Perhaps you should consider her feelings before you start to celebrate.'

'She'll get over it sooner than you think.'

'Please don't quarrel,' I cried. 'Lucas – your father is dying . . . '

His eyes were cold as he looked at me. 'I am aware of that but I'm not prepared to pretend he was a saint all of a sudden. He was a bad-tempered devil and much as I regret the way it happened, this is a relief for everyone.'

'I refuse to listen to this, Lucas.' Alice was angry, now. 'If you can't show suitable respect, please go away.'

'As you wish.'

He shrugged and walked out.

I felt awful and wished I hadn't said anything. It was horrible to see Alice and Lucas quarrel like this. 'He was only thinking of you,' I said as the door closed behind him.

Alice sighed, looking suddenly drained and defeated. 'I know. He's feeling guilty. Lucas is like that: he says and does things without thinking, then suffers agonies of regret afterwards and that makes him even more moody. I shouldn't have snapped at him but . . . '

She bent her head as the fight went out of her, and all at once she was weeping, great gulping sobs that were forced out from deep down inside her.

I went to cradle her in my arms, rocking her as all the pain and grief poured out. 'Don't cry, dearest Alice. I know you cared for him, and so does Lucas in his own way. He shouldn't have said what he did but he does have a point . . . it wasn't much of a life . . . '

'To think that his last few days were made so miserable,' Alice said, her tears easing as anger surged. 'If I thought that woman had hastened his death . . . '

'But you can't prove it,' I said. 'It might have happened even if – if Henry had still been looking after him.'

'If I hadn't gone away . . . ' Alice took out her handkerchief and wiped her eyes. 'I feel it's my fault for leaving him. I was so tired of always being here, of always doing my duty, but now . . . '

'You mustn't blame yourself,' I comforted her as best I could. 'If I hadn't gone for a walk in the garden . . . if Lucas hadn't engaged that nurse . . . '

Alice blew her nose. 'It would probably have turned out just the same,' she said. 'Doctor Miles told me months ago that Charles's heart was beginning to give out.' She gave me a rueful smile. 'We are none of us to blame. I shall apologize to Lucas later.'

'He'll understand,' I said, praying that I was right. 'You're upset. Everyone is.'

'Yes.' Alice squeezed her hand. 'Of course you're right. We're all upset . . . '

I tried to apologize to Lucas the next time I saw him. He looked straight through me, his expression cold and remote.

'You're like Alice,' he said. 'You blame me for what happened to Father.'

'No, of course I don't. It could have happened anyway – no one blames you.'

'Don't they?' He raised his brows. 'Excuse me, Nellie, I have things to do.'

He walked away from me, leaving me feeling hurt and bewildered.

I stood with Mrs Jermyns and Janet at a respectful distance

while the heavy oak coffin was lowered into the ground by four strong bearers. Alice had wanted me to join the family for the service but I'd refused.

'It wouldn't be right to intrude on Lady Amelia at the moment,' I said. 'She won't like it when Lucas tells her about us, but he won't, not yet . . . '

'If he ever does.'

The words were in my mind though I did not speak them aloud.

I had hardly seen Lucas since his father's death. When I tried to offer consolation he had brushed me aside, and after that had seemed to avoid me. I was not sure what I'd done to make him so angry with me and it caused me some heart searching, but so far I had not cried.

For days we had all been busy cleaning and cooking for the guests who were sure to come up to the house after the funeral, but each night I had gone to bed expecting Lucas to come to my room: he had not and his absence distressed me – what had I done to make him turn against me?

I wished so much that he would come, that he would share his grief with me so that we could comfort each other, but he didn't and as each day passed the pain inside me grew stronger. If he really loved me, surely he would not stay away from me at a time like this?

My eyes never left his face as he stood by his father's grave, but he didn't look at me or at anyone else. He was pale and withdrawn, seemingly unaware of what was happening around him, as though he were cocooned in his own little world. Was he ill? He didn't look at all well, though perhaps that was due to his grief and guilt. I wished I could go to him, hold his hand, show him that I understood and that I cared. Convention held me back as he walked with Alice and his mother to the big black car drawn up outside the churchyard. He helped his mother to get in, then, for one brief moment, he glanced back at me. I gave him a small, shy smile but it was not acknowledged.

He was staring at me as if I were a stranger, as if we had never made love, never held each other close in the darkness, whispering of love and of spending the rest of our lives together . . .

184

'Don't take it to heart so,' a voice said and I turned to see Tom Herries watching me. 'He's just upset . . . '

'What do you mean?'

My cheeks were warm as I looked into Tom's eyes. Were my feelings written so plainly on my face?

'Nay, lass,' he said. 'It's because I know you so well.'

'I'm all right . . . '

'Don't pretend with me.' Tom gave me a long, straight look. 'I've business away from the Dales for a few days but I'll be back a week Friday if you need me.'

I stared after him as he walked away, then followed on behind Mrs Jermyns and the others as they left the churchyard. Tom's words had cheered me despite myself. Perhaps he was right . . . perhaps Lucas was just grieving for his father. Maybe tonight he would come and tell me that he still loved and needed me.

'What do you mean – Lucas has gone?' I stared at Alice in disbelief. 'He was here when I cleared the tea-tray after everyone had left. He smiled at me and said he was sorry . . . ' I drew a sharp breath. 'I asked him what he meant but he just shook his head.'

'He left me a note. It seems he blames himself for his father's death – and has gone away to think things over.'

'Did – did he say anything about me?' I felt the sting of tears but refused to cry. There was nothing to cry about, Lucas would come back: he had to! 'He didn't leave a letter for me?'

'Not as far as I know. I'm very sorry, my dear.' Alice made a movement towards me then stopped. 'I'm sure he will come back very soon – or perhaps he will write to you from London.'

'Has he gone to London?'

'His show is being held there next week. I expect he will be staying at the house for a while. I'll give you the address. You could telephone him there if you wish.'

'No . . . No, I'll wait for him to come back for me. He will when he's ready, he's just upset.'

'Yes, of course,' Alice agreed. 'I'm sure you're right. Lucas has always had these moods. I imagine he'll return in a few days and everything will be sorted out.'

185

'Yes, I expect so,' I said and turned away.

My heart felt as if it were cracking right down the middle and I didn't know how to bear the pain. I longed to believe that Lucas would come back for me, but there had been something final about the way he had said he was sorry, almost as if he were saying goodbye. I'd thought it odd then, but it had never occurred to me that he would simply go away without telling me.

And yet he had once before. But that was different – that was before he had told me he loved me, asked me to be his wife . . . made love to me.

How could he just go like that? I could have understood if he had only had the courage to face me, to tell me it was all a mistake, that he had discovered he didn't love me enough to alienate his mother and friends by marrying me. I would have been hurt but I would have accepted it, but this . . . this cruel desertion was tearing me apart. Night after night I lay awake, the pain gnawing at my insides – but still I hadn't cried. I wasn't going to give way to self-pity.

'I'd best go and give Doris a hand with the washing-up,' I said and turned away.

'Wait just a moment.' Alice delayed me. 'I – I have something to tell you.'

I glanced back, sensing that she was reluctant to add to my grief. 'It's all right,' I said. 'You can tell me.'

'Amelia wants to go away – to France. She says she can't bear to stay here and the warmer climate will help her to recover her health. Of course I shall go with her.'

'To France?' I was surprised. I wasn't much of a one for reading the newspapers, preferring the women's magazines with their features on cooking and knitting, but I'd seen and heard enough to know that there was a great deal of political unrest in Europe. 'Will it be safe there?'

'Oh, yes, I think so,' Alice replied. 'Mr Chamberlain says the Germans don't really want war. Besides, we'll be in the south of France, far away from any of the danger zones even if there is trouble in parts of Europe.'

'I suppose it will do you both good to get away.'

'I would have asked you to come with us but – but Amelia has asked Mabel. You remember Miss Parkinson, of course?'

186

'Yes, I remember. She's not taking Janet then?'

'No. That will be a disappointment for Janet, too.'

Janet would be very upset but at least she hadn't had her heart broken.

'Old loyalties die hard,' I said with a shrug. 'Her ladyship can please herself now. I dare say she was upset when Sir Charles made her dismiss Miss Parkinson like that.'

'Yes, she was.' Alice sighed. 'And it was all so unnecessary . . . I'm sorry, Nellie. You won't mind that I can't take you? But you will want to stay here in case Lucas returns, won't you?'

'Yes.' I forced a bright smile. 'Don't you worry about me. You do what you have to do.'

'If . . . if Lucas shouldn't . . . ' Alice faltered. 'Of course he will but if he didn't, would you stay on here?'

'I don't know. I might write to Mrs Jones, see if her sister needs any help in the kitchens of her hotel.'

'Perhaps you should,' Alice agreed. 'I know you stayed here for my sake but I don't think you should waste your life in service, Nellie. You should make something of yourself.'

'Yes. Perhaps I shall.'

I went out hastily. It was obvious that Alice didn't think Lucas meant to come back for me – that she thought it had all been a mistake and was sorry for me.

'What's wrong?' Tom asked. 'If I've done something to offend you say so – though I can't for the life of me think what it is.'

'You haven't done anything.'

We were alone in the kitchen. I was beating eggs into my cake mixture and refused to look at him. Tom saw too much. He had sensed my unhappiness at the funeral and I was afraid he would guess that Lucas and I had been lovers.

'I've got a lot to do, Tom.'

'Yes, I'd best be on my way.' He picked up his baskets and started for the door, then swung back with an accusing look. 'It's him, isn't it? Lucas Harrington. There was something between you. That's why you've changed towards me.'

'Of course there wasn't,' I muttered, but my cheeks were on fire.

187

'Don't lie to me, Nellie. I can see it in your face.'

My head went up then. What business was it of his? I was close to tears, my eyes gritty from lack of sleep.

'Yes, I love him, if that's what you want to know. Not that it's anything to do with you! I'll thank you to keep your nose out of my affairs.'

Tom looked so hurt that I instantly wished the words unsaid. He'd been a good friend to me and didn't deserve this. Even as I tried to force out the words of apology he moved away.

'If that's the way you want it,' he said and went out.

I stared after him and my throat ached with the pent up emotion I was trying to control. Lucas had deserted me and now I'd lost Tom's friendship. At that particular moment I wasn't sure which hurt the most.

Damn him! Damn both of them!

I went back to beating the eggs with a vengeance.

Janet was very upset that Mabel Parkinson was to accompany Lady Amelia and Alice on their trip to France. She came into the kitchen after being told that she wasn't to go and burst into tears.

'It isn't fair,' she said. 'I've done everything for her – everything! – and this is what I get.'

'You've only done your job,' Mrs Jermyns said. 'Anyone would think you had been slighted in love.'

Doris looked at me with a malicious delight. I turned away to move the kettle on to the hob of the range.

'Well, I'm not putting up with it,' Janet said. 'I shall find myself a job somewhere else – in a shop or a hotel. I've had enough of being in service anyway.'

'That's foolish talk,' Mrs Jermyns said. 'I know the wages are better but by the time you've paid your keep you won't benefit.'

'Why shouldn't Janet go if she wants?' I asked. 'It wouldn't surprise me if her ladyship closed this house up and went to live abroad permanently.'

'You don't really think so?' Mrs Jermyns looked anxious. 'Maybe we should all start to look for other posts.'

She was really worried and I was sorry I'd spoken so

thoughtlessly. With her hearing the way it was Mrs Jermyns would have difficulty in finding another job.

'I expect she'll come back in the spring,' I said. 'Miss Alice said they were going away for three or four months, that's all.'

'I shall speak to her myself,' Mrs Jermyns said, 'ask her what my position is here.'

She was duly reassured by Alice that at the moment there was no thought of closing Beaumont House for good.

'We shall certainly come back in the spring. Any decisions about the future can be left until then, Mrs Jermyns. And until then we shall be relying on you to see that everything is as it should be.'

Her assurances pleased Mrs Jermyns, who rather liked the idea of being left in sole charge of the house.

Janet sulked for a few days, especially when Miss Parkinson arrived and she was relieved of all her special duties. She helped me with the packing for Miss Alice but never stopped grumbling. I held my own disappointment inside, though as each day passed and there was no word from Lucas the pain became harder and harder to bear.

Ten days after the funeral Alice, Lady Amelia and Miss Parkinson left to catch their train, Alice's car almost sinking beneath the weight of their combined luggage as it drew away from the front of the house.

Before they left Alice invited me up to her sitting room for a last cup of tea.

'I'm going to miss you so much,' she said. 'I do wish you could come with us, Nellie.'

'It's better this way. I shall be here when Lucas gets back.'

'I thought he would have written by now,' Alice said. 'He is staying at the house. I telephoned but he was in a hurry to go out. You could try phoning yourself, Nellie.'

'He knows where I am if he wants me.' I could hardly bear to look at her. If Lucas cared about me he would have been in touch by now.

'He does love you, he told me so. I don't know what to say to you – it is too bad of Lucas to behave this way. I can't think what has got into him.'

189

'He's just grieving,' I said. 'Don't you worry about it.' I hesitated then asked, 'What about Mr Gerald?'

'I'm hoping to see him in France,' Alice said. 'Amelia needs me for the moment, but I shan't let her stop me seeing Gerald. I think she will come to accept the situation in time and then we shall marry.'

'I'm glad. It's what you should have done a long time ago.'

'No.' Alice shook her head. 'I'm glad I did as I did. I have nothing to reproach myself for – and neither has Lucas. I've written to him and told him so, and I've told him it's time he stopped sulking, so I hope you will be hearing from him soon.'

'He'll come when he's ready,' I said. 'You'd better go down now – you don't want to keep Lady Amelia waiting.'

'No, I suppose not.' Alice stood up and reached for her coat, smiling as I helped her on with it. 'Now, you're sure there's nothing I can do for you before I go?' She turned and kissed my cheek. 'If you need me Mrs Jermyns has the names of the various hotels we shall be staying at.'

'I shall miss you.' My throat was suddenly tight. 'But it will soon be spring.'

'Yes, of course. I'm not going away for ever – and if you're still here when I return I may have something nice to tell you.'

She meant that she might be married to Gerald, of course. I took the used tea things down to the kitchen, then joined Mrs Jermyns and the others at the head of the long gravel drive to wave goodbye.

'Well,' Mrs Jermyns said as the car disappeared from view, 'that's that then. I suppose we can think ourselves lucky we still have jobs – and there'll be far less to do than there was. I don't know about you, Nellie, but I could do with a nice cup of tea.'

'I'll get it,' I said. 'I've made some macaroons if you fancy one.'

I wiped my face with a damp flannel, then rinsed my mouth with water and spat into the toilet. I had just been sick for the second time in twenty minutes and for the third morning

190

running. Looking at my pale face in the rather spotted mirror of the downstairs toilet I saw that there were shadows beneath my eyes. I hadn't been sleeping well for the past few weeks – and now I had something else to worry about.

At first I hadn't been sure. Even though my periods had always been regular I hadn't really worried when I missed the first one. I'd thought it might be because I was upset, and I'd still hoped then that Lucas would write or come down, but it was nearly two months now and I could no longer doubt that I was carrying his child.

'What are you going to do, Nellie Pearce?' I asked my reflection. 'You've got yourself into a nice pickle, haven't you?'

One thing I was certain of was that I couldn't go home. I'd visited a couple of weeks back and been relieved to see that my father looked better in himself, but his business was suffering because another shoe-repairer had set up in the village in opposition and money was shorter than in previous times, which hadn't improved my mother's temper. I could just imagine her face if I went home with a bastard in my belly.

I wasn't going to try and get rid of it as Iris had either. I placed protective hands over my gently rounded stomach and smiled as I thought of the new life growing inside me – my child and Lucas's. I could never destroy something so precious. So what was left? If Alice had been here I might have asked her for advice, but she was in Provence and having a wonderful time. I'd received three letters, all of them full of glowing descriptions of the countryside and the people she was meeting.

There was no point in writing to Alice; it would sound so awful in a letter, so sordid and nasty. I was just going to have to make up my own mind. I could go down to Bournemouth and see Mrs Jones, but she had warned me about trusting the gentry and I felt awkward about going to her when I was in trouble. Perhaps if I stayed on here for a little longer and saved my money . . . when I had to leave I would go up to London. I might try to contact Lucas. Even if he didn't want to marry me he would probably help to support me until I'd had the baby.

191

It went against the grain to contemplate asking Lucas for assistance, but I might have no alternative. The one thing I did not even consider was asking Tom Herries for help, though I had no doubt that he would have given it; he would probably have asked me to marry him.

Or perhaps not. He'd been avoiding me since our quarrel and that had hurt me. One thing I couldn't bear was to see the look in his eyes when he knew I was carrying another man's child.

'You've been sick again. I heard you in the toilet,' Doris said as I returned to the kitchen a few mornings later. Her eyes were full of a mixture of spite and triumph. 'I reckon I know what's wrong with you, Nellie Pearce. You've got your comeuppance at last.' Doris had a cold and she wiped her running nose on her sleeve. 'That's what you get for making up to your betters.'

'It's none of your business, Doris,' I replied. 'I don't know why you should hate me but . . . '

'You ain't no different from me,' she cried angrily. 'Yet you've been mollycoddled by them all from the start – too good to work in the laundry with me you were. You had to be Cook's favourite and have your picture painted, then you were taking tea with Miss Alice in the parlour as if you were gentry. Well, see where it's got you now. You're pregnant and . . . '

My patience suddenly snapped and I slapped her face. 'Shut up!' I cried. 'If I were having a child it would be my business, not yours.'

Doris pressed her hand to her cheek, tears of anger starting to her eyes. 'Well, we'll just see about that! You wait until I tell Mrs Jermyns. She'll send you packing so fast your feet won't touch the ground.'

'Say what you like. I'm leaving anyway.'

I walked out of the kitchen and up the stairs towards the housekeeper's room. Doris's spite had forced me to make up my mind. Rather than stay here to be dismissed and sent away in disgrace, I would give in my notice now and leave before my pregnancy began to show.

*

192

'I'm disappointed in you, leaving us in the lurch while Miss Alice is away. I'm sure I don't know what she would think of all this . . . '

Staring out of the train window at a meaningless blur of trees, fields and hedges, I recalled the housekeeper's parting words. Mrs Jermyns had been stiff and disapproving; I wasn't sure whether Doris had told her of her suspicions or not but she hadn't mentioned anything, seeming to accept my excuse that I wanted to get away and see a little more of the world.

'You're like all the young ones today,' Mrs Jermyns said with a sniff. 'You all think the grass is greener somewhere else. Well, don't expect me to take you back when you discover what it's really like out there.'

'I won't,' I promised, a smile flickering round my mouth. 'And if I were you, Mrs Jermyns, I should go to the doctor and have your ears looked at – it might just be wax, you know. My grandfather almost went deaf once from too much wax in his ears.'

'My hearing is perfectly all right,' the housekeeper replied indignantly. 'If people would speak up and not mumble all the time I could hear as well as anybody.'

'It was just a suggestion. Well, I'd best be off then. Thank you for everything.'

I had arranged for a lift to the railway station with the baker's delivery boy in his van; I gave him two shillings for his trouble, which left me with seventeen pounds and sixpence in my purse after paying for my train fare to London. It wasn't exactly a fortune but it would see me through for a few weeks, long enough for me to find a job and somewhere to live.

Before I left I'd sent a note down to the vicar's wife telling her I wouldn't be able to help out with the cooking lessons in future. I thought that if I'd wanted help Mrs Roberts might have been the one to talk to but I was determined to find my own way out of this mess.

I still hadn't made up my mind whether or not I ought to speak to Lucas; if I could find work in the kitchens of a hotel or a restaurant I wouldn't need to ask for his help – but perhaps he should know that I was carrying his child. It wouldn't be fair not to tell him, would it?

A part of me still kept thinking that it was all a temporary misunderstanding and that eventually everything would turn out right. Lucas had seemed to mean it when he said he loved me . . . but why had he gone away without a word?

Chapter Twelve

It was a little frightening arriving in London on my own. Everything seemed so big and so fast, people hurrying everywhere as if they hardly had time to live – and the traffic! I'd never seen anything like it, cars, buses and trams: so much noise that it almost deafened me. For a moment I stood outside the station clutching my suitcase and feeling confused as I shivered in the bitter wind and wondered where to go now that I was here; I couldn't just turn up at Lucas's house so perhaps I had better look for somewhere cheap to stay.

It took me a couple of hours of walking round the streets before I found somewhere that was both clean and cheap. I smiled to myself as I remembered Mrs Jermyns's warnings about girls who thought the grass was always greener somewhere else – little did she guess that at this moment I was wishing myself back in the big warm kitchen at Beaumont House.

My landlady had been polite when she showed me the room but not exactly friendly, and as I unpacked my things and stared at the single bed, with its candlewick cover and the religious picture above the head, I realized for the first time how lonely it was going to feel with no one to talk to. I should miss the busy life I had led for the past few years – and I should miss the people, even Doris and Mrs Jermyns.

'Now don't start feeling sorry for yourself.' I spoke aloud, wanting to break the silence. 'You got yourself into this, Nellie, and you're just going to have to get yourself out.'

'Thank you, keep the change,' I said as I gave the taxi driver two florins and a shilling. It was extravagant of me but I would never have found this place without him, and he had just told me where I could catch a bus to take me most of the way back to my lodgings.

'Ta, lass.' He grinned at me. 'Look out for yourself now.'

I smiled as he drove off; he had talked non-stop all the way here and I'd been glad of it – it helped to keep my mind off what I was about to do. Three days alone in London had been enough to convince me that it would be sensible to contact Lucas and tell him about the child. He was thoughtless and selfish at times, but I didn't believe he would be deliberately cruel. If he knew I was in trouble he would help me.

Once the taxi had gone I approached the building and checked the number with the address Alice had given me; it stood in a row of old-fashioned houses faced with stucco and was three storeys high. I pulled the cast-iron bell pull and waited. Nothing happened. I rang again but there was still no reply. This must be the right place, the taxi driver had assured me it was and the street name was the one Alice had given me. Lucas must be out.

'Did you want something?'

A voice startled me as I was about to turn away. I swung round to find myself facing a man of perhaps forty; he was tall with dark hair, slightly greying at the sides, a pleasant, friendly face and brown eyes, which were just now regarding me with interest.

'I – I thought this was Lucas Harrington's house,' I said as I saw the key in his hand. 'I must have made a mistake.'

'No, there's no mistake,' he said and smiled. 'I'm Jack Henderson, a friend of Lucas's. Can I help you?'

'I was hoping to see him . . . '

'He's away. I was about to let myself in and check his post.' His eyes went over me, their colour intensifying as he suddenly exclaimed, 'Good lord! You're her – the "Innocence and Knowledge" girl.'

'Nellie Pearce,' I said and blushed. 'Lucas told me about you once. You're his agent, aren't you?'

'Yes. Look, Lucas really isn't here at the moment. He popped over to Paris with some friends a couple of weeks ago – for an exhibition of his work, in fact – but I'm expecting him back any day. Give me your address and I'll tell him you called.'

The muted roar of the traffic mingled with a blackbird's trilling song as I hesitated. I was feeling very uncertain about intruding into Lucas's life. He had said that he loved and wanted to marry me, but how could I be sure? He might be angry if he thought I'd followed him to London.

'I could come back another day,' I said. 'When are you expecting him home?'

'By Friday at the latest,' he said. 'Yes, come Friday afternoon and I'll make sure Lucas is here.' His eyes were thoughtful as he looked at me. 'Is there anything I can do to help in the meantime? You're not in any trouble?'

'No. No, thank you,' I said quickly. 'I'll be back on Friday then. Goodbye.'

'Goodbye, Miss Pearce.'

I walked away, my emotions veering between anger and embarrassment. So Lucas was in Paris with friends; he had probably forgotten me and the promises he had made me such a short time ago. How careless and selfish he was sometimes! And what kind of a fool was I to love him the way I did?

For the remainder of the week I was torn with indecision. Should I go back to Lucas's house or not? Perhaps it might have been better if I'd simply left my address with Jack Henderson, then Lucas could have come for me or not as he pleased.

In the end I decided I would go back once more but if Lucas wasn't there I would simply leave a letter telling him where I was living; I wouldn't mention the fact that I was carrying his child.

Throwing caution to the winds I had my hair marcel waved and spent twenty-five shillings on a fitted blue wool suit. I wanted to look pretty for Lucas and after some hesitation I bought a lipstick from Woolworth's; it was a bright crimson and I wasn't sure whether or not it suited me but I wore it anyway. I wanted him to see that I could be more than the simple country girl he had known.

My stomach was tying itself in knots as I walked up to the

door that afternoon. I noticed that there were three expensive cars parked along the kerb and hesitated, wondering if he had guests, but then I made up my mind that it was now or never. I had to see Lucas, if only for my own peace of mind.

The door was opened by a young woman. She was very beautiful with long, thick golden hair and blue eyes. She was also exquisitely clothed in a figure-hugging dress of yellow silk that swirled into fine pleats about her hips, and she wore a string of thick creamy pearls about her swanlike neck.

'Is Lucas in?' I asked. 'Jack Henderson told me to come.'

'Sure, everyone's here,' she said. 'It's a party to wish Lucas *bon voyage*. Come on in, the more the merrier. I'm Natalie Lawson by the way.'

She spoke with an American accent and had that air of absolute assurance which comes from breeding and wealth. As I followed her into the hall I caught a breath of her expensive perfume. The hall itself was thickly carpeted with Persian rugs and the furniture reminded me of the special pieces in Alice's room; pretty, dainty things made of satin-wood and newer than the furnishings at Beaumont House. I recalled Iris saying once that the family's London house was much posher than the country one and now I saw that it was true.

'Don't you mean a welcome home party?' I asked as the girl beckoned me on. 'I thought Lucas had just returned from Paris.'

'He has.' She laughed and flicked her hair out of her eyes. 'But I've persuaded him to come to New York with me. We're sailing next week.'

'Oh, I see.' My stomach clenched and for a moment I felt faint. I must have shown some sign of distress for she gave me a considering look.

'Are you all right? Haven't I seen you somewhere?'

'No . . . no, I'm sure we haven't met before.'

'I'm certain I know your face.'

She seemed to be thinking hard but at that moment a door opened at the end of the hall and someone came out. My heart jerked and I almost stopped breathing as I saw Lucas. He looked towards Natalie, then beyond her to me.

'I heard voices . . . Nellie!' For a moment there was a hard

198

glitter in his eyes and my heart sank. 'Where on earth did you come from?'

He was angry! I should never have come. I stared at him, too miserable to answer.

'Jack invited her,' Natalie said, 'at least, that's what she told me.' There was suspicion in her face now. 'What's going on here?'

'Nothing. Nothing that concerns you,' Lucas replied. 'Go back to the party, Natalie. I'll talk to you later.'

She threw him a sulky glance, then walked past him. As the door opened again I caught the sound of voices, laughter and tinkling glasses.

'Don't be long, darling,' Natalie said with a meaningful look and closed the door behind her.

For a moment there was total silence, then Lucas walked towards me; his eyes went over me, taking in the new hairstyle and the lipstick.

'What the hell have you done to yourself?'

I touched my hair defensively. 'Don't you like it?'

'I prefer it natural – and that lipstick makes you look like a cheap tart.'

I felt as if he had struck me in the face and it made me defiant. I stared him straight in the eyes.

'Maybe that's what I am.'

'Don't be ridiculous.' He glared down at me, then as I continued to meet his eyes his expression changed to one of what could only be guilt. 'I was going to phone . . . '

I wished myself a thousand miles away. 'Alice went to France with your mother,' I said, half defensive, half proud. 'It isn't the same there now.'

'No, I don't suppose it is.' He hesitated, then, 'I've been away, Nellie.'

'Jack told me. Didn't he say anything about me?'

'We've hardly spoken since I arrived. I only got back a couple of hours ago and Natalie had arranged this party . . . '

'She must be a good friend of yours.'

'We've known each other for a while.'

There was a strained silence between us.

'I wanted to talk but perhaps this isn't a good time?'

'Don't look like that.' He was angry and guilty and it

didn't suit him. 'I would have been in touch if you had waited. I know I behaved badly, leaving the way I did. There were reasons . . . '

'What reasons? I should like to understand, Lucas.'

'I'd rather not talk about it – not just yet.' There was an odd expression in his eyes and I suspected that he was hiding something from me. 'I've been busy.'

'I'm sorry. I shouldn't have come.' I was hurt and humiliated, and so obviously in the way.

'Well, as you did, you might as well come to the party.'

'No.' I started to shake my head but he gripped my arm and half-pushed me towards the door through which Natalie had disappeared. 'I don't want to, Lucas. I'll come back when your friends have gone.'

'You're staying,' he said and his manner was back to its old autocratic style. 'We'll talk later. You've got to meet everyone sooner or later. It might as well be now.'

I wasn't dressed for a party, not this sort of a party. One look at Natalie had made me aware of how dowdy I looked; besides, I was still smarting from his criticism of my hair and lipstick.

The room was crowded and I was painfully aware that everyone turned to look as we entered.

'She looks like a waitress or something. Lucas was furious . . . ' As the shrill tones of Natalie's voice died away there was an awkward silence.

My cheeks were on fire and I wanted to run from the room, but Lucas had a firm grip on my arm. His fingers were digging so deeply into my flesh that it was all I could do to stop myself crying out.

'I want you all to meet Nellie,' Lucas said in an odd, angry voice. 'She was my model for the "Innocence and Knowledge" portraits.'

'Good lord!' Jack Henderson clapped his hand to his forehead. 'I forgot to tell you Miss Pearce was coming.' His eyes met mine in an expression of apology. 'Please forgive me.' He crossed the room in quick, easy strides. 'May I get you something to drink?'

'Thank you . . . perhaps some tea.'

'Nellie will have champagne, she likes it,' Lucas said, then

200

dropped his voice so that only Jack and I could hear. 'Try and get rid of this crowd as soon as you can, Jack.'

'No, please don't,' I whispered. 'You mustn't – not because of me. They're your friends, Lucas.'

'He's such a moody devil it's a wonder he has any,' Jack murmured with a wicked grin at me. 'Come with me, Miss Pearce. I should like to talk to you for a while. You can let go of her, Lucas. She isn't going to run away – are you?'

'No.' I was warming to him. He had a genuine smile and he was being kind. 'I really would prefer tea, Mr Henderson.'

'Then you shall have it – and I should like you to call me Jack. Perhaps I might use your name, Nellie?'

'Yes, of course.'

Lucas was scowling at us. Jack tucked my arm through his. 'Shall we see if we can find someone to make our tea? I think I could do with a cup myself.' He drew me through the room, nodding to various people as he did so and saying, 'No, no, you can have your turn later. I want Nellie all to myself for a while.'

We went through a smaller reception room into what was obviously a conservatory. It was light and warm, far less formal than the other rooms. Jack rang a bell as he gestured to me to sit down in a cane chair which was made comfortable with piles of fat, squashy cushions in bright colours.

'Mrs Rawlings will bring us tea here,' he said. 'I hope I did right, Nellie? You looked as if you might be going to faint at any moment.'

An elderly woman had come in answer to his summons. She looked curiously at me, assented to Jack's request for tea with a nod and then went away again.

'Now, tell me all about yourself,' Jack said, turning back to me. 'How old are you – seventeen, eighteen?'

'Sixteen and a few months. I was fourteen when Lucas painted those pictures.'

'They're the best work he's ever done but he refuses to sell them. I used to wonder why but now I think I understand.'

'What do you mean?'

Jack looked into my eyes. 'You're carrying his child, aren't you?'

201

My cheeks flamed and I didn't know where to look. 'Does – does it show that much?'

'It doesn't show in that way at all.' His expression was kind and his voice gentle. 'Please don't be embarrassed. I guessed, that's all.' He paused. 'Have you told Lucas yet?' he asked then.

'No. I was going to but now I'm not sure if I should.'

'Why?'

'He's going to America, isn't he?'

'Yes. He has been offered a show there with an important gallery – but I still think you should tell him.'

'I wouldn't want him to feel that he had to give up his trip for my sake.'

'You owe him the choice, don't you? Besides, there's a good reason why he should know. It's not my place to tell you but . . . '

He would have gone on but we were interrupted by the return of Mrs Rawlings with a tea tray. She set it down on a little cast-iron table, then looked at Jack.

'There is a telephone call for you, sir. You could take it in the library if you wish.'

'Thank you,' he said and glanced regretfully at me. 'Please make a start. I'll join you as soon as I can. There is something I think you should know.'

'What? Please tell me.'

'I'll be back soon.' He smiled at me, then followed the housekeeper from the room.

I hesitated, then poured myself a cup of tea. I drank that, poured another and ate two small cucumber sandwiches. Jack had been gone a long time and I was beginning to feel uncomfortable. I got up to gaze out at the garden, which was looking rather sad and neglected, the roses blackened and dying on the bushes.

'Are you still here? I thought Jack had got rid of you ages ago.'

I recognized the voice and turned to face Natalie. Her eyes were openly hostile, signalling her dislike of me.

'Jack will be back soon,' I said, pretending to misunderstand her. 'He went to answer the telephone.'

'I saw him leaving five minutes ago. Can't you take a hint? You're not wanted here. Why don't you leave?'

'You're very rude. This isn't your home. You have no right to tell me to go.'

'It may not be my house yet . . . ' She paused, a smile of satisfaction in her eyes. 'But it's only a matter of time.'

'What do you mean?'

'Use your imagination – if you have any, of course.'

I wanted to hit her, to wipe the smile from her lips, but I couldn't hit a woman who was a guest in Lucas's house; I was too much aware of the difference between us. She was gentry and until recently I had been a servant.

'Excuse me,' I said. 'I think I'll go and find Lucas.'

'You won't get your claws into him!' She flung the words after me. 'Men like him don't marry tarts like you.'

'He'll be a fool if he marries a bitch like you!' I was driven to retaliation at last and felt a certain satisfaction as I saw the fury in her face.

I had hit out at her in my distress but I believed every word she'd said: this was obviously what Jack Henderson had been going to tell me.

I walked swiftly through the next two rooms, which were thankfully silent and empty, no sign of Lucas or his guests anywhere. All I wanted now was to escape before anyone saw me. I should never have come.

I was at the door when I heard Lucas call my name.

'Nellie – where are you going? I was just coming to find you. We have to talk . . . '

I looked up at him and all the hurt and pain I was feeling was there for him to see in my eyes. 'No,' I said quietly. 'I don't think we have anything to say to one another. I don't think I want to speak to you ever again.'

'Nellie!'

I heard his cry but was close to tears and had to escape before they could fall and shame me. I ran out into the street, and, seeing a taxi pulled up at the kerb across the road, I dodged in front of a lorry and pulled at the cab's door.

'Please,' I said breathlessly. 'Take me away from here quickly!'

Lucas had come out on to the pavement but the traffic was too busy for him to follow me. I heard him call and saw him wave his arms above his head but I closed the door after me.

'Hurry, please,' I said. 'He mustn't stop me.'

'Like that, is it?' the taxi driver said with a grim look as he drew away from the kerb. 'You want to go to the police, luv. Them sort always think they can take advantage of innocent young girls like you.'

'No, please.' I choked as the tears almost blinded my eyes and saw Lucas running behind us as if he thought he could somehow make me change my mind. 'I just want to get home.'

I wept into my pillow all night and in the morning I felt drained and ill. Lucas wanted to be free. He had regretted his promise to me just as Alice had forecast; he had realized that his feelings for me were not strong enough to overcome the differences between our two worlds.

I believed that he had meant his promises when he had given them but after he left the Dales he had begun to see how impossible it had always been ... and then he had met Natalie again. She was beautiful, sophisticated, and she belonged in his world. No wonder he preferred her to me.

I should have known that it would end like this but that did not stop it hurting. My heart ached as I remembered the sweetness of his kisses. Lucas might be selfish and thoughtless, he might be moody and arrogant, but sometimes he could be wonderful. Even now, in my wretchedness, I did not regret having loved him.

I soaked my pillow with tears for three nights, but on the fourth morning I washed the salt from my face and decided that I was not going to be a fool. Crying would not mend something that had been beautiful but was now broken.

After breakfast I left my lodgings and spent the whole day looking for somewhere cheaper to stay. The room I eventually found was clean but not as nice as the one I'd first had. It was however near a fish and chip shop where there was a job advertised for a counter assistant, which I was offered and accepted.

Unfortunately, I was forced to leave after only two weeks because the smell of frying fish made me feel queasy. It was

204

longer this time before I found work and as my meagre stock of money began to dwindle I regretted not having waited to ask Lucas for help. He would surely have given me something to help tide me over, but it was no use going back to his house. He would be in America by now and thinking of his marriage to Natalie.

The next place I found was in a newspaper shop and I was offered a room in the back as part of my pay. I'd barely moved in before I discovered that my new employer had ideas about my sleeping arrangements and I left in a hurry.

I found another lodging house but work was elusive, though I was offered a few hours scrubbing out offices in the early mornings. It was hard, unrewarding work and after two days I left. I was not yet so short of money that I was forced to accept drudgery and I wanted to take my time. I was searching for something worthwhile, somewhere I could begin to put down roots and make a new life for myself – and my child.

Time passed slowly now that I wasn't working. I felt numbed, as if I were going through the motions of living. Perhaps that was my way of coping with my pain.

Christmas came and went. I brought a sprig of holly, then wept as I recalled my first Christmas at Beaumont House.

I'd been so young and innocent then. It was a cruel awakening to find myself alone and pregnant in an unfriendly world.

Sometimes I felt that I must have been half asleep for most of my life; in the solitude of the Dales I'd let time drift by, unaffected by what was happening in the rest of the world. The harsh realities of a cold winter in London were to say the least painful, and as I held my reddened and chapped hands to the pitiful heat of a single bar gas fire, I often longed to be back in the warm kitchens at Beaumont House.

And yet there was a part of me that welcomed my new-found freedom. I spent most of the first few weeks of 1939 walking the streets, staring at the brightly lit windows of fashionable shops and wandering inside the big department stores, like Selfridge's and Peter Robinson's, where the heat warmed my hands and feet, and I was bewildered by the variety of goods on offer. This was a whole new world to me and would have been enjoyable if it had not been for the ache in my heart.

If Lucas had only been honest with me at the start . . . but there was no point in going over and over it in my mind. I could not undo what was done.

'What cannot be cured must be endured.'

'I beg your pardon?'

I had been staring at a notice in the window of a large department store. It was advertising the opening of 'The British Industries Fair' on 20 February 1939 – just three weeks away – and it said that everyone was cordially invited to attend the stand where a tub that did its own washing would be demonstrated. A tub that did its own washing!

'Doris should see that!'

'What did you say?'

I became aware of the woman standing next to me. 'I'm sorry,' I said. 'I was talking to myself. I do sometimes.' It was a habit I'd dropped into since coming to live alone in London. The woman gave me an old-fashioned look and moved away, as if she feared contamination.

It was time I was at work! I quickened my steps as I turned down the narrow, cobbled alley which led to the tearooms in which I had recently found employment.

Hurrying in through the side door of the small shop, I took off my coat and donned the white apron I wore over my plain grey dress. As yet I had been unsuccessful in my search for a position as a cook, but I'd found work as a waitress at Maud's Tearooms; at two pounds a week it was not as well paid as it might have been but the owner was friendly. She greeted me with a smile as I went into the kitchen, which though small was clean and modern with a gas stove, a big, rather noisy refrigerator, bright red cabinets around the walls and a scrubbed pine table.

'I was beginning to think you weren't coming in today.'

'I wouldn't let you down, Mrs Bristow. I'm sorry I'm late. I stopped to look at a poster about a new washing tub – it does all the work for you.'

My employer was a plump widow in her late-forties with tightly waved greying hair, a mild manner and a tendency to forgetfulness, especially where her reading glasses were concerned. She was forever laying them down and then forgetting where she had left them.

'Whatever will they think of next?' Maud Bristow shook her head in wonder. 'One of these days they'll put a man on the moon. Mark my words, Nellie, we'll all be going there for our holidays soon.'

I laughed. 'Not me! You wouldn't get me up in one of those spaceships folk claim to have seen.'

'Martians as high as skyscrapers!' Maud said, chuckling at the joke. 'That caused a right old panic in America last Hallowe'en – the switchboards were jammed with calls and people were running out on to the streets in fear. Still, you'd expect that over there, wouldn't you? Fancy them thinking it was a real newscast!'

'I think I remember reading about it in the paper,' I said. 'It was that novel by H. G. Wells, wasn't it? Broadcast by Orson Welles . . . '

'You should read it,' Maud started to say but the bell went in the shop. 'Customers. You'd best get on, Nellie. We can't stand here gossiping all day.'

I went through to the tearoom with its oak panelling on the walls, neat tables covered by white lace cloths and a welcoming fire in the old-fashioned iron grate. Two women had come in; they took seats by the window, ordering tea, crumpets and a plate of cakes.

For the most part Maud's customers were regulars, visiting at least two or three times a week. Maud's cakes were homemade and very popular – especially the layered angel cake, which was light and moist, and sandwiched together with a delicious buttercream.

As the tables began to fill up I was kept busy serving until nearly five o'clock when the last lingering customers finally paid their bills and left. Once the shop was empty Maud locked the door and we washed up together, using an enamel bowl and the nice new packet soap powder Maud preferred to washing soda. I liked it better, too, because it didn't sting my hands so much, and it was easy to tip the water away down the sink when we wanted fresh – much nicer than the old, deep stone sinks at Beaumont House.

The kettle was whistling on the gas stove. I poured boiling water into the big brown pot Maud liked best and we sat down for a cup of tea ourselves.

'Well, that's that for another day,' she said with satisfaction as she hung a linen tea towel up to dry.

I looked at her thoughtfully. 'Haven't you ever thought of opening up for morning coffee – or for lunch?'

'It would be too much for me,' said Maud. 'I can manage tea but for anything else I should have to take on extra staff and it might not pay. Besides, these are tearooms. I should need a licence to sell wine if I wanted to do lunches – and I don't hold with alcohol of any kind.'

'We could do morning coffee though. Just from ten until twelve, couldn't we?'

'Well, I suppose we might.' Maud looked doubtful. 'I usually spend the morning baking . . . '

'I could help with that – and with the coffees.'

'I couldn't afford to pay you much extra . . . perhaps ten shillings.'

Ten shillings would make all the difference. With an extra ten shillings I could put something by for when I wasn't able to work.

'I'm sure it would pay,' I said. 'We could try it, couldn't we? I make very good rock cakes. Tom Herries used to say they were the best he'd ever tasted.' I thought wistfully of those happy days and then blushed as Maud looked at me with interest.

'Is Tom your young man?'

'Just a friend,' I said, unwilling to meet her curious gaze. As yet I had managed to hide my condition under a full skirt but within a few weeks it would begin to show – and I wasn't sure how Maud would feel about employing me then. Unless I could make myself indispensable in the meantime . . . 'We could serve treacle tart and hot custard in the mornings. I reckon that would bring them in on cold days like this.'

'We could try it, I suppose.' Maud began to sound interested. 'But you'll have to be in by eight if we're to have fresh tarts ready by mid-morning.'

'I don't mind that,' I said. 'It's nicer here than in my room.'

'I'll put a notice in the window. We'll try it for a week and see how it goes.' Maud smiled at me. 'Are you going anywhere special this evening? Out with your friend perhaps?'

'Tom doesn't live in London.' I couldn't help sighing. 'I thought I might go to the library on my way home and take out that book you were talking about. Most evenings that's all I do, read or listen to the wireless.'

'Reading broadens the mind. I've noticed that you like books,' Maud said. 'But you mustn't spend all your time alone in your room. You ought to get out, Nellie, meet other young people – have some fun. I would ask you to come to a concert with me, but I don't suppose you like classical music, do you?'

'I don't know,' I said truthfully. 'But if you were wanting company one evening, I should be pleased to come.'

'Well, then, let's make an arrangement for Friday night. I would have asked you before, but I know you young things like all this modern jazz music.'

'I'm not sure what I like. I've never thought about it. To be honest, Mrs Bristow, I've never given much thought to a lot of things.'

'Then it's about time you did.' Maud shook her head disapprovingly. 'Books aren't everything. An intelligent girl like you should make the most of her opportunities. Learn about life, Nellie, that's what I say. I left school to go into service when I was fourteen but I went on trying to learn everything I could. My husband used to say I knew more than many a college student, God rest his soul.' She sighed heavily. 'I'm not sure what good it's done me to have my head stuffed full of facts – but at least I've managed to run my own business since Fred died, and there's many another in my place who couldn't have done it.'

'I think it was brave of you to set up in the first place.'

'Fred left me a little money,' Maud said, 'but it wouldn't have been enough to support me in my old age. The tearooms have enabled me to live as I please and save for later. I've done well enough but if your idea about the coffee works out I wouldn't say no to a little extra.'

'I'll be off then,' I said as Maud turned off the gas heater. 'I'll be sure to be in nice and early in the morning.'

'Don't forget those books on the way home. And don't just take fiction. It never did anyone any harm to learn a little about real life.'

'I won't forget. See you in the morning. 'Bye.'

I walked to the end of the road and then caught the trolley bus that would take me a part of the way to the library I meant to visit before going home. If I hadn't been so naive perhaps Lucas wouldn't have found me so easy to deceive. It wasn't just myself I had to think about now; soon I would have a child – Lucas's child – and I wanted it to be proud of its mother.

I spent an hour in the library picking out books. I was in no particular hurry to return to my dreary little room and the library was warm. I'd discovered it when I was looking for work and wasn't the only one who came in for more than something to read.

I found the book I was looking for, took another on world history and a copy of Mrs Beeton's *Household Management*; I'd read this before, but it wouldn't hurt to look through it again, just in case the chance of a proper cook's job came along.

As I handed in the books to be stamped by a serious-looking young woman behind the counter I noticed a magazine about art. Opening it, I flicked idly through the glossy pages, then my heart jerked as I saw a photograph of Lucas. The accompanying article was about some pictures he had painted which had sold for rather a lot of money.

'This brilliant young artist seems to go from strength to strength,' I read, then the words suddenly leapt off the page at me. 'At the moment Lucas Harrington is enjoying great success in New York and there are rumours of an imminent engagement to Miss Natalie Lawson, daughter of . . . ' The words blurred as tears misted my eyes.

'Your books, Miss Pearce.'

I stared stupidly at the woman behind the counter; I could hardly breathe and felt as if I'd been punched hard in the stomach.

'Thank you.' I picked up the books and left.

Natalie had been telling the truth. I blinked back my tears

as I ran for my bus. I wasn't going to cry. He wasn't worth it. I would forget about Lucas and think only of myself and my child.

My treacle tart and hot custard were an instant success, so much so that by the end of the second week I'd added apple and cinnamon pie and chocolate sponge pudding to the menu for mornings.

Our morning customers were very different from those who came regularly in the afternoons; mostly men who popped in for a late breakfast or an early lunch and often ate two or three helpings at a time.

'Like little lads they are,' Maud said. 'They would rather indulge their sweet tooth than eat a proper meal.' She looked round in bewilderment. 'Now where did I put my glasses?'

'By the till,' I replied with a smile. 'You can't blame them for liking our puddings; they're working men for the most part and probably don't get much chance of home-cooking at midday. Besides, our prices are much cheaper for them than a proper meal.'

'You're a better cook than I am,' Maud admitted without rancour. 'Perhaps I should serve tables and let you take over in the kitchen.'

Maud had meant it as a joke, but it made me think. It wouldn't be long before my condition began to show and then it might be difficult for me to continue as a waitress. I had never pretended to be married, thinking that I would only get caught out if I lied, and some of Maud's customers – especially the afternoon ladies – might be offended when my pregnancy could no longer be hidden.

I'd been to a concert and to a play at the Shaftesbury Theatre with Maud; we had been out for a fish and chip supper together afterwards and enjoyed a close relationship at work. Maybe it was time for the truth, before it became obvious to everyone.

'Perhaps I should do more in the kitchen,' I said. 'If you paid me a bit less you might be able to afford another waitress.'

'Pay you less?' Maud looked at me over the top of her gold-rimmed spectacles. 'My takings have more than doubled

211

since you suggested opening in the mornings. I ought to be paying you more.'

'You may not think so when I tell you . . . ' I took a deep breath. It was now or never! 'I should have told you before but . . . '

'That you're expecting a baby?' Maud's eyes were gentle, without a hint of reproach. 'I guessed weeks ago. There's no chance of him marrying you, I suppose?'

'None at all – though he promised he would. Now he's engaged to someone else, someone more suitable.' A note of bitterness had crept into my voice. 'I was a fool to believe him when he said he loved me, but I did.'

'I suspected as much.' Maud looked upset. 'You're not the sort of girl who gives herself lightly.' She hesitated. 'What will you do when the baby is born?'

'I'm going to keep it . . . somehow. I don't know whether my landlady will let me stay on; she said no children or men in the rooms. But I'll find somewhere.'

'You couldn't go home?'

'My father would have me, but Ma would make me pay for it every second of the day.'

Maud nodded, her expression thoughtful. She seemed about to say something but the bell went and I took my order pad into the front shop. I was nervous as I served a rush of customers. What would Maud have to say to me when she had thought about what I'd told her? I hoped she wouldn't sack me straight away: it wouldn't be easy to find another job I liked as much as this one.

We were very busy the whole morning and it wasn't until we closed at past twelve-thirty that we had a chance to talk properly.'

'You know I live over the shop?' she said. 'Well, I've got a spare bedroom and I've never cared much for living alone.'

'Are you offering to take me in?' I couldn't believe my ears.

Maud laughed at my astonishment. 'We always wanted children, Fred and me, but we couldn't have them. It would be nice to have a baby to fuss over – and you could have the room cheap, to make up for that cut in wages. I could take on another waitress then, because you won't be able to serve once it shows. My ladies wouldn't like that. If we keep you out of sight in the kitchen it won't offend their sensibilities.'

'You're so kind.' To my horror I found I was crying. 'Sorry – but I've been dreading this. I thought you would give me notice.'

Maud handed me a white handkerchief. 'I'm a fair judge of character, Nellie. If you'd been the wrong sort I'd have sent you packing weeks ago – but as it is, well, I've taken to you. Let's try it, see how it works out for now, shall we?'

'Yes, please,' I gulped. 'I'll work hard. I shan't let you down, I promise.'

'That's the last thing on my mind. It's all this talk of free air raid shelters for Londoners that worries me. If there is a war the city won't be a safe place to bring up a child.'

'Do you think it will happen?'

'I pray it won't,' Maud said. 'I remember the previous one too well for my liking. I had three brothers killed in the trenches and it was the war that gave Fred his bad chest. He might have been alive today if he hadn't served two years at the Front.'

'You must feel very bitter about that?'

'No, not really. We had a few years together and there's a good many who didn't. I'm not bitter and nor should you be. You've been let down, but you're young and healthy; there's still time to make something of yourself – and one day you may find someone else to care for.'

'I'm not sure that I want to. It hurts too much when you find out that love isn't what you thought it was.'

'You've been unlucky.' Maud's eyes misted with tears. 'My Fred was a good man, a decent man.'

Tom Herries was a decent man, too. He'd offered to marry me but I'd turned him down and given my heart to a man who didn't really love me. I plunged my hands into hot, soapy water. I might be a fool but I couldn't hate Lucas, no matter how I tried.

I moved into Maud's spare room the next day. It was much larger than the one I'd been renting and heated by a big iron radiator that kept it warm all night. For the first time in my life I was able to take steaming hot baths in a proper

213

bathroom with running water – and without having to ask permission.

'You're to make yourself at home,' Maud told me. 'It's going to be a pleasure for me to have you here.'

'It's like being in Heaven,' I cried rapturously. 'I keep pinching myself to make sure I'm not dreaming.'

'You deserve a bit of luck. Besides, it's company for me. I've always kept myself to myself, other than for business, and that can be a bit lonely sometimes.'

'I know how that feels since I came to London. Still, I'm happy enough now. I feel I've come home since you took me in, Mrs Bristow.'

'Then something good has come out of all this – and you can call me Maud, except when we're in the shop.'

We had become friends; I liked and respected my employer, who had helped to fill a large gap in my life.

I had not yet been able to bring myself to write to Alice, who was in all probability back at Beaumont House now that spring was on its way. I had sent a Christmas card to my parents, though, enclosing a short note telling them not to worry but no return address. If Sam had known where to find me he would have got on the next train to London to fetch me back. One day I might go on a visit of my own accord, but not yet; I wasn't ready. The pain of betrayal was still far too raw to expose it to my mother's sharp tongue.

As if reading my thoughts Maud said, 'You're sure this is what you want? I shan't mind if you change your mind and go home.'

'One day perhaps,' I replied, 'but not for a while.'

'Well, I shan't push you. To be honest I should miss you if you went – and so would my business. I've been thinking that we might try a few lunches once the baby is born . . . '

'CONSCRIPTION DETAILS!' the stall holder cried. 'Get your papers here. Conscription age-limit – find out how you stand with the new laws. Get your papers here.'

I bought a paper, frowning as I saw that men of twenty were being called up for training. It was a grave and unprecedented step for the Government to take, which showed how serious things were.

214

Maud had been increasingly worried by the events of the past weeks.

'You might do better to go home,' she'd said more than once. 'I think you should at least write to your parents – test the water a little in case you change your mind.'

'Are you going to close your business then?'

'Oh, no, I couldn't do that,' she said. 'It's all I've got. But you should think of your child.'

'It hasn't happened yet.' I sighed. 'All I can think about at the moment is having the baby. I can't wait for it to be over.'

My back was aching by the time I reached the library. It had seemed like a good idea to walk, but I would take the bus back. I felt so huge and awkward – and there were almost another two months to go yet.

I chose my books quickly. I couldn't concentrate and suddenly all I wanted was to be back in the kitchen having a cup of tea with Maud. Perhaps I would look for a taxi, I thought as I left the library with my books hanging from my wrist in a string bag; it was extravagant but I felt so tired. I took my purse from my coat pocket, opening it to see if I had enough money for the fare.

It all happened so quickly that afterwards I couldn't remember very much. I felt a sharp push in the middle of my back, then, as I tried to recover my balance, my purse was snatched from my hand and I was knocked to the ground, where I lay winded until a small crowd gathered and a man helped me to my feet.

'Are you all right, madam?' he asked politely and handed me the books I had dropped. 'Good lord! Nellie ... I saw that rogue attack you but I didn't realize it was you.'

I was shaken as I found myself looking up at Jack Henderson.

'Are you hurt?' His expression was concerned. 'What happened exactly?'

'I didn't notice him. I was tired and – my purse! He's stolen my purse.'

'Was there much in it?'

'Just a few shillings. I – I was going to take a taxi home ...'

'I'll take you, my car is just here.' He smiled and held my

arm. 'Please, Nellie. I've wondered about you so many times.'

'You're very kind. It's not far – Maud's Tearooms, down Commercial Road and on your . . . '

'Yes, I do know it,' he replied. 'I haven't been this end of town for months, but I've had tea at Maud's once or twice in the past.' We had reached a large black Rover. He opened the passenger door for me to get in. 'Are you sure you're all right? You look very pale – and in your condition . . . '

'I was shaken,' I admitted, 'but not hurt. This is really very kind of you.'

'The least I can do – and a pleasure.' He started the car and we drove in silence for a while. 'I've just come back from New York,' Jack began. 'Lucas isn't happy over there but Natalie insists. Damn' fool . . . '

'I beg your pardon?'

He glanced at me and laughed ruefully. 'I was thinking aloud.' He suddenly stopped the car and turned to look at me. 'Why didn't you tell him, Nellie? About the baby.'

'I couldn't. I think I should go.' I tried to get out of the car but he caught my arm. 'Please, let me out.'

'I'm sorry,' he said. 'It's none of my business, of course, but I don't like to see Lucas making a mistake. Natalie isn't the wife for him. If you'd only told him the truth . . . '

'Lucas made his own choice. I didn't tell him then and I would rather he didn't know now. Please don't say anything.'

'If that's what you want. I'll take you home now.'

We lapsed into silence. Neither of us spoke again until we stopped outside the tearooms.

'You were going to tell me something,' I said. 'That day at Lucas's house. But you didn't come back.'

Jack frowned at me. 'I didn't come back because I'd had a row with Lucas. I thought you should know and he was furious because I said I was going to tell you . . . '

'Tell me what?' I stared at him. 'That he was going to marry Natalie, I suppose?'

'Good lord, no,' Jack said, looking surprised. 'I know that's what Natalie wants but I'm sure he had no idea of it then. Not until you ran out on him, in fact.'

216

'I went because she told me they were practically engaged.'

'She always was a little bitch.' Jack took a deep breath. 'Lucas may kill me but I think you should know he went to New York for other reasons besides his show.'

'What reasons?'

'You know he suffered with terrible headaches?'

'Yes, of course.' I remembered Lucas coming to his father's room the afternoon of his death looking unwell and tired and my heart caught. 'He isn't ill, is he?'

'He thought he might be,' Jack said. 'The migraines had got suddenly much worse and he'd had some dizziness. Lucas thought he might have a tumour . . .'

'No!' I cried and clutched Jack's arm. 'He isn't dying, is he?'

'No. No, Nellie, it's all right. He saw a specialist in New York and was told there was no tumour.'

'Why didn't he tell me?'

'He didn't want you or Alice to know. He was afraid of what might happen if the tumour was there.'

'That was why he went away without telling me.' Tears stung my eyes. 'He should have told me. I had a right to know.'

'Yes, that's what I said to him but he wouldn't hear of it. We argued and I left the house in a temper. Afterwards I regretted not telling you anyway.'

'I would have stood by him whatever happened.'

'That was what he was afraid of, my dear.' Jack looked at me sadly. 'It was pride . . . foolish pride.'

I took the handkerchief he was handing me and blew my nose. 'Thank you for telling me now.'

'I could give you his address if . . .'

'No. If Lucas wants me he'll find me here. You can tell him if he asks . . . but only if he asks.'

'Yes, I understand.' He took a card from his pocket. 'If you should ever need anything, I should like to be of help.'

'I shan't need help,' I said. 'It was good of you to bring me home. Goodbye.'

I got out of the car and walked into the tearooms.

'You should have gone to the police,' Maud said. 'To knock

you down like that in broad daylight – whatever next? I don't know what things are coming to these days.'

'I didn't think about it. I was upset and when Mr Henderson offered to bring me home I accepted.'

'At least there are some decent folk left,' Maud said, still indignant but calmer. 'You sit down and have a cup of tea. I don't suppose the police would have caught him anyway – unless you got a good look at his face?'

'No.' I eased my aching shoulders. 'I'd just come out of the library and I was feeling tired. I never saw him at all.'

'It's over now,' Maud said. 'I don't like to think of that rogue getting away with it, but it's just one of those things. It won't happen again.'

'No. At least, I hope not.' I smiled wearily. 'I shan't be going far for a while anyway.'

I was glad when she left me alone so that I could think about what Jack had told me. If Lucas had left Beaumont House without saying goodbye to me because he thought he might have a malignant tumour on his brain . . . but no, I mustn't let myself think like that. I mustn't start to hope. I was beginning to get over my hurt and enjoy my new life.

I mustn't let Lucas back into my heart.

I ventured only as far as Victoria Park in the next few weeks. It was a warm afternoon towards the end of May. I sat on a bench in the sun watching children playing with sail boats at the edge of the lake and enjoying the scent of flowers carried on the soft breeze.

As I walked slowly home afterwards I was aware of a nagging ache in my back. Surely it must be soon now! I was so tired of waiting for my child to be born.

My pains started in the middle of the night. At first I lay still, catching my breath to stop myself crying out and disturbing Maud in the next room, but as the sharp stabbing pain intensified I realized what was happening and went to wake her.

Maud had insisted that the child must be born in hospital where both the baby and I would receive the best attention. I agreed because it would have been too much work for her if I'd stayed at home, and so the arrangements had all been

218

made and a taxi was soon speeding me to a maternity ward. The hospital was old and a little grim with dark cream walls and long narrow wards, but when I was forced to endure a long and gruelling labour, which took some minor surgery to bring to a successful conclusion, I was grateful I had taken Maud's advice.

'I never knew anything could hurt that much,' I said afterwards when the pain was only a memory and I was sitting up in bed enjoying the sweet black grapes she had brought in. 'Still, it was worth it – she's beautiful, isn't she?'

'Absolutely perfect,' Maud agreed. 'What are you going to call her?'

'Samantha,' I said, 'for my father.'

'A nice name; I approve,' said Maud. 'But don't you think you should let your father know he has a namesake?'

'Perhaps.'

I glanced at the child in the cot beside me. I couldn't have gone home while I was pregnant but now that Samantha was a living, breathing being it was somehow different.

'I'll write and tell him I have a child,' I promised. 'I might visit in a few months' time, but I shan't go home to live. I would much rather stay with you. Unless I'm in the way?'

'You know you're not,' Maud said. She bent over the cot, her face lighting up as Samantha's tiny fist curled about her finger. 'I can't wait for you to bring this little love back to the flat.'

I relaxed and popped another grape into my mouth. I was feeling happier than I had in months; the pain of losing Lucas had eased to a dull ache now and I was aware of a new optimism springing up inside me. I had a child I adored and I'd found a good friend in Maud: the future looked promising, providing I didn't let myself think about Lucas and what might have been if only he hadn't been so proud and stubborn.

Chapter Thirteen

In thinking that the future looked promising I had over-looked the threat of war, which loomed oppressively over us until the crisis was reached in early-September. For months Maud had been gloomily forecasting the inevitable clash with Germany but I'd gone on hoping that it would somehow blow over.

The papers seemed to be full of dire stories of fighting in Europe, IRA bombs going off in English cities and streams of worrying new regulations that would come into force once the war began; it wasn't easy to find something cheerful to talk about – other than Samantha, who was the light of our lives – but I did my best.

'Did you see that picture of Judy Garland in the paper?' I asked Maud one morning in August. 'I should like to see The Wizard of Oz, wouldn't you?'

Maud looked up from the official letter she was reading and frowned. 'What worries me is how we're going to manage once they bring in this food rationing. It will be sugar before long, you'll see, and then where shall we be? You can't make cakes without sugar.'

'It hasn't happened yet,' I said. 'Besides, we've been stock-ing up for months.'

'That won't last for ever. We'll never make the tearooms pay, not on what they're talking of allowing us.'

'No, perhaps not.' I was thoughtful. 'But we can still open up in the mornings.'

'Your puddings need sugar, too.'

'We can vary the menu,' I said, determined not to let

Maud's despondency defeat me. 'We could try different things . . . something new.'

'Like what?' She took her glasses off. 'You haven't been through a war, you don't know how bad it can get.'

'I've thought about this. We could do all kinds of snacks – hot jacket potatoes with pickles, potato scones, brawn, vegetable soups, our own breads, maybe even a few fatless sponges.'

'No one will come in for food like that,' Maud objected. 'This place has always been known for quality cakes with lots of cream and chocolate fillings.'

'I know it will be different. But we have to try and adapt otherwise we may have to close down if things get too tight.' Samantha had begun to grizzle. I picked her up, rocking her gently in my arms. 'Why not let me see what I can do?'

'But I can't cook that sort of food,' Maud said, clinging to her principles. 'I've always enjoyed baking fancy cakes. I don't even know how to make brawn.'

'I do. You would be surprised what I've found in some of the books I get from that library – recipes from the last war that sound awful but actually taste good. We shall still be able to get offal and tripe even if the best meat goes on ration – you leave it to me, Maud. I'll get up early and scour the shops and markets for anything that's going and then we'll improvise, have a "Special" every day.'

'You can't cook and serve tables – and we can't afford extra help.'

'You once suggested that we should reverse our roles. I know you were joking, but it would be a way out of our problems. While Samantha is still sleeping most of the day I can keep her with me. We'll have to see what happens when she starts to run around.'

'The little darling,' Maud said and held out her arms. 'Give her to me. If you're sure you know what you're doing we may as well start to make the changes straight away – we can conserve what sugar and treacle we have, then we might be able give all our regulars a treat now and then.'

'You won't regret this. I promise I'll make a go of it somehow.'

'If the worst comes to the worst I'll sell up, go off to the

221

seaside and live in a cottage,' Maud said. 'But we'll try your ideas first, Nellie. Now where did I put my glasses?'

'On top of your head.' I laughed. 'Life doesn't come to a full stop just because there's a war, Maud. Look on the bright side, it might turn out better than you think.'

I was still smiling as I went to write a notice for the window, my head buzzing with plans and ideas for the future. It was going to be a struggle to keep the restaurant going but I liked the idea of a challenge. It might even be fun.

It was on a spring morning in 1940 that Alice came back into my life. Maud had been urging me to contact my family and friends for ages and in the end I wrote to Mrs Jones, telling her where I was working and that I had a child; she wrote back at once, inviting me to come and see her – and she must have written to Alice, too, because it was a week later when she came into the tearooms, which happened to be empty for once.

For a moment we stared at each other, then she came towards me, taking both my hands in hers and gazing at me with faint reproach.

'Why didn't you let anyone know?' she asked. 'We've all been so worried about you.'

'You were in France. I couldn't write,' I said awkwardly. 'Besides, I wanted to make a complete break.'

'From me?' she asked, sounding hurt. 'I thought we were friends, Nellie.'

The bell clanged as customers came into the shop. 'We can't talk now,' I said. 'Perhaps we could meet later?'

'May I come this evening? I would like to talk to you, and to see Samantha – if you will let me?'

'Yes, of course. Come at about six, before I put her to bed.'

Alice went away and I took the customers' orders, feeling a little confused and uncertain. Now that Alice had gone I wanted to ask her so many questions and the evening seemed a long way off.

I spent the day between excitement and anxiety, and my mood must have communicated itself to Samantha because she was fretful. However, she quietened soon after Alice arrived and she was able to nurse her for a while before I put her to bed.

'She's a beautiful child,' Alice said. 'I do wish you'd told me, Nellie. I could have helped you.'

'I didn't need help.'

'Don't be proud,' Alice said. 'I didn't mean that I would offer you charity. We were friends – and Samantha is my niece, isn't she?'

'Yes.' My cheeks were hot. 'Please ... don't tell Lucas about her.'

'Don't you think he has a right to know?' Alice looked solemn. 'I know he behaved badly but ... ' She hesitated. 'He did have his reasons ... '

'Yes, I know. I met Jack Henderson a few months ago and he told me. Lucas thought he was ill.' I gave her an angry glance. 'But we had a right to know. I had a right to know.'

'Yes, of course you did.' Alice looked sad. 'Please don't be angry with me. I feel much as you do but you know what Lucas is, how stubborn he can be.'

I also knew that several months had passed since I'd talked to Jack and Lucas had still not been to see me.

'Please, don't let's talk about Lucas. Tell me about you. Are you and Gerald married yet?'

'We were married in France last year,' she said, a smile of happiness in her eyes. 'Gerald is working with a Government department at the moment, so we're living in London. My sister-in-law sometimes lives with us but stays at our country house with Mabel most of the time.'

'So everything turned out right for you after all? I'm glad.'

'And you ... are you happy?'

'Yes, of course,' I replied but could not quite meet her eyes. 'Is – is Lucas married to that American girl?'

'No.' Alice was upset. 'He's still in New York, though. I hardly hear from him. I don't know whether he intends to marry her or not. I quite thought he wanted to marry you.'

'Perhaps he changed his mind.'

'He should have thought more carefully before making you empty promises.' For a moment she sounded angry. 'Sometimes I wonder what gets into him.'

223

'You mustn't blame him too much. I always knew marriage between us was impossible.'

'He should have been more responsible.'

'The same could be said of me.'

'But you were younger. He was thoughtless and careless.'

I told her about my visit to his house and she looked thoughtful. 'So you see, he did try to talk to me. If I had asked for help he would not have refused me.'

'You won't let me write to him about Samantha?'

'I would rather you didn't. If he comes back . . . perhaps one day I'll tell him myself.'

'I must and will respect your wishes,' Alice said. 'But I think you're wrong. At the very least Lucas should provide for you and his daughter.'

'That's exactly what I don't want!'

'Oh, Nellie!' Alice cried with a rueful laugh. 'You're so proud. Between you, you and Lucas are the most stubborn people I know.' Her smile faded. 'You will keep in touch? Promise me you won't disappear again.'

'I'll keep in touch,' I said. 'But in return you must keep my secret.'

'Then of course I will,' Alice said. 'Besides, Lucas may decide to stay in New York, especially if he does marry that girl.'

Later, much later, long after Alice had gone, I lay in bed and shed a few tears into my pillow. Despite everything I'd always hoped that Lucas might keep his promise to come back to me, but now I saw how foolish I was.

He would never have stayed away this long if he loved me.

'Are you sure you can manage?' I asked for perhaps the hundredth time. 'I feel as if I'm deserting you.'

'Absolute nonsense,' said Maud. 'You deserve a rest after the way you've been working for months on end. I thought we might as well close up when we had to stop afternoon teas, but your snacks have run the pair of us off our feet. I won't hear of you giving up your holiday. I shall stick to soups and our special breads until you come back; I can manage them, and that new girl – what's her name? Janice, I keep forgetting – you wanted her to help out with Samantha sometimes, well, she can serve tables for a couple of days while you're away.'

Maud was a kind, motherly woman and her generosity made me feel even more guilty, though there was absolutely no reason why I shouldn't go away for a few days.

'It's just that Mrs Jones was good to me,' I said. 'She taught me the basics of cooking and gave me those recipe books.'

'The ones you've almost worn out?' Maud nodded. 'Of course you must go. The least you can do is to visit, especially as she's a bit poorly.'

'That's the only reason I'm going. I think she's really ill, Maud. It might be my only chance to see her again before . . .' I stopped and blinked away the sudden tears. 'But I still don't feel easy in my mind. I've left an order with all our regular suppliers – and you won't forget to have the gas man round to that cooker, will you?'

'You wrote it down on the list,' she said. 'Now where . . . ah, yes, here it is. He's coming on Tuesday, in the morning.'

'Yes, I made the appointment myself. I'm not happy with the way it's working, though sometimes it's fine. Anyway, he'll sort it out for you. Oh, don't forget to check the blackout curtains are shut at night. We haven't had any bombs here yet, but there's always the first time.' I kissed Maud's cheek, then held my daughter up to do the same. 'Say bye bye to Aunty then, Samantha.'

She planted a wet kiss on Maud's cheek and mumbled something in her baby talk. She had delighted us both a few days earlier by saying her first words, and since then Maud had been eagerly listening for her own name.

She stood in the doorway to wave us off before going back inside to start preparing the first batch of spiced bread for the morning's customers.

I wheeled Samantha's pushchair to the bus stop, waiting patiently for the right number to take us to the station. I was still uneasy in my mind as the conductor helped us on board and punched the fare into his ticket machine, winding them out with a little handle as I settled down with Samantha on my lap. I was worrying for nothing: Maud would manage if she stuck to a simple menu for the few days I was away; the

225

customers might be disappointed not to see some of their favourite "Specials" chalked up on the daily board, but they all knew I was going away for a while – just as they all knew it was I who had kept the place running through these first months of the war.

It was almost a year since the war had started and rationing had begun to bite, but I'd discovered that if you were out early when the markets were only just beginning to stir there was always a chance of finding something extra. I'd become a regular at various butchers and wholesale greengrocers and they looked out for me, saving all kinds of things for me; it might be bones or offal to make my soups tastier or it might just be a rare shipment of fruit that had come in overnight and from which I would be allowed to take my pick. Sometimes there was a big bag of suet, which allowed me to make all kinds of puddings, both sweet and savoury, a side of bacon or something under the counter that was even more of a find, like extra sugar or fresh eggs. It was a marvel what you could do with very little if you tried, and I had no patience with some of the women I met as I queued at the shops, women who seemed to do nothing but complain about the shortages.

We couldn't change things by moaning, we just had to make the best of things – use some imagination.

Sitting in the train with Samantha asleep in my arms, I wondered how my parents were coping with the shortages. Maud had coaxed me into writing to Sam a couple of times; I'd told him I was well and sent him a photograph Maud had taken of Samantha with her little box camera, but I hadn't sent a return address. Perhaps I ought to think about visiting home soon. It would mean swallowing my pride but Maud said that sometimes other things were more important and she was so often right.

I had at last accepted Mrs Jones's invitation to visit her and her sister Jean and so here I was, beginning to look forward to what would be my first real holiday at the seaside.

The sun was shining when Samantha woke me. She had been a little fretful the past couple of days. Margaret's sister Jean thought it might be the change of air but I suspected another tooth was the cause of her trouble. I picked her up, soothing her in my arms until her cries ceased.

I'd decided that I would take Samantha on the beach that morning, and I put on a plain blue cotton dress; it was the new shorter fashion that we were all wearing to help save material for the war effort, with a square neck and puffed sleeves, and Margaret Jones told me I looked about fifteen in it.

'Not a day older than when you first came to the house,' she said. 'But prettier. I like your hair longer, Nellie. It suits you.'

'Thank you.' I blushed at her praise. 'I'm taking Samantha for a picnic on the beach, but we shall be back before tea.'

'Make the most of the weather,' she advised. 'You know which bits of the beach are safe and those you're not allowed on, don't you?'

'Yes. Don't worry. We'll be fine.'

Samantha had a little tin bucket and spade, which she alternately clutched possessively and then threw down. I left her in her pushchair by the reception desk while I went to collect our picnic basket from the kitchen, and the young clerk – who like all Jean's staff adored her – promised to keep an eye on her.

In the large kitchen I lingered for two minutes to exchange greetings with the cook, then picked up my basket and went back to the foyer. As usual Samantha seemed to have collected several admirers; there was the receptionist, one of the chambermaids – and a man dressed in cream flannels and a smart navy blazer. He was standing with his back to me, his attention all for my daughter who was keeping him occupied retrieving her bucket and spade and chuckling for all she was worth.

Something about the set of his shoulders made me catch my breath. Surely it couldn't be . . . then he turned towards me and for one dizzying moment the world stood still.

'Lucas,' I breathed. 'I . . . '

'Nellie.' For a moment he seemed just as dumbstruck as I, then he came towards me. 'Forgive me. I had to come once I knew where you were.'

227

'Who told you – Alice?'

He shook his head. 'Jack told me where you were working – and your friend Maud told me the rest.'

'I see.' It was just like Maud to do that.

The remembered scent of him – musk, shaving soap and cedarwood – set off a sharp, aching nostalgia. I knew I ought to be angry but all I could do was stare at him.

'Mummy . . . Mummy . . . ' Samantha called fretfully, breaking the spell.

I bent to pick her up, kissing her cheek as I struggled against the wave of emotion that threatened to overcome me. 'Yes, darling,' I whispered against the softness of her hair. 'We're going to the beach soon.'

'So this is Samantha?' Lucas's voice had a humble, almost awed note. 'She's enchanting, absolutely enchanting.'

'Everyone says that. I'm afraid she's rather spoilt.'

'I wouldn't say that . . . not at all.' He looked at me wistfully. 'So you're going to the beach?'

There was such longing in his eyes that I almost invited him to come but checked myself just in time. It would be madness!

'We must go,' I said as Samantha started to struggle in my arms. 'She's getting impatient.'

'Yes, of course.' He let me walk away, then followed with quick strides to catch me at the door. 'Please – may we talk? I know I have no right to ask, but it would mean so much to me.'

My heart felt as if it were being squeezed and it was difficult to breathe. It would have been more sensible to refuse but I had never been sensible where he was concerned.

'I suppose we could talk,' I said. 'Jean will keep an eye on Samantha when she's in bed.'

'We could have dinner – here or somewhere else?'

'I would prefer to stay here.'

I would feel safer in the hotel. There was a flash of the old humour in his eyes, as if he had read my mind, but he sounded sincere as he said, 'Thank you. I shall look forward to this evening.'

He let me go then. I walked away, my basket lodged against the handle of Samantha's pushchair as we left the

228

grounds and walked down the hill towards the town and the beaches. The sun was warm on my head, making me feel it was good to be alive – or was there another reason for the way my heart had suddenly begun to sing?

But I mustn't let myself hope. Just because Lucas had come to find me . . .

It was at about half-past one that I saw him walking along the beach towards us; he was carrying three ice-cream cones which had started to melt and trickle down his hand.

'You had better eat these quick or they will run away,' he said, handing me two. 'It took longer to find you than I thought.'

I held one of the cones for Samantha, who had deserted her sand games at the prospect of such a treat. Lucas squatted down on the sand beside us; he was still wearing his cream flannels but had abandoned the blazer for a casual open-necked shirt.

For a while we sat in silence, enjoying the cool creaminess of the cones and avoiding each other's eyes. It was very peaceful with the sound of the waves rippling lazily against the shore and an occasional cry from a gull.

'I shouldn't have come,' he said at last. 'But I couldn't wait until this evening – and I wanted to see her again. I can't believe how beautiful she is.'

'It doesn't matter.' I wiped my own hands and Samantha's protesting face on a damp towel. 'I would have asked you to come but . . . '

'Of course. I understand.' His eyes seemed to move over us with such hunger that it set my heart racing. Why was it that he could still make me feel this way with just a look? 'I'm not asking for anything you don't want to give, Nellie. I don't even have the right to this . . . '

'No, you don't – but rights don't come into it. She's your daughter. I've often wished you could see her.'

'Not as often as I've wanted to see you.' He cursed softly as I turned away with a gasp of pain. 'That wasn't fair of me. I'm sorry.'

'You should be!' I cried. 'You had no right to go away without a word to me, Lucas. It broke my heart.'

229

He glanced at me then away, his eyes brooding as they followed the flight of a gull swooping over the sea. 'There were reasons. But Jack told you . . . '

'Yes.' My fingers clenched in the sand. 'That wasn't fair, I had a right to know if you were ill.'

'I wanted to spare you the consequences if . . . ' He gave me a rueful smile that seemed to beg for understanding. 'Obviously you don't see it my way, but that was the one unselfish act of my life, Nellie.'

'Why didn't you tell me when I came to the house?'

'You didn't give me the chance.' His gaze narrowed intently. 'Why did you run away like that? You heard me calling when you got in that taxi. I know you did.'

'What did you expect?' I gave him a resentful look. 'Natalie had just told me you were going to marry her.'

'So that was it!' He seemed angry. 'She had no right to say such a thing. I did have a brief affair with her but that was before I came back to the Dales, before we . . . I had never made a commitment to her.'

'She seemed to think you were going to marry her.'

'Yes, she made that clear. It was difficult when you came to the house, Nellie. I had the shadow of my illness hanging over me and there were other considerations. Her father owns an influential gallery in New York . . . '

'Your work was more important than the way you felt about me, of course!' I cried, though I knew I was being unfair. In keeping his secret fears to himself he had tried to save both Alice and me from pain.

Lucas looked uncomfortable. 'My work has always been important to me, but I didn't know about the baby. I would never have left you to fend for yourself alone in London if I had. You must believe that if nothing else.'

I jumped to my feet and walked down to the water's edge, staring blindly out to sea as my eyes pricked with tears. I was angry and upset, the pain inside me so intense that I wanted to scream. Lucas had no right simply to walk back into my life when he chose.

'Nellie.' He touched my shoulder. 'I'm sorry. I didn't mean to hurt you.'

I whirled on him then, anger flaring. 'You didn't think it

230

would hurt me? You made love to me, promised me we would marry, then simply went off to New York and forgot me. Yes, you did, Lucas, don't deny it. Jack told me months ago that the specialist had cleared you of having a tumour – where have you been since then? If you'd wanted to see me you could have found me ages ago.'

'Put like that it sounds pretty damning, I must admit.' There was a rueful look in his eyes. 'I did employ a private detective to try and find you before I left for New York.'

'He couldn't have tried very hard.'

'No, he didn't,' Lucas admitted. 'He sent me a couple of negative reports then disappeared with the money I had given him.'

'You could have come home yourself.'

'Things were going well for me in New York . . . but I know that's no excuse.' He had the grace to look ashamed. 'I was a bloody ass. Believe me, I've regretted the way I behaved when you arrived at the house that day. I was surprised and reacted badly. I've wished I'd behaved differently a thousand times.'

'I don't believe you – you say things without meaning them. You don't care how you hurt people.'

Tears were wetting my cheeks. He attempted to take me in his arms but I pushed him away. He stood back, his expression a mixture of frustration and guilt.

'I'm going back to the hotel. Forgive me, Nellie. I didn't intend this. I only wanted to see you and Samantha before . . . I'm sorry.'

I turned away, looking out towards the sea, my feelings too raw and painful to be faced just yet. His footsteps crunched in the sand as I stood with my arms wrapped around me, fighting the storm of emotion raging inside me.

Samantha had started to scream. I saw she had fallen over and grazed her knee on something hidden in the sand. Picking her up I kissed the pain away, wishing I could ease my own as easily.

'Mummy kiss it better. All better now.' I set her down again as the tears dried by magic. 'Let's paddle in the sea, shall we? See if we can find a crab?'

Her eyes were so like her father's as she gazed up at me

231

that my heart jolted with pain. After the way he had behaved I should hate him, but I didn't.

'So what are you going to do?' Margaret asked as we drank tea from dainty porcelain cups that afternoon. 'Will you have dinner with him this evening?'

'I don't know.' I sighed. 'I still care about him – but I'm afraid of being hurt again.'

'Men like Lucas are a law unto themselves.' She looked at me with concern. 'They don't fit into the ordinary mould. You can't change them – but perhaps they wouldn't be so attractive if you could.'

She was right. Lucas couldn't be chained. He wasn't like Tom who had wanted only to marry me, Tom who would have done anything rather than hurt me.

'Sometimes you have to risk pain to be happy,' Margaret said. 'But don't see him this evening if you would rather not. We can tell him you have a headache. Jean could ask him to find other accommodation, pretend she made a mistake in the booking.'

'No, please don't ask her to do that,' I said. 'I can't run away this time. Whatever happens I have to face it.'

'I thought you might change your mind about dinner,' Lucas said, his eyes assessing me with approval. 'I'm glad you didn't.'

I was wearing blue again, but a pale turquoise this time which I thought made my eyes look greener. My hair was longer than it had been when I was sixteen and waved softly about my face. The expression in his eyes told me that he liked it.

'You look lovely,' he said. 'Is that a new blouse?'

'Almost. Alice gave it to me for my birthday. This is the second time I've worn it.' I gazed up at him. 'She wanted to tell you about Samantha months ago, but I made her promise not to. You shouldn't be angry with her.'

'I'm not angry with anyone except myself.'

'Perhaps it was partly my fault. If I'd told you that day at your house it might have changed things. I always knew you would have helped me if I'd asked.'

232

'Thank you. You are as generous as ever.' His smile was warm, embracing. 'Shall we have dinner?' He offered his arm, his brows arching as I hesitated.

'Are you hungry?'

'No – why?'

'I know I suggested eating here but could we go for a walk or a drink or something? I don't feel like eating yet.'

'I have my car. We could drive along the coast, then stop for supper later if you like?'

'Yes, please. I would prefer that.'

'Jean won't mind if we change our mind about dinner?'

'I told her we might.'

'Shall we go then?'

I took his arm and we went outside.

Later that evening we found a quiet pub which served fresh sandwiches and delicious local beer, and sat outside to eat and drink in the warmth of late-summer, enjoying the perfume of night-scented flowers carried on the air.

'These are very good,' Lucas observed. 'Or perhaps it's the company.'

'Compliments?' I laughed. 'I'm not used to them from you, Lucas.'

His eyes were soft and teasing. 'I've used you shamefully, haven't I, Nellie? It's a wonder you don't hate me – but you don't, do you?'

'No, why should I?'

'Some women would – after what happened.'

'If you mean Samantha, I think she's the best thing that ever happened to me.'

'She is rather wonderful.' A sigh escaped him.

I looked across the table at him. 'Those headaches . . . are they better now? Did the specialist discover what was wrong?'

'He thought it might be stress or something in my diet, but I've discovered that one of the paints I was using seems to bring it on. Since I've stopped using that particular type I've been better.'

'I'm glad.' I touched his hand. 'You should have told me, Lucas.'

'I know, but you were so young. I didn't want to ruin your

233

life but I almost did it anyway.' His fingers entwined themselves with mine. 'I do love you, Nellie. I can't expect you to believe that after the way I went off and left you, but it's true.'

'Is it?' I gazed into his eyes, wanting so much to believe him.

He stood up and took my hands, pulling me to my feet and into his arms. As his mouth took possession of mine I felt myself melting, my resistance ebbing away as I surrendered to the urgent throbbing of my senses. I was a fool. Lucas had hurt me once and I was just beginning to rebuild my life . . . but I couldn't help myself. This feeling between us was too strong for me to fight it.

'Nellie,' he breathed and I knew what he was asking. 'My darling.'

'Yes, Lucas,' I whispered. 'Yes.'

The room Lucas found for us in the inn was homely with a large, old-fashioned bed plumped by a feather mattress and piles of pillows.

'You're quite sure about this?' he asked as he reached for me, his fingers gently caressing my cheek, moving over the fullness of my lips.

'You asked me that once before.' I smiled as I went into his arms. 'I may be a fool but I still love you.'

'Oh, Nellie . . . Nellie.' He swept me into his embrace. 'I've missed you so much.'

And then he was kissing me and nothing else mattered. We were swept away by a tide of passion that seemed to take all the pain and bitterness with it.

After we had made love I lay with my head against his shoulder and wept. He held me in silence, his lips brushing softly against my hair.

'It's all right,' he whispered. 'Don't cry, my darling. I never meant to hurt you.'

I looked up, smiling through the tears. 'I'm crying because it was so beautiful – and because I don't want to lose you again.' I felt him tense and turned my head on the pillow to look at him. 'What is it, Lucas? What's wrong?'

A nerve flicked at the corner of his eye. 'I should have told you . . . I have to go away again soon.'

I sat up in bed and looked at him. 'Back to New York?'

He hesitated, his eyes not quite meeting mine. 'For a while.'

'I see.' My voice and eyes were filled with accusation.

'It isn't what you think. It has nothing to do with Natalie.'

'Do you expect me to believe that? But of course you do. I'm such a fool where you're concerned, aren't I?'

I started to leave the bed but he caught my arm and held me back. I resisted vigorously and for a moment we fought, then he held me imprisoned beneath him.

'Little cat,' he said as he felt the sting where my nails had scratched him. 'I'm not going to marry Natalie. I'm not in love with her and I never was.'

'But you're going away again,' I cried, and tears were close. 'You shouldn't have deceived me, Lucas. You let me believe you cared and now . . . '

'I do love you. This isn't the end,' he promised. 'I shall come back to you and Samantha, I promise. When this is all over.' There was something odd in his eyes then and I stared up at him uncertainly.

'What do you mean? Has your trip got something to do with the war? You're not really going to New York, are you?'

'If I wasn't, I couldn't tell you,' he said, and drew me back into his arms. 'Let's talk about when I do come back.' His fingers traced the line of my throat. 'You will marry me then, won't you? No more of this nonsense about not being good enough – no rubbish about my friends looking down their noses at you?'

'Oh, Lucas,' I whispered chokily. 'All I ever wanted was for you to love me.'

'How can you doubt that I do?'

He bent over me, his lips touching one corner of my mouth then the other, flicking at me with his tongue until I opened to him. He moaned low in his throat as the desire raged between us once more, then he was kissing my breasts, teasingly, tantalisingly, moving lower and lower over my quivering flesh to seek out the essence of my femininity. A groan broke from me as he delicately probed and licked, my back arching as my hips rose to meet him.

Then his body was covering mine, his hot, silky smooth penis lancing into my moistness as I opened to welcome him, my frantic cries arousing him to ever harder thrusts. I writhed beneath him, losing myself in wave after wave of sensation and screaming his name aloud as we reached a shattering climax together.

Afterwards, satiated, too tired to talk, we slept in each other's arms.

It was the following Sunday. Our brief time together had fled in sunlit days on the beach with Samantha and breathless, passionate nights that were never long enough. Now we were at the station in Bournemouth and time had speeded up beyond all reason as Lucas thrust the huge bunch of flowers he'd bought into my arms. I was already loaded with baskets of fresh foods and preserves Jean had insisted on giving me.

'It was lovely to see you,' Margaret Jones had said, kissing me before I left the hotel. 'You'll forgive me if I don't come to the station with you – but Lucas will see you off.'

Tears stung my eyes as I embraced her. 'Goodbye, Margaret. I'm glad I came.'

'You must come again,' she said. 'Come to see Jean even if . . . but we shan't talk of that. I want you to have these. I always thought I might have them published one day – but perhaps you'll do it for me.' She gave me a large parcel of recipe books, all written in her own neat hand.

'That's a wonderful idea, Margaret, but you would have done it better. I'm not clever enough to write a book.'

'You never know unless you try. Anyway, I want you to have them as a keepsake if nothing else.' She kissed me again. 'Good luck, Nellie. I hope it all turns out the way you hope with Lucas.'

I was quiet as he drove me to the station. He glanced at me several times and his expression became grimmer.

'What are you thinking?'

'Why do things always have to be so horrible? Margaret is dying and you're going away again.'

236

'Margaret is ill,' he said, a nerve flicking in his throat. 'I have to go, Nellie. It's not something I can change.'

'I wasn't suggesting you could.'

Lucas hadn't told me that his imminent departure had something to do with the war . . . the horrible, hateful war that seemed to drag on and on and was responsible for so many deaths, so much unhappiness on all sides . . . but in my heart I knew it.

My train was waiting at the platform. Lucas carried all my parcels into a carriage and I settled Samantha in her chair. We stared at each other, both outwardly calm.

'Will you write to me sometimes, Lucas?'

'Not for a while. It won't be possible – but I'll be in touch as soon as I can. Just trust me, Nellie.' I nodded, holding back the tears. He brushed his lips across mine, his fingers smoothing my cheek. 'I love you – always believe that.'

The guard was slamming doors. Lucas got off the train, looking up at me with a strangely naked look in his eyes. His words reached me through the open window.

'If for any reason I shouldn't come back, remember I loved you. Always.'

'Lucas!' I cried as the guard blew his whistle. 'You promised . . . you promised . . .'

'I love you,' he called as the train began to move off. 'I love you.'

'Lucas . . . Lucas . . .'

I was crying now as I pressed myself against the carriage window, my fingers splayed over the glass as if I could touch him. 'You have to come back. I love you . . . I love you . . .' I wasn't sure if he heard me but he stood watching as the train pulled away, his face pale and strained. 'You have to come back, Lucas,' I whispered when I could no longer see him. 'I need you so much . . . so much . . .'

When I got to London the station seemed to be more crowded than usual. A young sailor helped me off the train with all my baskets and Samantha's pushchair and a porter took my luggage to the taxi rank.

A soldier had just taken the last one and I caught a glimpse of his face as he was driven away – could I be

237

mistaken or had it been Tom Herries? It was possible that Tom was in the army now.

Sitting in my own taxi a few minutes later I thought about Tom and about my parents. Now that I'd seen Lucas again I realized how unfair it had been of me to go off without a word the way I had. Lucas had wanted to see Samantha and so would Sam.

'We'll go and see Grandad soon,' I said, kissing the top of my daughter's head, 'but not just yet – that wouldn't be fair to Maud. I can't leave her in the lurch again. She's been so good to us both. I don't know what I would have done without her . . . '

A short time later I stood staring in disbelief at the pile of rubble where Maud's Tearooms had been. My head was spinning and I felt sick. What had happened? Surely it wasn't possible for a gas explosion to make this much mess? It couldn't have happened that way. It couldn't! Surely it was a mistake? It must have been a bomb!

One of our regular customers had seen me pushing Samantha's pushchair down the road and come rushing to stop me; he told me what had happened and begged me to go into his shop for a cup of tea, but I'd wanted to see for myself.

'It must have been a bomb,' I said. 'It couldn't have been the gas . . . '

'Come away, Nellie,' the man said, taking my arm. 'You can't do any good here. It was a mercy you and the little one were away.'

'No! Don't say that!' I glared at him. 'If I'd been here it wouldn't have happened. I warned her to get that cooker seen to.' I was overcome with grief. 'Oh, Maud . . . Maud, I should never have gone. I should never have left her. It's my fault.'

'It's her own fault. The gas man came to mend it once but she told him it was the wrong time and asked him to come back when the shop was closed. It happened the next day, went off with a bang. We thought the Germans had started bombing us instead of the airfields.'

Somehow it was worse because it wasn't a bomb. If I'd been able to blame the war it might have been easier to bear but this was such a shock. Both Maud and Janice had been

238

killed outright . . . as I might have been, would have been, if I hadn't been away.

'Where is she?' I looked at him through my tears. 'I want to see her.'

'Not much left to see,' he replied. 'We're burying her tomorrow. She hadn't got anyone else and we look after our own round here.'

For the next few days I was so numbed with grief that I hardly knew what I was doing. I managed to find temporary accommodation but the room was dark and cramped, not at all suitable for a child; there was only a small basin to wash her clothes and nowhere to dry them. We should have to move on soon and I would need to find some kind of work, but all I felt like doing was weeping. Maud had been such a good friend and I was going to miss her so very much.

I was still undecided about going home, but, ironically, the bombs that Maud had worried about for months began to fall in London's East End a few days after her death. The first planes attacked a power station, the docks, a gasworks and the city. More came in during the night, setting off a sea of flames that was terrifying to witness. Many of us went out on the streets after the all clear; we felt shocked and dazed as we saw the red sky and smelt the awful stench of burning, our minds struggling to take in what was happening. What we didn't know that first night was that it was to be the start of an intensive campaign against us.

The bombing brought me out of my apathy; I was terrified that something would happen to my child, perhaps when I had left her in someone's care to go shopping, and realized that we could not go on like this: it was time we went home. I was under no illusions about the reception I would receive from my mother (she would lose no chance to remind me of the shame I had brought on my family) but Samantha's safety was more important than my pride. She was all I had and Maud's death had made me very aware of how vulnerable we all were. I would bear anything rather than risk my little girl's precious life.

If I was going I might as well make it now, while I still had my train fare and a few pounds to spare. I felt guilty because

I was leaving, as though I were deserting people who had been my friends and neighbours, but what choice did I have? Alone I would have faced the bombs and whatever hardship fate cared to throw at me, but I had my child to think of now. I had lost my best friend and did not know if I would ever see Lucas again, but somehow I would come through this; I would make a new life for my daughter.

The train was crowded with women and children that morning; like me other mothers had decided to take their loved ones to safety, though many of them were determined to return to their homes.

'No bloomin' Jerry's going to make me stay in the country with a lot of bleedin' cows,' one pretty young woman told me cheerfully. 'I'll be back as soon as I've delivered young Ronnie to his cousins. I expect you'll be doing the same – can't let the side down, can we?'

'I'm not sure,' I replied vaguely, and blushed as I saw derision in her eyes.

She thought I was afraid of the bombs but she didn't know that it was taking far more courage to go home than it would to have stayed in London. It wasn't going to be easy facing all the gossip, meeting people I had known all my life and seeing the scorn in their eyes as they realized I had an illegitimate child, but the thought of just dumping Samantha and leaving appalled me.

I glanced out of the train window, trying to ignore the growing feeling of dread inside me. I was doing this for Samantha and no matter how much it cost me personally I would carry it through.

Chapter Fourteen

'So you've come scurrying back then,' my mother said as I walked in at the back door. 'I wondered how long it would take you now that it's not so comfortable for you up there.'

There was such bitterness in her voice that I almost wished I hadn't come. Perhaps Jean could have found me work in her hotel, though I knew she was finding it harder and harder to keep going because of the war.

'It's just for a little while. Until I can get on my feet again,' I replied defensively. 'I won't be a burden to you longer than I can help. I just need somewhere to stay until I sort myself out.'

She looked at me with dislike, her expression cold and ungiving. I'd known she wouldn't exactly welcome me back but I'd hoped for a slightly warmer reception than this.

'I hope you're not expecting us to keep you? Your father's business hardly provides for the rest of us these days. We can do without another two mouths to feed.'

'I've earned my own keep since I left school – the day I left school,' I reminded her pointedly. 'I've not asked anyone for a penny I haven't earned since, and I shan't.'

'That remains to be seen.' Her eyes flicked towards Samantha. 'I wonder you've the gall to come back with a child everyone will know is a bastard.'

'Samantha can't help her birth,' I replied, anger making my voice rise. 'And I'll thank you not to use that word in her hearing.'

'You're such a fool,' she said bitterly. 'After what happened to me I should have thought you would have learned

241

your lesson, my girl! I should have thought you'd more sense than to get yourself landed with a child out of wedlock.'

'I was in love with her father,' I said, my head lifting with pride. 'As a matter of fact, I still am. I might marry him one day. And as for my keep – I've a few pounds put by. I'll earn what I can and I'll leave as soon as . . . '

'You're not to talk of leaving when you've this minute set foot in the house.' My father came downstairs, still fastening his collar stud. He brought the fresh scent of soap with him and had obviously been up to wash off the dirt of his working day. 'And you'll keep your money in your purse while you're under my roof. No matter what your mother told you, I can still afford to feed my own family.' His face softened as he saw the child in my arms. 'So this is the little lass then? I'm glad you've brought her to see us at last.'

'Samantha . . . ' I said, a catch in my throat as he took her from me. She stared at him with her innocent eyes, then patted sticky fingers against his cheek. 'Ganda . . . Ganda . . . '

'On the train I was telling her she was going to see her grandad. She's that bright and clever you wouldn't believe it, Da – far cleverer than her mother.'

'You're bright enough yourself, lass,' he said, catching the child's fingers in his mouth as if to bite her and making her laugh. 'You've done the best you could, despite everything. I've always been proud of you and I still am . . . '

'Proud! Of her bringing a bastard into this house?'

We both turned at the sound of Mother's shrill voice.

Sam frowned at her. 'Yes, because she's had the courage to do it, despite knowing what sort of a reception she would get from her own mother. You've reasons enough of your own to show a little compassion, Rose. You know as well as I do that our Nellie isn't a bad girl. If she has made a mistake we should give her love and support, not make her feel ashamed.'

'Oh, Da.' The tears streamed down my cheeks. 'I've wanted to see you so bad. Maud got me to write you . . . ' I choked on a sob of despair. 'She's gone, Da. Dead . . . blown to pieces.'

'In the air raids?'

'No. It was a gas explosion – just ripped the whole place to pieces. She had been afraid of the bombs, but they didn't start until after . . . '

My father sat Samantha down in a chair, then drew me into his arms to comfort me. Beneath the sharpness of the soap the remembered scents of leather, glue and body musk lingered on and I breathed them in, going limp with relief. His big, work-stained hands moved gently in my hair, caressing the nape of my neck as I poured out my grief – not only for Maud but for everything that had hurt me so deeply.

'There, lass, cry your heart out if you want. You've had a bad time, but you're home where you belong now – and you can stay for as long as you want. You mustn't think of leaving until you're sure you're ready.'

I glanced over his shoulder at my mother. The expression in her eyes warned me that this could only be a temporary refuge. Nothing had changed between us. She could never forgive me for being the child of the man who had raped her; it was a shame she was forced to bear – a shame she found so horrible that she had never revealed the name of her attacker to anyone, not even to the man who had married her.

'I lost it,' I said. 'Grandad's watch. It was in Maud's safe. I should have put it in the bank but I didn't think . . . ' I'd lost the kettle Tom had given me as well as the bulk of my possessions, but it was the watch I missed most.

'It's a pity about the watch but we must expect these things to happen,' Sam said, then bent to pull some onions.

We were standing in the allotment. It was even more important to grow what you could these days and, between them, my father and Bob had put up a chicken run on part of the ground so that they would have their own eggs.

'I just wish I'd been there.' Tears stung my eyes. 'I keep thinking it might not have happened if I hadn't left her alone. She was so forgetful . . . '

'You shouldn't torture yourself, lass. If you had been there you and the little one might have been killed. I'm grateful you weren't.'

'Oh, Da . . . ' I swallowed hard. I loved him so much and

243

his kindness moved me. 'You've lost weight again – are you ill?'

'I can't seem to keep any flesh on my bones and it's not for want of trying.' He smiled wryly. 'But I'm well enough. A few aches and pains of a morning, nothing more.'

I wasn't sure that he was telling me the truth, but he would not have complained even if he felt ill. I reached up to kiss his cheek, feeling a surge of love and pride. Sam Pearce ran deep just the way Grandad had told me years before.

He had never mentioned the fact that I was not his child. I doubted very much that he had ever spoken of it to my mother after she had married him, but surely he must have felt it inside? He must have wondered about the man who had hurt the woman he loved, turning her from an innocent young girl to the hard, bitter woman she had become.

Yet still he had managed to love both my mother and me. It made me even more aware of just how good a man he was and of how much I cared for him.

'A man came to the shop looking for you after you went off,' he said suddenly, and I knew who it must have been.

'Was it Tom Herries?'

'Yes – did you think he would?' Sam rubbed the bridge of his nose where the glasses he wore for work had made a permanent red mark. 'I heard that he was one of the first to join up.'

'Was he? I should have thought he would have waited to be called, because of his business interests.' I blushed as my father stared at me. 'We – we were friends. He asked me to marry him but I turned him down.'

'Samantha isn't his then?'

'No, she isn't.' I looked at a point somewhere beyond his head. 'She – she's Lucas Harrington's.'

'You were in love with him, weren't you?'

'I still am.' I lifted my head proudly. 'He promised to marry me, Da.'

For some reason I couldn't bring myself to tell him about those last few days in Bournemouth. Now that they were over I had begun to doubt again, to wonder if I was a fool to go on loving Lucas. It hadn't been fair of him to come back into my life only to leave again so soon. Fortunately, I knew that there would not be a child this time.

Father looked sad. 'You're not the first lass to have been betrayed that way. You won't let it make you bitter?'

'No, I won't.' He was thinking of my mother and the way she had let a terrible experience overshadow her life. 'It hurt me and . . . and I shall never forget Lucas, but I won't let it make me bitter. He's promised to come back for me. Maybe he will one day.'

I smiled at him and tried hard to banish the doubts. Lucas had said he loved me and promised to come back. I had to believe that he would keep his word.

For the next few weeks there was an uneasy truce between Mother and myself. I tried looking for work but there was very little available in the village and Sam wouldn't hear of me going into town to the munitions factory.

'You're not going there – nor back to London while the blitz is on,' he said firmly. 'Give yourself time to think what you want to do with your life, Nellie.'

'I should like to find work as a cook,' I said. 'I've been reading the recipe books Margaret Jones gave me and she's right, they do deserve to be published. Maybe I'll do something with them one day.'

I'd already begun sorting them out into sections and discovered that I enjoyed the act of writing them down, of actually forming the words and sentences. Through Alice I'd embraced what would be a lifelong love affair with books and I'd started to think that Margaret Jones was right when she'd said I could make a book of her recipes.

'You've heard nothing from Lucas?' Sam asked as I was silent. 'He hasn't written to you?'

'No . . . he said I wouldn't hear, not for a while.'

I'd made arrangements in London for my post to be sent on and had written to Alice, telling her I was living at home for the time being. No letters had come.

'Well, maybe you'll hear soon.' Sam gave me an encouraging look.

'Yes, perhaps I shall.' I smiled at him as I put my daughter into her pushchair. 'I've promised to meet Mary Hopkin. You remember? We were friends at school.'

He nodded. 'Off you go then, lass. It's a lovely day for a walk.'

It was a lovely day; the sun was warm but not hot and the sky a clear azure blue. In summer the village came to life with children playing in the narrow lanes, gardens blazing with colour as old-fashioned flowers rioted in the borders and vegetables flourished in the allotments. Only bees droning and birds singing disturbed the tranquillity, and the war might have been a million miles away as I walked to meet my friend near the common.

'She's beautiful,' Mary said as she looked into the pushchair. 'You're so lucky, Nellie, you always were. I can't wait to have a baby – but Joe says it wouldn't be fair until the war is over.' Her eyes clouded. 'I get so worried when I don't hear from him. What if he's killed? I'll never have his baby then . . . '

'You've only been engaged a few weeks, Mary.'

'On Joe's last leave,' she agreed, and sighed. 'We're going to marry next time he comes home. My parents still think I'm too young but I'm almost eighteen – that's old enough to be married, isn't it?'

I hadn't been quite seventeen when Samantha was born, but it was different for me. Mary's parents had always fussed over her, keeping her a child longer than necessary.

'It's old enough if you love him,' I said, and kissed her cheek. 'Don't worry, Mary, I'm sure Joe will write soon.'

I was thoughtful as I left my friend to walk home. Mary was right, I was lucky to have Samantha. Sometimes I remembered the nights of passion I had spent in Lucas's arms and longed to feel his body close to mine once more. Where was he and what was he doing? Was he thinking of me? If only I knew . . . if only he had told me where he was going . . . if only I could be sure that he truly loved me.

It was about two months later when my questions were suddenly answered in the most terrible way. Mother and I had just begun to whitewash the scullery that morning; she looked at me in annoyance as someone knocked at the back door.

'If that's for me I'm busy.'

An elderly neighbour had been unwell recently and her daughter was always coming to fetch Mother out. I was expecting another tearful request for her services so it was a shock when I opened the door and saw who was standing there.

'Alice,' I said. 'What a lovely surprise. Will you come in?'

'Who is it?' Mother called, wiping her hands as she came in from the scullery. 'Oh . . . Miss Harrington. What are you thinking of, Nellie? Ask Miss Harrington into the parlour.'

'It's Mrs Simpson now,' Alice said in her gentle way. 'I would like to have a few words in private with Nellie, if that's convenient?'

'Yes. Yes, of course. Please go through, Mrs Simpson.'

Mother looked pleased and I realized she thought Alice had come to offer me a job. I led the way through to the kitchen, then glanced at Alice.

'Would you prefer the parlour?'

'No, this will be fine.' Alice's voice sounded a little odd and I suddenly sensed that she was very upset. 'Nellie my dear, I don't know how to tell you . . . '

'You're crying.' A coldness was creeping over me. 'It's Lucas . . . something has happened . . . '

'We've just heard the most terrible news . . . ' Alice choked back a sob. 'Lucas . . . Lucas has been arrested by the Germans as a spy.'

'A spy! What are you talking about?' I stared at her in bewilderment. 'I don't understand. How could . . . where . . . he was supposed to be in New York . . . ' But he hadn't gone to New York. I'd known that was a lie even as he'd spoken.

'He was working for British Intelligence in France,' Alice said. 'He couldn't tell us, of course, but I knew because Gerald has friends who arrange these things. We've been told about his arrest unofficially.'

'In France . . . arrested?' I sat down as my legs turned to jelly. 'That's why he was so strange at the station . . . that's why he looked at me that way . . . '

247

Suddenly I understood his last words: 'If I shouldn't come back . . . remember I loved you . . . '

My heart felt as if it were being squeezed and I couldn't breathe properly as I asked, 'What happens now? What will they do to him?'

'I . . . Gerald says he will have been given a cyanide pill in case of arrest. Our people are told to take them rather than risk torture.'

'No!' I cried. 'No, not dead. He can't be dead, Alice. He can't be . . . he can't . . . '

I leant my elbows on the table, covering my face with my hands as the agony of my grief swept over me. Lucas couldn't be dead. I wouldn't believe it. It wasn't possible – not Lucas.

'He can't be dead . . . he can't . . . ' I went on repeating the words over and over. 'Why, Alice – why? Why did it happen?'

'I don't know, my dear.' She shook her head, her face drawn with grief. 'Except that this is typical of Lucas. They turned him down for the army because of those recurrent migraines so this was his answer – he wanted to do something and he speaks fluent French and German so I suppose he was ideal material for this kind of work.'

'He should have told me!' Anger mixed with the grief now. 'He had no right to do this without telling me. It was selfish and cruel. He knew he might never come back. He knew . . . '

It was the same thing all over again. Lucas had believed he was being noble by hiding his fears of a terminal illness, when in fact he had inflicted unnecessary pain. Now he had volunteered for a highly dangerous mission without thinking of the grief his death might cause to others. He had such certainty, such belief in his own actions, that it made him careless of others – or perhaps he simply did not think.

'He is always so selfish!'

Alice stared at me helplessly. 'Lucas is a law unto himself, my dear. He knew the risks, of course, but he has always been so stubborn, so unpredictable. That's why . . . '

'You warned me not to love him,' I cried wildly. 'I should have listened. Damn you, Lucas! You had no right to do this to me . . . to Samantha . . . ' All at once my anger waned as a

248

wave of grief washed over me. 'Oh, Alice, I love him so much . . . so much.'

'I know, dearest. I know.' She took me into her arms, rocking me as I wept into her shoulder. 'It's such a waste – such a stupid waste. This whole war . . . such a waste of young lives.'

Afterwards, I had no memory of Alice leaving or of my own return to the scullery to help finish the cleaning, though I believe that's what I did. I was numbed, moving in a daze as I held my grief at bay by refusing to believe it.

Lucas couldn't be dead. It was all a terrible mistake. Soon I would wake up and discover it had been a nightmare.

But the nightmare continued throughout a restless night and for many nights after. I could fill my days with work – and I had at last managed to find a job helping a local farmer's wife cook for her army of land girls – but the nights were unbearable. My moods swung from a terrible, tearing grief to angry rages when I cursed Lucas and wished that I had never met him.

As the days and then weeks passed I lost weight and the shadows grew darker beneath my eyes, causing Sam to look at me in concern and shake his head.

'If you go on like this much longer you'll kill yourself,' he said one spring morning in 1941. 'You accuse Lucas of being selfish but you're not thinking of Samantha. It's time you pulled yourself together and got on with your life. You loved Lucas but other women have lost their husbands and lovers. You're not the only one.'

I had never heard Sam speak so harshly and it made me realize that I had been going through the motions of eating, sleeping and caring for my child. Looking at Samantha building brick castles and knocking them down again, I saw that she was too quiet, too subdued.

'You're right,' I said. 'I'm sorry, Da. I'll try to do better.'

'I know it hurts, lass,' he said in a softer tone, 'but life goes on.'

It was true. I had been dealt a harsh blow but that was no reason to lay down and die. I had my child to think of. If anything happened to me she would be completely alone.

Sam's words brought me to my senses and after that I spent more time playing with Samantha, taking her for walks or simply cuddling her. Sometimes it hurt unbearably when she looked at me with her father's eyes but my love for her was so deep that I knew I must make a good life for her. In future I would live for her. She was all that mattered to me now.

It was only a few days after my father spoke to me that Jean rang to tell me that her sister had died.

'She passed away peacefully in her sleep. The night before we sat up late talking – mostly of you. Margaret was so fond of you, Nellie. She thought of you as the daughter she never had.'

'I was fond of her, too, Jean. I'll come down for the funeral.'

In some strange way my grief for the death of my friend helped to ease the pain of losing Lucas. In supporting Jean through her time of sadness I began to find a way for myself, a way to live again.

'Margaret wanted you to have these,' Jean said when I was preparing to leave again. 'As a keepsake.'

I opened the box she gave me, exclaiming as I saw the pretty gold brooches and diamond rings. 'But you should have these, Jean!'

'She left me something, too.' Jean smiled. 'Take them, Nellie. She wanted you to have them.'

I was thoughtful on the train journey home. Margaret's dearest wish had been to have her recipes published in a cookery book. I promised myself that I would make it happen. Somehow. I might try writing down some of the special wartime recipes I'd invented for Maud's tearooms, too.

It would be a challenge, something to do during the long, restless nights when I could not sleep.

Summer was almost on us. The air had a gentle warmth as I left the farm, walking across a meadow with long grass that almost reached my waist and was filled with wild flowers. We had been busy all morning baking and cooking; the land girls were always starving when they came in for their meals, their noisy, friendly chatter filling the kitchen as they talked of their lovers, who were away fighting with one of the services.

I was feeling wistful, thinking about what the girls had been saying, especially those who had received letters telling them their loved ones would soon be home for a visit. My lover would never come home.

Perhaps because of the nature of my thoughts it was even more of a shock when I reached the lane leading to my parents' house and someone stepped out from behind a tree to block my path. I looked up to see a man in army uniform.

'Tom . . . ' I felt the blood draining from my cheeks. 'What are you doing here?'

Tom Herries stared at me with a strange, half hungry, half angry expression. 'I was wounded in the arm. It's just a scratch – got me home for a bit, though.' He moved his left arm stiffly.

'As long as it's getting better,' I said, feeling awkward. He looked different . . . older, harder, almost a stranger. 'Tom . . . '

'I heard you had a child.' There was bitter accusation in his voice, bringing a flush to my cheeks.

'Yes – a little girl.' It wasn't easy to meet his eyes but I managed it. 'She's two now. My mother looks after her while I'm at work.'

'It was him . . . Lucas Harrington.' His eyes held smouldering resentment. 'He took you away from me. You were mine and he stole you!'

'Tom, that isn't fair . . . ' My protest died because I knew it was fair. I had half promised to marry him before Lucas came home. 'I'm sorry. I didn't mean to hurt you.'

'You said you cared for me.'

'I did – I do care for you, Tom. What happened . . . you don't understand. Lucas was . . . ' I stopped, unable to put my thoughts into words. How could I explain that my love for Lucas had been something special? A dream that I had known was impossible even while I lay in his arms.

Tom's eyes went to my ringless left hand. 'He didn't marry you then?'

'No, he didn't marry me.' I wasn't prepared to talk about

251

Lucas! I tried to go past him but he moved to stop me. 'Please let me go. I have to get back.'

'Don't go like this,' he said and there was a note of pleading in his voice. 'Come out with me this evening. I need to talk to you – please, Nellie.'

'There's no point, Tom.'

'Please . . . I still care for you. Just talk to me. I think you owe me that much.' He was angry and yet there was a look of appeal in his eyes that held me. I did owe him something. 'Please, Nellie.'

'All right,' I said at last. 'I'll meet you this evening – but don't come to the house. I'll tell my mother I'm going to Mary's and meet you near the green.'

'I thought you saw Mary Hopkin yesterday?' Mother said, a suspicious note in her voice. 'Why do you need to go round there this evening?'

'We're going to cut out a dress pattern for her.' I averted my head so that she couldn't see my face, because she would have known I was lying. 'I shan't be long.'

'Let her go,' my father said. 'She doesn't go out often and the child is never any trouble once she's asleep.'

'I didn't say Samantha was a nuisance.' Mother turned to me. 'Just behave yourself, that's all. We don't want another mistake.'

'Leave her alone, Rose. Off you go, lass – and have a good time.'

I picked up my coat and hurried from the house, feeling wretched about lying to Sam. If it had been possible I would have told him I was going to meet Tom Herries but my mother would have made so much fuss. She had never approved of Tom's family and she certainly wouldn't approve of my going out with him, even if it was perfectly innocent.

Tom was sitting in his van when I reached the green. He got out and opened the door for me, his expression oddly unsure and defensive.

'I was afraid you wouldn't come.'

'I said I would.'

'Shall we go to a dance? There's one on in Hanlith church hall.'

252

He had abandoned his uniform and was wearing a smart, dark navy suit, his hair slicked back with brilliantine and his shoes highly polished.

'I would rather we just went for a quiet drink somewhere – not in the village.' He helped me into the van. I noticed his arm was very stiff. 'Are you sure you can drive?'

'My arm is fine now, just a bit awkward. I've got six weeks' leave for a rest. No doubt they'll send me off again once I report back.'

'What's it all for, Tom? I know what the papers say, what the Government's official line is – but why do people want to fight each other?'

'Sometimes you have to, because it's right.'

'Is that why you joined up?'

'I had my reasons.'

He drove on in silence for a while. I wondered if it was because of me, because I had let him down, but I couldn't find the words to ask.

We had been driving for twenty minutes or so when he pulled the van into a farm lane and shut down the engine. For a while he stared into the darkness lit only by a pale moon half hidden by cloud, then he turned towards me.

'I was hurt when you went off like that, angry, too. You could have told me, Nellie.'

I reached out to touch his hand, then hesitated and drew back. 'I'm sorry, Tom. I couldn't face you. I was confused, scared . . . ashamed . . . '

'You should have told me! I would have stood by you – you knew that, Nellie. I would have married you.'

'Perhaps that's why I didn't. It wouldn't have been fair to you, Tom. I couldn't saddle you with another man's child.'

It was what my mother had done to my father but I didn't tell him that. Sam had known that she was carrying the child of a rapist when he married her, but even so it had been between them all their lives, ruining their chance of happiness.

'Why did you do it, Nellie? You must have known he wouldn't marry you – that sort never do. They know how to use girls like you.'

'It wasn't like that!'

'What was it like then?'

I couldn't answer him because I didn't know the truth myself. Lucas had sworn he loved me but I would never be sure now – never know if he'd really meant to come back for me.

'I thought he loved me,' I said at last, and then I was crying as the hopelessness swept over me. 'He said he loved me . . . I couldn't help it, Tom. It just happened and now . . . and now . . . ' I choked and couldn't go on. Lucas was dead and I was so alone.

Tom stared at me in silence, then he moved towards me, drawing me close. He stroked my hair, whispering words of comfort and forgiveness, then, as I gazed mistily into his face, he kissed me very gently on the lips.

'Don't cry, lass,' he said. 'You've been hurt. We've both been hurt – but it isn't the end of the world. We can get over it.'

'I'm such a fool.' I reached for my hanky and blew my nose. 'I shouldn't be crying all over you.'

'I've got broad shoulders. Besides, I love you.'

I could hardly see his face in the dim light but I touched my fingers to his lips. 'You can't love me,' I said huskily, 'not after what I've done. Don't say it, Tom. Please don't say it.'

'Because you still love him?'

'It's over . . . the dream is over,' I whispered. 'I loved him but he left me – and now he's dead. He – he was killed in France.'

'Then give me a chance. Let me try to make you happy.'

'I don't know. Supposing . . . '

'Don't turn me down.' He didn't give me time to finish and there was desperation in his voice now. 'I'll be going back out there soon – don't send me away without hope. Give me something to come back for, Nellie. I need you. I don't care what happened in the past. We are the future.' His voice cracked and I realized he was crying. 'Please, Nellie. I'm begging . . . '

'Tom, don't, my dear. Don't.' My heart felt as if it were being torn apart. I did love him in my own way and I hadn't wanted to hurt him like this. I drew his head down to mine and kissed him. 'My dearest Tom.'

Suddenly he was holding me crushed against him so hard that I could scarcely breathe. His mouth covered mine, demanding, passionate and yet tender. He was trembling.

I wound my arms around his neck, wanting to comfort him and wanting comfort in return. The urgency of his kisses awakened a stronger need within me, a need I had repressed for a long, long time. This feeling deep inside me was not the heedless passion I had known with Lucas but a warmer, softer giving that made me cry helpless tears.

Tom's kisses intensified, his hand moving to caress my breasts, slipping inside my blouse. His breath rasped against my ear.

'Let me love you,' he begged hoarsely. 'I need you, want you so much. We'll be married before I go back, I promise. Please . . . please don't stop me.'

His hand was between my legs, his fingers stroking, invading, thrusting into the soft moistness of my flesh; then he was fumbling at his buttons and I felt a surge of panic, trying to stop him, to call a halt now, but his kisses smothered my cry. He was in me, hard and eager, plunging into me with such desperate need that nothing could have stopped him. I lay helplessly beneath him until it was over, my mind numbed; it had happened so quickly and was over before I'd had time to clear my thoughts.

Afterwards, he lay with his head against my breasts. 'I'm sorry,' he mumbled. 'I wanted you so badly. I couldn't control myself.'

My fingers tangled in his dark hair. I felt sad and I wanted to cry but I held the tears inside me. It wasn't his fault that I hadn't been able to respond completely – that a part of me had held back from him, clinging to my memories as a frightened child might cling to a worn blanket.

Tom was a decent man. He loved me and wanted to marry me. Perhaps it was for the best. I wanted to make a new life for myself and Samantha and Tom would provide us with a home of our own. Sam was right, I had to start living again.

'It's all right, Tom love,' I whispered. 'It's all right . . . just give me a little time.'

*

My father had gone to bed when I got home, but Mother was sitting in her chair by the fire, her back ramrod straight as she waited for me to come in.

'Where have you been?'

'To Mary's – I told you.'

My cheeks burned as I lied to her but I hadn't yet agreed to marry Tom and I didn't want her to know that I had been meeting him.

I'd asked Tom for a few days to think things over.

'I know I've rushed you,' he'd said as he let me out of his van at the top of the lane. 'But I love you, Nellie. I don't want to lose you again.'

'You won't,' I promised. 'I just need a little while to get used to the idea, that's all.'

I wanted to be quite certain this time, and when I was I would talk to Sam. I knew he liked Tom and was sure he would approve, no matter what my mother thought. Her eyes were stabbing at me like little knives and I knew she was suspicious.

'If I find out that you're lying to me, I'll make you wish you were never born.'

'The way you do?' I asked. 'It wasn't my fault, Ma. I don't know who he was – the man who hurt you so bad – or why it happened, but it wasn't my fault.'

'I would have got rid of you if I could,' she said. 'Sam wouldn't let me. You've always come between us, always.'

'Only because you wouldn't let yourself forget. Sam never held it against you, Ma. If I ruined your life it was because you wouldn't let go.'

'I'm warning you,' she said. 'Don't give me cause to be more ashamed of you than I am.'

'Good night, Ma,' I said and walked on past her up the stairs.

Alone in my room I lay on the bed without undressing and stared into the darkness. When I'd left Tom I hadn't been sure it would be right or fair to marry him, because a part of me was still grieving for Lucas, but my mother's bitterness had shown me that I would have to leave this house soon. It would not be easy to bring Samantha up alone . . . but could I marry Tom because my daughter needed a father?

256

I closed my eyes as the tears overflowed. Lucas was dead. Even if he had lived he might never have come back for me. It was time to put the past behind me, to stop crying for the moon and take what life had to offer.

Next time we met I would tell Tom that I was ready to marry him.

Chapter Fifteen

It was starting to rain as I left the farm to walk home, not hard but a soft mizzle that was enough to take the curl from my hair and wet the grass. One of the land girls had just told us she was getting married soon, inviting us all to her wedding.

'You'll come, won't you, Nellie?' she'd said, lingering after the others had gone back to the fields.

'Yes, if I can, Amy,' I replied. 'I – I might be going away soon myself.'

I hadn't dared to tell anyone yet that I was going to marry Tom, because I hadn't been able to catch my father alone before he went to work. Mother had hung around the kitchen all the time, almost as though she suspected something – but she would have to know soon. If Tom managed to arrange the wedding before he went back to his unit I should move into the rooms above his shop in Malham as soon as we were married.

'If they don't send me back too soon I might be able to help you get the business running properly again,' Tom had said, a gleam in his eyes as he'd tried to persuade me to marry him. I'd promised him an answer soon and now I was ready to give him the one he craved.

He was full of plans for the future. I was still not quite sure I'd made the right decision – mainly for his sake – but it was what he wanted. Besides, I wanted a decent life for Samantha and I believed that marrying Tom was the best way to secure that. My daughter was going to have the best I could give her – and she needed a father.

As I turned into the lane that led to my parents' cottage I was conscious of a feeling of unease, though I wasn't sure why. Mother was in the back kitchen, muttering to herself as she wrung out some woollens she had washed by hand. She gave me a resentful glance as I entered.

'You've got a visitor,' she said. 'Mary Hopkin insisted on waiting for you – she's been in the kitchen for ages. I've taken her some tea in but I was too busy to talk.'

'I'll go in to her now,' I said. 'Where's Samantha?'

'With your visitor – being spoiled silly with sweets and presents.'

Now I understood the reason for her mood. She was always annoyed when Mary brought Samantha sweets, though I'd never known why.

I went through to the parlour. Samantha was sitting on Mary's knee playing with an expensive doll. It had hair, a painted china face and eyes that opened and closed; the clothes it was wearing must have cost the earth.

'You'll spoil her,' I said, but with a smile. 'Thank you, Mary. It's beautiful.'

She glanced up, a flush in her cheeks as Samantha scrambled off her lap and came toddling towards me. I caught her up, hugging and kissing her until she clamoured to be set down to play with her doll. It was only then that I saw how agitated Mary was.

'I've had a letter from Joe,' she said. 'It has been censored in places but we have our own special code . . . ' She faltered and was obviously very upset.

'What's wrong, Mary?'

'I think Joe is ill,' she said and the tears were very close. 'He's been in the thick of the fighting for weeks and I don't think he can take much more.'

'Oh, Mary . . . '

'You're the only one I can talk to. My parents don't understand. They think I'm too young . . . but I love him, Nellie. I love him so much.'

'Of course you do.'

I tried to comfort her but there wasn't much I could say. She was afraid for Joe and she had every right to be. Too many loved ones would never come home.

We talked for several minutes then my mother came in.

'There's some ironing needs doing,' she said, giving me a pointed look, then to Mary, 'Did you get your dress finished last night?'

'Dress?' Mary was puzzled. 'What dress?'

'The dress Nellie came to help you with last night.'

Mary went bright red as she saw my face. She tried to recover, saying, 'Yes, yes, I'd forgotten,' in a fluster, but it was too late. I had seen the look in my mother's eyes.

She started on me as soon as Mary had gone.

'So you're a liar as well as a slut!' She glared at me. 'I knew you'd been with a man all the time. It wasn't Mary you went to see last night.'

'No, it wasn't.' I got to my feet, forgetting to be cautious as the anger boiled over. 'I did go to see a man – a man who wants to marry me.'

'You little slut!'

'I'm not a slut, Mother. Tom is a decent man. He's arranging the banns and we'll be married before he returns to his regiment.'

'Tom? Tom who?' she demanded. 'I suppose he's the filthy devil who gave you one before?'

'No, he isn't. Tom Herries has always wanted to marry me but . . . ' The words drained away as I saw the look on her face. 'I know you don't approve of his family but Tom isn't like the others. He had his own business even before the war and I'm going to help . . . '

'Over my dead body!' She was furious now. 'You'll never marry a member of that family. Never!'

'You can't stop me. I know I'm still too young to marry without permission but Da will give it to me – and if you stop him I'll go away with Tom. I'll live with him without getting married.'

I wasn't sure why I was pushing her so hard. It would have been better to walk away, leave things for a while, until she'd had time to calm down, but there was a little devil inside me driving me on. For once in my life I wasn't going to let her dominate me; I wanted to hurt her as she'd hurt me so many times in the past.

'You can't marry that tinker trash. I won't let you.'

The mantle clock's tick seemed loud and harsh in my ears – or was it the beating of my own heart?

'Why?' I challenged. 'Give me one good reason why I shouldn't.' My blood ran cold as I stared at her. 'You're not telling me that Tinker Herries is the man who raped you . . . my father . . . are you?'

For a moment there was indecision in her face and I sensed that she was tempted to lie.

'No . . . ' she said at last in an odd, harsh tone. 'No – Tinker didn't rape me, that was a stranger, a man I'd never seen but once before. But I blame Tinker . . . ' Suddenly her eyes were blazing at me. 'Oh, yes, I blame him for what happened that day.'

'Why, Ma? Tell me. Tell me, what did happen?'

It was important that she broke her long silence. Perhaps then she would be able to conquer her bitterness.

She seemed not to hear me. She was reliving it all second by second, feeling the pain and humiliation as if it were happening now.

'We saw them that afternoon as we walked across the common, Janet and I, Tinker and a tall swarthy-skinned brute of a man I'd never seen before. We were laughing and teasing each other the way young girls do. Tinker was watching me with those bold eyes of his . . . '

'Go on, Ma,' I urged as she hesitated.

'He was a handsome devil in those days. I wasn't the only girl to think so.' She took a ragged breath, her brow creased with pain. 'God forgive me but I fancied him. I'd been warned by my father to stay away from him but he called out to me, asked me to meet him later in the woods . . . teasingly like.'

She hesitated again and I saw she was regretting having told me anything. She mustn't stop now! I had started this in anger but now I felt it was something she needed to do. She had kept it inside her for far too long.

'Go on, Ma. You went to meet Tinker, didn't you?'

She nodded, harsh furrows about her mouth as it drew into lines of bitterness. 'I was courting Sam. I had no right to look at another man but Tinker had a strange fascination for me so I went to meet him, but he wasn't there.' Her eyes

261

were bleak as they suddenly made contact with mine. 'The other one was waiting. He'd been with Tinker, heard him ask me. It was getting dark. He taunted me, called me a whore and then . . . I fought him. Oh God, I fought with all my strength but he was too strong. He battered me and used me and all the time . . . all the time he was laughing.'

'Oh, Ma.' My throat caught with emotion. 'I'm so sorry. So very sorry.'

She had kept the humiliation and guilt inside her, letting it fester and become poisonous over the years, blighting her own life and ours. But she had suffered too. How she had suffered!

'You weren't to blame,' I cried. 'Just because you went to meet a man you liked.'

'But it was a betrayal of Sam, don't you see?' She stared at me with wild eyes. 'I've regretted it every day since. Sam's been good to me. He's a decent, honest man and I love him now . . . but I didn't then. It was Tinker who'd turned my head and because of that I ended up with a bastard in my belly.'

A strangled sound from behind her startled us both. Neither of us had heard the back door but it must have opened because Sam had come in – and he'd heard her saying that she hadn't loved him when they were wed. He was staring at her as if he'd never seen her before.

'You swore it was a stranger,' he said in a queer, hushed tone. 'You lied to me, Rose. All these years . . . '

'Sam!' she gasped and the colour drained from her cheeks. 'Oh, no! Sam, no, please. I didn't mean . . . '

'It was that Tinker bastard. All the time you knew. You went to him of your own accord and he raped you. Why didn't you tell me the truth?'

'No, Sam. You don't understand. It wasn't . . . '

She was close to tears, her hands reaching out as if to implore him for understanding. 'I couldn't tell you. I was afraid . . . ashamed. Besides, I knew you would have gone after him. You would have killed him or he you.'

She was making it worse with every word, compounding the misunderstanding.

'I'll kill the bastard now!'

'No! You've got it all wrong,' she cried. 'It wasn't Tinker. I blamed him for not being there, for letting it happen – but it wasn't him. It was a stranger.'

'I don't believe you. You're lying to me again, just the way you always have.'

'Sam, come back!' she screamed. 'Please listen . . . '

'Don't go, Da,' I called. 'It isn't worth it – not after all this time.'

He wasn't listening to either of us, his mind tortured with thoughts beyond bearing. I knew he would go after Tinker whatever we said now – and he would find him, because Tom had told me his father was camping on the common. Sam must have heard that, too. From the agonised expression in his eyes it was clear that he would kill or be killed.

'Please, Da . . . '

For a moment he seemed to see me and I recognized all the pain and suffering he had kept inside, the hurt pride, anger and frustration he'd suppressed over the years.

'I have to settle it,' he said and moved towards the door.

Mother screamed again and grabbed his arm, hanging on to him desperately as he struggled to free himself. She begged him over and over not to leave.

'Please, Sam . . . please,' she wept. 'Forgive me . . . forgive me . . . '

'Let go, Rose,' he said. 'It's time . . . '

We would never know what he meant to say for he made a choking sound in his throat, then his eyes rolled upwards and he staggered, falling against my mother.

'Sam!' She sent a frantic look towards me and I rushed to help her support him. 'Sam . . . '

Together we laid him on the daybed by the window. His eyes flickered then opened, looking at us both as we bent over him anxiously.

'It's all right, Da. It's all right. I'll get the doctor.'

'I love you,' he whispered. 'All of you . . . all of you . . . Rose . . . '

And then, quietly, without fuss, he was gone.

The silence of the house was unbearable during the three days before Sam's funeral. My mother and I were both grieving in our separate ways, but we could not talk to each other. Neither of us could really come to terms with the fact that the man we had both loved was dead.

He had been such a good, decent man, always giving more than he took. He had died as he had lived, with dignity and causing no trouble for anyone – but we hadn't wanted him to die like that, so suddenly, without warning. We wanted him back with us and the pain of his loss was so terrible that it could not be shared. We both wept alone during the long dark hours of night, neither of us able to reach out to the other. My mother hated me and I was wracked with guilt.

Why had I forced that quarrel on her? The truth was that I'd wanted to hurt her, to pay her back for all the years of neglect and hurt she'd inflicted on me but I'd ended by killing Sam.

'Oh, Da,' I sobbed into my pillow. 'I'm so sorry. Forgive me. I didn't want to hurt you.'

I'd forced my mother to reveal her secret and in doing so I'd broken Sam's heart. I would find it difficult to forgive myself for my part in his death. The next few days would be hard to face.

Mary Hopkin had offered to look after Samantha until it was all over and I had agreed; Samantha liked her because Mary made a big fuss of her – and it wouldn't be right for a small child to stay in this house of terrible mourning.

Bob was old enough to understand and did his best to comfort his mother, but she had locked herself away in a world of her own and in the end he came to me for comfort himself.

'Why did Da have to die, Nellie?' he asked, trying not to cry. 'He wasn't old, not like Grandad.'

'I think it was his heart. He hadn't been well for some time, Bob. He didn't tell us because he didn't want us to worry, but I think he knew he was very ill.'

'I loved him . . .'

His mouth trembled as he began to cry. I took him in my arms, kissing the top of his head and holding him until he was quiet.

'He loved you, too,' I said. 'But he wouldn't want you to be miserable. You have to think of Ma now. You'll be the man of the house, Bob. You'll have to look after her when I go.'

'Are you going away?'

'Not just yet but soon,' I said as he gazed up at me. 'You know Ma doesn't like me as much as she likes you.'

'She loves Samantha,' he said. 'I've seen her looking at Sammie when you weren't around, smiling and kissing her. Ma will miss Sammie and I'll miss you. Don't go, Nellie. Please don't go.'

'I'll stay for a while,' I promised. 'Now go and feed the chickens the scraps and see if there are any eggs.'

I watched as he ran off to do his chores and sighed. Everything was such a mess. My mother had not spoken a word to me since Sam's death. She stared at me with cold, unforgiving eyes and I knew she was blaming me for what had happened.

I wanted to see Tom but I'd asked Mary to let him know he must not come to the house or the funeral. I could not add to Mother's grief by flaunting Tom in front of her.

The future was fraught with uncertainty. Could I marry Tom now? I was confused and unhappy, unable to think about anything or anyone but the dear, good man lying so stiff and pale in his coffin.

After the funeral I should have to decide but I could do nothing until my da was decently buried.

Until I saw the people overflowing out of the church and standing outside in the drizzling rain to show their respect, I had no idea how much Sam had been loved by his friends and neighbours. They looked at us in sorrow and sympathy as Bob and I walked on either side of our mother, following the simple oak coffin into church.

My mother had refused support from either of us. She walked with her head up, her face closed and harsh behind the black gauze veil, but I knew that she wept when she was alone and I wished there was something I could do to help her. But she didn't want my help.

At my side the stone-faced woman stared in front of her throughout the service, giving no hint of the agony that must have been tearing her apart. My heart bled for her but I dared not offer to take her hand.

She stayed on at the graveside after Bob and I walked away.

As I reached the lane outside the church Mary came up to me. 'Tom gave me this,' she whispered, slipping a note into my hand. 'He wants to see you.'

'Tell him I'll try to get away later,' I said. 'I'll meet him by the green at about two if I can.'

Mary nodded, moving away as my mother came towards us.

As Bob, Mother and I drove back to the house in silence I came to a decision. For as long as I stayed here my presence would be a painful reminder for my mother of that last morning. I knew she would blame me for Sam's heart attack, for if I had not insisted that I would marry Tom Herries she would never have spoken those fatal words. It was best that I should take Samantha and go.

Perhaps then we could all begin to rebuild our lives.

Several of Sam's friends and customers came to the house to eat dainty paste sandwiches, drink tea and offer their sympathy. My mother seemed calm, almost serene as she listened to them telling her what a good man Sam had been and how much he would be missed, but I knew that inside her nerves were stretched almost to breaking point. I did my best to protect her from our well-meaning friends, but she stared through me. It was as though I wasn't there, as though I didn't exist. It wasn't until after everyone had gone that she finally looked at me.

'I want you out of this house in the morning,' she said. 'You can stay tonight but then out you go. I've written permission for you to wed. It's on the sideboard.'

'Thank you.' There was a terrible silence between us, then I nodded. 'Yes,' I said quietly. 'It's best I go.'

She turned away but I called after her.

'I'm sorry,' I said. 'I'm sorry, Ma. I didn't want this to happen.'

She swung round to face me, her eyes glittering with hatred. 'You killed him,' she said. 'You killed my Sam and I'll never forgive you.'

'That's not fair,' I whispered, and pressed shaking fingers to my lips. 'I loved him. You know I did. I never meant to hurt him.'

'He wasn't your father and as far as I'm concerned you aren't my daughter.'

She walked away, leaving me staring after her. The pain in my chest was intense and I knew I had to get out of the house. I had to see Tom – Tom would help me. I needed him because I was hurting too badly to cope alone.

I would see Tom, then collect Samantha from Mary's house. It was the first time I had been away from my darling daughter for more than a few hours and I couldn't wait to have her back again – but I had to talk to Tom before I did anything else.

When I reached the green there was no sign of him. I sat down on the bench beside the pond watching the ducks and shivering as the cold breeze struck through my coat. It was later than I had arranged and I wondered if Tom had been and gone.

'Are you 'er?' a voice asked and I became aware of a young lad looking at me curiously. 'Tom told me to watch out for a pretty woman sittin' 'ere.'

'Are you his brother?'

He had a look of Tom about him but he was small, his face pale and thin beneath the layers of grimed-in dirt.

'He's gorn to see me ma,' the urchin said. 'She's bin took bad and she asked fer Tom. He's the only one of the lot of 'em wot's ever done anyfing fer 'er.'

'Could you take me to see him please?'

'He said ter tell yer to come back at six tonight.'

'Please – I would like to see him now. Would you take me? It's very important.'

He hesitated then nodded, a smile very like Tom's playing over his mouth. 'Aw right, if yer want.' He offered a small and very dirty hand. 'I'll take yer – but if Tom belts me it's yer fault.'

'He won't hit you, I promise.'

He laughed in delight. 'I wus just jossing yer, missus. Tom ain't like that – not like me da.'

'Does your father hit you?'

His merriment vanished and something like fear flickered in his eyes. 'He's a right ole devil,' he said. 'As soon as Ma's better I'm gettin' out, the way Tom did. I hate the old bugger. One day I'll kill 'im.'

'You mustn't say things like that.' I glanced down at him. 'What did you say your name was?'

'It's Jerry,' he replied. 'I'm eleven – leastways Ma thinks I am but she ain't real sure 'cos she's had so many of us and some of 'em died.'

My heart was stirred with pity as I looked down at him. I would speak to Tom about the boy. Perhaps between us we could do something to make his future a little brighter.

As we approached the common I saw there was a caravan parked in the shelter of a clump of furze bushes and two horses grazing. Tom's van was near by. A fire had been lit earlier in the day but was smouldering now as if it had been allowed to die down; from somewhere behind the van came the sound of a couple of dogs barking furiously.

'Them's me lurchers,' Jerry said. 'I'd best see to 'em. You'll be all right now, missus. Me ma and Tom are in the van.'

The lad ran off in the direction of the barking and I stood looking at the caravan, feeling hesitant now. Once it must have been an attractive thing; there were traces of paint around the arched doorway as if it had been decorated with bright colours but the pictures had faded into a blur and there was an air of neglect about it as though whoever had painted them had given up caring.

For the first time I wondered about Tom's mother. The memory of Tinker Herries fighting at the jubilee party was firmly fixed in my mind, but his wife had always been a quiet, pale woman of whom no one ever took the slightest notice; from what Tom's brother had just told me I realized she must have had a miserable life and I wondered why she stayed with a man who treated her so badly – but perhaps she had no choice?

Walking up the three wooden steps that led to the door, I

knocked and waited. After a few seconds the door was opened by Tom, who stared at me in surprise.

'Nellie – I told Jerry to wait for you and explain . . . '

'He did. I asked him to bring me here, Tom. I have to talk to you, it's important.'

'You don't want to come in here.' Tom looked awkward. 'It's not fit for a pig.'

'Tom . . . who is it?' A woman's voice spoke from inside, then there was a choking sound and a rasping cough. 'Tom . . . '

He left the door open as he answered her cry. I followed him inside; it was dark and stuffy, the air smelt of stale unwashed bodies and vomit. For a moment my throat caught and I was afraid I would be sick but I held my breath, forcing myself to show no sign of my disgust. As my eyes became accustomed to the dim light I saw a woman lying on a narrow cot; she was covered with a patchwork quilt that had seen better days and looked very ill, her greying hair straggling about her face.

'It's all right, Ma,' Tom said as he bent over her. 'It's just a friend of mine come visiting.'

I went closer so that she could see me and felt a surge of pity as I saw the bruising on her face and arms: more evidence of her husband's brutality. She looked at me as I approached and tried to smile.

'You'll be Tom's girl,' she whispered. 'He's told me about you. He's a good lad . . . not like his father.'

She started choking again and clutched at her chest, so obviously in pain that I turned to Tom.

'Have you had the doctor to her?'

'She wouldn't have him and I haven't liked to leave her alone. Tinker has gone off somewhere to get drunk and there's only Jerry . . . '

I moved forward, hesitating before laying my hand on the sick woman's forehead. She was burning up.

'I'll stay with her while you fetch the doctor, Tom. Go on.' I gave him a little push as he hesitated. 'You know she needs one, don't you?'

He nodded, glanced at his mother and then back at me. 'I shan't be long, Nellie. I'll take the van and use the telephone in the village. You'll be all right here?'

'It's all right, Tom. I've helped with sick people before. Don't worry. Get off and ask the doctor to come at once.'

'I won't be long, Ma,' he said. 'Nellie will stay with you until I get back.'

He went before she could do more than shake her head. She didn't want a doctor but she was too weak to protest much and I had a feeling that if she wasn't helped she would die; perhaps she even hoped that she might, that her life of wretched misery might be over at last. I didn't know if it was right to interfere in another person's life but I couldn't just let her lie there in this state; she was Tom's mother and he loved her.

'Is there anything I can do for you?' I asked when we were alone. 'Can I get you something to drink?'

She shook her head wearily, closing her eyes for a moment, then as I turned away her hand touched my arm. 'Could you give me a little wash?' she asked as I looked down at her. 'I've been too ill to bother and I didn't like to ask Tom but if the doctor is coming . . . '

'Of course.'

I could see a jug and bowl in the corner of the van. Further investigation revealed a grimy flannel, a sliver of Sunlight soap and a torn towel; there was cold water in the jug but I could see no way of heating it.

'The water is cold.'

'I'm used to it,' she said, a faint smile in her eyes. 'Don't worry about heating it, I doubt you could get the fire going in time. There's a little talcum powder in the tin. I use it sparingly: Tom gave it me once.'

My heart twisted with pity for her but I tried not to show it, hiding my emotion as I brought the water in the bowl and set it down on the floor beside the bed. Slipping my arm beneath her I lifted her higher against the pillows; she was frail and thin and easy to move. First I washed her face, hands and arms, then she pushed the covers back; she was wearing a torn petticoat and nothing else. We slipped the straps off her shoulders and I washed her sagging breasts and beneath her arms, drying her and smoothing on the precious talcum powder. She asked for the flannel and washed herself below, then sighed as I cleared away the water.

270

'Just tip it outside, lass,' she said. 'Thank you. I feel much better now.'

'It was nothing,' I replied. 'I wish there was more I could do for you.'

'I doubt there's much any . . . ' Her words drained away, the colour leaving her face as she stared at something behind me.

I swung round and saw that a man was standing in the doorway blocking the light. A strong odour of stale sweat and whisky emanated from him and although I could not see his face clearly I knew it was Tinker Herries.

'Who is she?' he demanded in a belligerent manner, belching and swaying as he lurched towards us. 'I've warned you before, woman, I won't have strangers interfering in me business.' He turned his glaring, bloodshot eyes on me. 'Git out of 'ere, blast yer! What do you think yer doing in me home?'

'She's only helpin' me, Tinker,' Tom's mother cried. 'She ain't doin' no harm.'

'I'll not have these blasted do-gooders poking their noses in where they ain't wanted.' He belched again and I gagged on the evil stench of his breath. 'Git out afore I give yer a taste of me 'and!'

'I came to see Tom,' I said, my head going up stubbornly. 'Your wife is very ill, Tinker. She needs a doctor. I've just been giving her a wash.'

'Who the hell are you?' He peered at me through bleary eyes. 'Ain't I seen yer somewhere?'

He had obviously long forgotten the pretty young girl he'd asked to meet him in the woods. I was suddenly angry. If he had not called after her . . . if he'd gone to meet her himself . . . perhaps none of the terrible consequences need have happened. In a way he *was* to blame for ruining Ma's life and for Sam's death.

'You don't know me but you knew my mother. She was . . . '

'I don't give a damn who you are,' he muttered. 'Jest git out of me home and stop poking your nose in me business.'

'No.' I glared at him. Anger and grief welled up inside me, sweeping away all sense of reason. I needed someone to hate

271

and he was there, drunk and disgusting. 'I don't care what you want. You're a revolting, evil, selfish man and I'm not moving from here until the doctor comes. It's time someone stopped you . . . '

I should have known that bad temper is counter-productive, that it is always best to placate rather than confront, especially with a man like Tinker Herries – but I was too angry to think clearly. All I knew was that I hated this man who had helped to ruin my mother's life, contributed to my da's death, and was slowly but surely killing his own wife.

'You bloody interfering bitch!' He gave a yell of rage and struck out at me, catching me across the face. 'Evil, am I? I'll show you what I'll do to a . . . '

'Tinker . . . '

The cry came from behind me as I staggered beneath the force of the blow. I glanced round and saw that his wife had got out of the bed. As he lifted his hand to hit me again she grabbed at his arm, pulling at him weakly and screaming at him to stop.

'Don't hit her, Tinker. She's Tom's lass . . . '

'Stay out of this, woman!'

He hit her against the side of the head, felling her to the floor where she lay moaning, then started to kick her again and again until she lay still.

'Murderer!' I cried as I saw her face go a deathly white. 'You'll hang for this.'

He swung round with a great roar of rage, coming for me again with his huge, hammerlike fists. His eyes had a queer glazed expression as if he were beyond knowing what he was doing. I backed away from him, sure that he had killed his wife and was about to kill me.

'Interfering bitch . . . just like your mother. Jethro taught her a lesson she didn't forget and I'll teach you the same . . . '

He did know who I was! He hadn't forgotten my mother – and he'd known about the rape. He'd known but done nothing. Maybe he'd laughed about it with his friend afterwards. Now I truly hated him.

My back was against the wall. I stretched out my hands as the fear mounted inside me, searching desperately for a way of escape or something with which I could defend myself.

272

There was nothing ... nothing ... and he was going to kill me ... but he was untying the string at his waist ... he was going to rape me before he killed me ...

My searching hands encountered something cold and heavy. It was an axe someone had used for chopping wood earlier. My fingers curled around the worn wooden handle as I lifted it, swinging it back.

'Get away from me,' I cried. 'Stay away or ... '

He grunted and flung himself at me, obviously believing that I didn't have the strength or the courage to carry out my threat: that was his mistake. Mine was that I had not realized how heavy the axe was and I swung wide. He grabbed my arm, twisting my wrist as he tried to force me to drop the weapon; we struggled wildly, crashing back and forth in the enclosed confines of the van, knocking over baskets of dirty clothes, stools and the bowl of water I had not emptied. It spilled over on the floor and he slipped, jerking backwards as he fought to keep his balance, his hand still clasping my wrist. My fingers opened and the axe fell uselessly to the ground.

I retreated as he got to his feet, my breath coming in short gasps as I realized there was nothing more I could do. My strength was exhausted and he knew it. He was leering at me as he lurched towards me, intent on having his way, on subjecting me to his will.

I was still standing there, frozen in horror, when the caravan door opened and Tom came in. He gave a startled shout, stopping Tinker in his tracks.

'You evil bastard! Touch her and I'll thrash you.'

Tom knelt briefly by his mother and saw that she was beyond his help, then got to his feet, staring at his father with a terrible hatred in his eyes.

'I'll kill you for this.'

'Tom ... ' I cried but there was no way I could have stopped them. Years of hatred had been building between them to an inevitable conclusion. 'Please don't ... '

Tinker had forgotten me as he lunged towards the son he had thrashed into submission so many times over the years.

'I'll teach you, runt,' he muttered thickly. 'Teach you good.'

I watched in sick fascination as they circled each other in the crowded confines of the small van, then they were at it, fists flying, pounding each other with bone-crunching ferocity, crashing into everything in their way. I was unable to move, pressed back in terror against the far end wall. For several minutes they fought fiercely, rocking the van with the violence of heaving bodies, then Tinker landed a blow that sent Tom sprawling, staggering backwards out of the door and down the steps.

I screamed, thinking such a fall must have killed or badly injured Tom, but he was on his feet again as Tinker launched himself into the attack once more.

Once they were outside the fight changed. Tom shook his head as if to clear it. He was thinking now, dodging the hammer fists, moving and ducking, waiting until he was able to dart in and deliver a telling blow.

I edged towards the door, my heart racing as I saw that Tom was gradually gaining the upper hand. Tinker was reeling under the heavy, accurate punches, his head snapping back and his fists flailing wildly as he missed time and again.

'Stand still and fight,' he muttered. 'Cowardly runt . . . '

'You're the coward,' Tom retaliated. 'You only hit those who can't fight back. Well, I've been in the army now and I've learned a thing or two. You've thrashed me enough – this time I'm going to show you how it feels.'

As he spoke he landed a blow that sent Tinker staggering. It was obvious that the older man was finished, his strength gone as he reeled and buckled at the knees.

'Tom!' I cried, finding my voice at last as Tom went in for the final blows. 'Don't kill him. It isn't worth it.'

Tinker was on his knees but not finished. As Tom glanced at me he grabbed a piece of wood and hit out at Tom's legs. I screamed and Tom threw himself at his father. They rolled over and over together on the ground, then all at once Tinker lay still.

Tom bent over him, then got to his feet and turned to look at me, a flicker of pride and triumph in his eyes.

'Is he dead?'

'No, just stunned. He'll be all right in a few minutes.'

He came up the steps of the van towards me.

274

'Thank you,' I whispered. 'He – he killed your mother and I think he would have . . . '

Tom touched his fingers to my mouth. 'I shouldn't have left you here alone. I didn't dream he would come back while I was away.'

I had begun to shiver and shake. 'He ordered me to leave,' I said. 'I wouldn't. It was my fault, Tom. I called him names and he attacked me. Your mother came to my aid and he killed her.'

'She was dying anyway,' Tom said as he drew me to him, stroking my hair. 'Maybe it's a blessing for her to go quick instead of slow and hard. It wasn't your fault. Hush, Nellie. Hush, my love.'

'What can we do for her?'

'I'll see to her when I come back,' Tom said. 'We'll just cover her up for now.'

Together we went into the van. Tom knelt beside his mother and kissed her cheek, then lifted her in his arms, laying her on the bed with infinite tenderness. He covered her with a patchwork quilt and turned to me.

'I'd best take you home now.'

'Yes. We can talk on the way.'

As we left the van Tinker was stirring.

'I'll be back for her,' Tom said grimly. 'She's going to have a decent funeral.'

Tinker stared at him sullenly but said nothing.

'Don't be here when I get back,' Tom went on. 'You deserve to hang for what you've done but she wouldn't want that. God knows why but she cared about you until the last. I won't turn you in but if you interfere I'll make you rue the day you were born.'

'Don't tell me what to do,' Tinker muttered. 'You beat me this time because I was drunk – but I'll have you for it. Watch yourself. I'm warning you, I'll have you.'

Tom took a step towards him but I caught his arm. 'Don't Tom. Please. There's been enough death for a while. Come away and leave him.'

'I'll be back for her so make yourself scarce.' Tom gripped my arm so hard it hurt. 'Come on, Nellie. Let's get out of here before I kill him.'

Chapter Sixteen

Tom stopped outside Mary's house and looked at me in the half-light as I finished my story.

'I knew Rose Pearce scorned us as a family,' he said, 'but I had no idea why. I'm sorry, lass. Sorry that you've had to suffer all these years for something Tinker did . . . '

'It wasn't really his fault,' I said, calmer now. 'Rose knows in her heart she was asking for trouble when she went to meet him – a married man, or as good as – but she blames him because it's easier than admitting the truth.'

Tom nodded, his expression thoughtful. 'You said Tinker mentioned someone called Jethro?' I nodded and his brow creased. 'There was someone he hung around with by that name but he was killed years ago in a drunken brawl – nasty brute.'

'If he's dead I'm relieved but it makes no difference. It's over, Tom. Ma should have told Sam the truth years ago and got it out of her system. The shock of it killed him and now . . . '

'She blames you.' Tom was silent for a while, then, 'Well, I can't change that but I can solve your immediate worries. You can live above my shop. The rooms are empty again.'

'Was someone living there? I thought you'd probably closed everything up when you joined the army.'

'I left someone in charge of the shop and he was living there, but I threw him out when I got back. He'd been cheating me and my customers. I was going to find someone else to manage the place.'

'I could look after it for you if you show me what to do –

just until the war is over and you're back for good.'

'I was thinking the same way.' He smiled at me. 'It will give you time to mull things over – to decide if you want to marry me or not.'

'Tom . . . ' I touched my fingers to his mouth. 'I've made up my mind.' Then as I sensed the apprehension in him I leant over to kiss him, a soft, brief kiss but full of promise. 'I want to marry you, Tom – if you'll have me?'

'If I . . . ' He laughed and grabbed me, giving me a swift, fierce hug that took my breath away. 'Daft woman! You don't think I'd let a chance like this slip through my fingers? I've wanted you for years, Nellie Pearce.'

'Then it's settled.' I smiled at him as he released me. 'I'll just fetch Samantha.' I hesitated as an unwelcome thought crossed my mind. 'You'll not mind that she . . . you won't . . . turn against her?'

Tom's expression hardened as if my words had offended him. 'Nay, don't think that of me,' he said. 'She's yours, Nellie. I'll love her as I love you – with no regrets, no recriminations for what's gone.'

Tears were stinging my eyes as I left him and went to fetch my daughter. Tom was such a good man and I wanted to make him happy as he deserved.

Mary saw my tears but accepted them as a sign of my natural grief for Sam.

'I'm so sorry about your da,' she said. 'Is there anything I can do?'

'You've done it already by looking after Sammie.' I hesitated. 'I'm going to marry Tom. He's taking me to live over the shop. I'm leaving in the morning.'

'I suppose it's best, considering.' She looked at me sadly. 'You will keep in touch?'

'Of course I shall – and you must come and visit us when you can.' I picked up my daughter. Mary came to the door to wave us off. ''Bye. Thank you for having her.'

'I loved it. Take care, Nellie.'

Tom took a sleepy Samantha from me, waiting until I was settled in the van to hand her up to me.

'She's a bonny lass,' he said as he climbed in beside me. 'Just like her mother.'

I smiled at him but said nothing. Samantha had her father's eyes but if Tom wanted to believe she was like me, I wouldn't argue.

We drove in a comfortable silence, exchanging only a few words until he drew up outside the house.

'I'll see you safe to the door,' he said as he helped me down.

'There's no need.'

'I prefer to be sure.'

He was determined and I let him have his way. It was good to have a shoulder to lean on and I liked being looked after for once in my life.

Tom carried Samantha through the covered passage and then stopped. As I caught up with him I saw what he was staring at so fixedly. My mother had piled all my belongings outside the back door, the bags and baskets packed anyhow as though she had thrown everything together in a fit of temper.

'She said I could stay the night.' I was upset by this last betrayal. 'To just throw me out like this . . . '

'Take Samantha back to the van. I'll bring this lot.' Tom's mouth thinned into a hard line. 'Don't let her hurt you, lass. She's not worth it.'

He was right, of course, but it hurt just the same.

Tom piled everything into the back of the van and we were off again, neither of us speaking much during the journey. We had both been hurt that night in our separate ways and we didn't feel like talking. Besides, Samantha was fast asleep in my arms.

The street was in darkness when we finally arrived. Tom parked his van in the large yard at the back of the shop and we felt our way towards the kitchen door in the gloom.

'Watch the step,' he warned as I stumbled. 'Are you all right?'

'Yes. I just stubbed my toe, that's all.'

Once we were inside the kitchen Tom drew the heavy blackout curtains and switched on the light. I glanced round at the deep stone sink with its wooden drainer, the open fireplace – which would be cheering when a fire was lit – and the tall pine dresser stacked with blue and white crockery.

There was a warm, friendly atmosphere and a homely smell about the place, which came from the bunches of dried herbs hanging next to the dresser.

'This is nice, Tom.'

'Not bad,' he replied with a grimace. 'You'll make it better once you've settled in.'

'I lost your kettle,' I said, a lump in my throat. 'When Maud was killed.'

'I'll buy you a new one,' he promised, and squeezed my waist. 'Things will get better from now on, lass. Take the babe upstairs and have a look round while I put the kettle on.'

'Electric – you've got electric. I'm glad about that.'

'I wanted it modern,' he said. 'It was always for you, Nellie. I wanted the best.'

I nodded, my heart too full to say much.

There was a plain brown fitted cord carpet all the way up the stairs and along the landing, not fancy but the sort that lasts for ever. It softened the sound of my footsteps and made it seem cosier than just the boards and rugs in my parents' house.

I came first to the living room which was large and square, furnished with surprisingly good pieces, some of them as good as the Harringtons owned. A fine mahogany dining table, four chairs with striped brocade seats and a handsome sideboard set with a fancy brass clock and matching candlesticks took up most of the space, but there was a high-backed wing chair and a Chesterfield settee by the fireplace.

The bedrooms were also well furnished with pretty wardrobes and chests in a pale, satiny wood with inlay round the edges. I wondered how Tom could have afforded all this stuff, then remembered that he had cleared several houses before the war. One thing was certain: he knew what to keep and what to get rid of.

I was settling Samantha in the room with two single beds when Tom came in to see how I was doing.

'The linen is aired,' he said. 'I had someone come in last week and give the place a good clean.' He watched my face eagerly. 'So what do you think then?'

'It's lovely, Tom. You've made it a real home.'

'It's not finished yet but it soon will be.' He smiled his satisfaction. 'It's just a start, Nellie. After the war we'll have a house with a garden for the little one . . . ' He glanced at her. 'She's still sound asleep then?'

'Yes. She'll sleep through till morning. Let's go down and have that tea. I shall hear her if she wakes but she hardly ever does once she's away.'

I followed him downstairs, my eyes moving round the large kitchen once more. Tom had done well but already I was planning improvements.

'This is my first real home,' I said. 'You won't recognize it once I get going.'

He grinned at me. 'I've got a while yet before I have to report back to camp. We can sort out what you need to know about the shop . . . ration books and suppliers you can trust not to cheat you.' He set down his empty cup. 'If you're comfortable I'll leave you to sort things out your own way.'

I gazed up in surprise as he rose to his feet. 'Where are you going? I thought you had been staying here?'

'I have but there's a cottage I've bought down the way. I'm getting it ready to let. I can sleep there until we're wed.'

'Tom, there's no need.'

'The other night . . . ' He pulled a wry face. 'I rushed you, lass, and it wasn't right. Next time we'll do things properly. I'll arrange a licence and we'll spend a couple of days at a hotel, make a bit of a splash. Mebbe Mary would have the lass for us?'

'I'm sure she would.' My throat was tight with emotion. 'If that's what you want, Tom?'

'I want things right,' he said, and grinned at me in his old bold manner. 'You just leave it to me, Nellie.'

I nodded and he kissed me briefly on the lips, then released me, walked to the door and went out. After I heard the van start I locked the door.

It was what Tom wanted so I'd let him go, but I felt uneasy as I put out the lights and walked upstairs. I wished he had stayed.

Samantha was a little fretful in the morning. She wouldn't eat her breakfast and she asked for Mary and her Ganda. I tried to explain that we had a new home but she was too young to understand; she only knew that once again she was in strange surroundings and clung to my skirts as I moved about the kitchen.

When Tom arrived she stared at him suspiciously but he won her over with a lump of barley sugar from a jar in the shop and a paper windmill on a stick that had lain forgotten in the dark recesses of a back shelf. He showed her how to blow at it and she giggled delightedly as the brightly coloured sails whirred faster and faster.

Tom's shop was packed full of the most amazing things. He had stacks and stacks of boxes in the storeroom containing everything from odd ounces of different coloured knitting wools, cotton reels, needles for wind-up gramophones, bootlaces and flypapers to first aid kits, blotting pads and pencils.

'I bought everything I could lay my hands on for months before the war started,' he explained. 'Thought I might find a use for this lot – but to tell the truth, I've forgotten half of what's here.'

'I'll sort it all out,' I promised, and pounced gleefully on a box of knicker elastic. 'This is like gold dust. You can't buy it anywhere these days.'

'Put a penny or two on the old price then,' Tom said. 'We don't want to cheat anyone but it's not easy to make things pay at the moment.'

'I can put sixpence a yard on your price,' I replied, 'and they will be glad to pay it. This is like Aladdin's cave, Tom – those notebooks will come in handy for my recipes. I'm writing down some of the most popular ones from Maud's . . .'

'I'd like to see them.' Tom looked interested. 'Well, do you think you can manage if I go off on my rounds? I'd like to talk to some of my old customers, let them know you'll be here in future.'

'Yes, of course I can manage.' I touched his arm as he turned away. 'Your mother?'

'All taken care of. She'll have everything the way she would have wanted.'

'And your father?'

281

'No sign of him. Don't you worry, Nellie. He won't trouble us again.'

Tom seemed confident and I let him go. There was so much to be done and the first customers were already coming into the shop. I was obviously going to have my hands full from now on and I would enjoy it. There would be no time to worry over something that might never happen . . . nor to dwell on the past.

It was just over two weeks later when Tom laid a pile of little booklets on the shop counter and grinned at me in triumph.

'What do you think of them then? I've had a hundred printed to see how they go – but we can soon get more if we want them.'

'Tom!' I stared at the bright red cover of the top booklet and saw my name flashed boldly in thick black letters. 'What have you done now?'

'It's your recipes,' he said with a grin. 'See the title – *Wartime Recipes* by Nellie Pearce.'

I was astounded. I'd given him a few of my recipes to look at only ten days before, never imagining he was planning anything like this. He'd said he just wanted to show them to a friend and now here they were all printed up in black ink on white paper just as if they were proper books.

'But you're never expecting to sell these? I only scribbled them down for my own use. They're nothing special, Tom.'

'I reckon they're good. Just what folk need to help them make the most of what they have these days. You put some on the counter and I'll take the rest on the van with me. See what happens.'

'No one is going to pay a shilling for one of these. You're daft, Tom. You should have spent your money on something useful.'

'We'll see.'

He was about to go on when the shop door opened with a loud jangling from the bell. We both looked round expecting a customer but when I saw who it was I felt a tingle all the way down my spine.

'Mary, what's wrong?' Was Ma ill or Bob? I'd heard not a

282

word from them since the funeral, though I'd sent Ma a letter to tell her where I was living.

'Oh, Nellie,' she cried, her voice breaking on a sob. 'I had to come. It's Joe . . . I've had a telegram. He's missing . . . missing in action.'

'Mary love! I'm so sorry.' I moved to take her in my arms, rocking her gently as she burst into tears. 'Don't take on so, love. He may be all right. You don't know yet.'

'Take her through to the kitchen,' Tom said. 'I'll see to the shop for a while.'

I did as he suggested. Mary was obviously in a terrible state and we didn't want people walking in on her; we should be better alone in the kitchen where it was comfortable and private.

Samantha had been curled up asleep in a chair but she woke as we entered and came running, pulling at Mary's skirts and demanding attention.

'Leave Aunty Mary alone, darling,' I said but Mary shook her head.

'No, let her be,' she said and gave me a watery smile. 'I'll be better with her to fuss over. I came to you because I couldn't bear it at home. Can I stay with you, Nellie, just for a few days? Will Tom mind?'

'He isn't living here yet. Not until we're wed – and then he'll soon be off. He wouldn't mind anyway.'

'Can I stay then?'

'Of course you can. You'll be a big help to me with Samantha. I've more than enough to do here for the moment. The man Tom employed while he was away let things get in a terrible mess. I haven't half sorted it out yet.'

Mary was cuddling Samantha. Her tears had stopped as she looked at me over the child's head.

'I don't know what I'll do if . . . if he's dead.'

'The telegram said missing,' I reminded her. 'He may be a prisoner, Mary. I know how you feel – but don't give up hope yet.'

Mary nodded. 'You lost Lucas but now you have Tom,' she said. 'Are you happy, Nellie – I mean really happy, deep down inside? Have you forgotten Lucas?'

'I don't suppose I'll ever quite forget . . . ' I hesitated for a moment, then, 'Yes. Yes, of course I'm happy. Tom is a good man and I'm lucky.' Suddenly I sensed something and swung round to see Tom standing in the doorway watching us. 'Tom . . . Tom . . . '

'I'm off on my rounds now,' he said, his usual cheerful smile absent. 'I'll call in on my way back this evening.'

'Tom, please . . . ' I called after him but he turned away without answering. I looked at Mary. 'He heard and he's taken it wrong,' I said to her. 'He isn't Lucas but I do care for him, Mary. I care for him very much.'

'Go after him,' she urged. 'Don't let him leave thinking you're still hankering after Lucas.'

'Yes, I must stop him before . . . '

I hurried through the shop but when I reached the street Tom's van was already pulling away from the kerb and he didn't hear me call to him.

I watched him drive away and my heart was heavy. My life was with Tom now and I didn't want him to doubt me. The wedding was to be within a few days so why should we be apart? Tom's leave was almost over and we would have only a week of married life at most before he had to report back to camp – and then who knew where he might be sent.

Mary's arrival with her news of Joe having been reported missing had made me realize how short the time was. I wanted to be with Tom as much as possible and I decided then and there that when he returned that evening I would ask him to stay with me.

'I was wondering . . . ' Mrs Roberts paused to look at the pile of recipe booklets on the counter. 'These look interesting. I'll take ten for my classes.' She raised her eyes to mine. 'I know you're busy, Nellie, but if you could possibly help out sometimes? My classes are so much bigger these days. It's difficult to manage on the rations we all get and I'm trying to teach women who've never had to do without eggs and butter before, that's as well as my regular classes with the travelling folk.'

'I might be able to help,' I replied. 'Mary won't mind looking after Samantha.'

'I'm sure my niece would be happy to have your little girl

at any time.' Mrs Roberts paid for her purchases. 'You were so good with the gipsy women before, Nellie. I do my best but you have a gift for teaching. I've often thought . . . '

She stopped speaking as the door opened and a man in the uniform of a police constable came in. He looked from her to me then cleared his throat.

'Would you be Miss Pearce?' he asked. 'Miss Nellie Pearce?'

'Yes,' I said and my spine tingled. 'Why? Has something happened? Is it my mother?'

'Not your mother, miss.' He cleared his throat again. 'I've a bit of bad news. You're engaged to Tom Herries, I believe?'

'Something has happened to Tom!' I felt a sudden sickness in my stomach. I should never have let him go without sorting things out between us.

'In a manner of speaking.' The constable looked uncomfortable. 'We've had to take him into custody.'

'Tom? Why? What has he done?'

'There was a fight between him and his father. One of them pulled a knife and . . . well, Tinker's dead. Tom is in the cells. He's asked to see you and if you want to see him you'd best come soon. They'll be charging him in a day or so, I shouldn't wonder, then he'll be taken off somewhere else.'

'You mean he'll go to prison?' I stared at him in dismay. 'But it wasn't Tom's fault. Tinker must have attacked him. He'd sworn to have his revenge on Tom and this was it. It was Tinker who pulled the knife, not Tom.'

'Were you there then, miss? Saw it all, did you?'

'No.' I looked at him uncertainly. 'Not this time.'

'You've seen them fight before perhaps?'

'Yes. Yes, I have.'

I took a deep breath and poured out my story in a rush.

'That's quite a tale, miss. If it's true . . . ' He eyed me sternly. 'I take it you would be willing to swear to this in court if need be?'

'Yes. Yes, I would. It's the truth. Please believe me. I wouldn't lie over something like this.'

'I've always found Nellie very honest,' Mrs Roberts said,

fixing him with a straight look. 'You can believe her, Constable Rogers.'

He coughed and touched his helmet. 'Yes, ma'am, of course. Well, it might help him. It could mean a charge of manslaughter rather than murder.'

I clutched at the counter, feeling dizzy. 'Tom wouldn't kill his own father . . . not deliberately. He wouldn't murder him. He's not like that. You must believe me.'

The constable nodded. 'There was no love lost between them. Tom's been heard to say he would kill Tinker more than once. But with your testimony at least he can show he was provoked and if it was Tinker's knife . . . '

'But he didn't do it on purpose,' I cried. 'It must have been self-defence.'

'Maybe it was. It will all come out at the trial.' His expression showed sympathy towards me. 'You come to the station this evening, miss. I'll be on duty and I'll see you have a little time together. Just ask for Constable Rogers.'

He nodded to me, smiled at Mrs Roberts and went out. For a moment I was too shocked to say anything.

'He'll need a lawyer,' Mrs Roberts said. 'Can he afford a good one?'

'We'll find the money.' I wondered how much Tom had put by. He wasn't one for hoarding cash, preferring to spend it on property or goods. If there wasn't much money . . . I was worried until I remembered the diamond rings Jean had left me. 'We'll get the money,' I said with renewed confidence. 'But how shall I find a lawyer? Tom will need the best.'

'I'll ask my husband,' Mrs Roberts promised. 'You mustn't worry too much just yet, Nellie. This probably all sounds much worse than it really is.'

'I hope so.' I could feel a sinking sensation in my stomach. 'I do hope so.'

I couldn't bear to think of Tom in prison. He would hate being shut up with nothing to do; he would go mad with frustration.

Mary had heard some of what was being said. After the vicar's wife had left I went through to her in the back kitchen. Her eyes were dark with concern as I took off my apron and sat down at the table.

'You'd better get ready,' she said. 'Go and visit Tom and don't worry about Samantha or the shop.'

'Remember to check the list before you let anyone take goods on tick,' I warned, my mind dwelling on business as if refusing to allow the worrying thoughts a free run. 'Tom says they're not to have it if they owe more than two pounds.'

'I told you not to worry. You just get off and visit him. He'll be fretting until he sees you.'

'Yes, I know.' I caught back a sob then told myself I was a fool and went upstairs to get ready.

Shortly afterwards I took Tom's old bike from a shed in the yard and cycled to the police station. Constable Rogers was behind the desk and he smiled at me as I entered.

'You can see him for twenty minutes, then I'll take a statement from you, Miss Pearce – about what you told me earlier. I've made notes but we'll go through it together and you can sign it when you're satisfied.'

'Thank you.'

He was trying to be kind and I gave him a grateful smile but underneath the fear was tearing at me, gnawing like a rat at my nerves. I knew Tom had sworn he would kill his father one day but he hadn't meant it; it had been said in anger. Of course he wouldn't kill Tinker. He wouldn't! It had been an accident.

He was sitting with his head bent as we went through to the cells but he looked up, getting to his feet and putting on a show for my benefit.

'Nellie . . . you came then?'

'Of course I came.' I went to embrace him. 'Tom, oh, Tom, I'm so sorry. You must feel awful. I know Tinker wasn't perfect but he was your da . . . '

Tom's smile caught at my heart. 'No one but you would understand that. It's no wonder I love you, lass. He was drunk. He came at me with the knife. I was trying to take it from him and he fell on it. I swear it was an accident. I never meant to kill him.'

'Oh, Tom . . . of course you didn't. I know you didn't.' I reached out to touch his cheek. 'You mustn't worry. We'll get a good lawyer. We'll have you out of here soon.'

287

'Maybe.' He was no longer smiling. 'It won't be that easy, Nellie. They've made up their minds I did it.'

'But you didn't. We'll prove it somehow.'

'It was outside the Black Boar pub, Nellie. Someone must have seen Tinker pull that knife on me but unless they come forward . . .'

'We'll find witnesses,' I promised. I couldn't bear the thought of leaving him here. The air was stale and the cell smelt of urine and sweat. 'We'll get you out of this place as soon as we can.'

'You're a good lass.' His expression wrenched at my heart. 'I want you to know there's a few hundred pounds in the bank and I've made a will. It's for you – the shop, everything. I made it the day after we met again. If anything should happen . . .'

'Hush, Tom.' I pressed my fingers to his lips, holding back the tears with difficulty but knowing he mustn't see me cry. 'Don't say it. Nothing will happen.'

'It's not just this. I wanted you to be safe if I got killed overseas. We might not be wed yet but you're all I care about.'

'What about Jerry?'

'You'll do what you can for him? See he gets some schooling?' Tom combed restless fingers through his dark hair. I could see that he was afraid though trying to hide it, more afraid than he had ever been facing the German guns. It was the travelling man's worst nightmare, being shut in and not being able to get out. 'I told Jerry to come to you if he needs help but I've no idea where he is now. He ran off after Ma was buried and I've not seen him since. I went to the pub looking for him . . .'

'He'll be back,' I promised, my heart aching as I saw the frustration in Tom. He was hating every second of this, chaffing at the invisible bonds that held him. 'We'll take care of your brother, Tom. When you come home.'

'Aye, when I come home.' His eyes darkened and for a moment his voice cracked with emotion. 'I had such plans for us . . . such plans . . .'

'Don't, Tom!' I spoke sharply. 'You're talking nonsense. It was an accident. You were defending yourself and we'll prove it. I promise you. You've told me often enough to keep my chin up, now take your own advice.'

He stared at me, a reluctant smile dawning in his eyes. 'I've always thought you a brave lass. Aye, I'll heed me own advice, Nellie. I'll not give in to them while I've got you waiting for me.'

'I'll be waiting, Tom,' I promised. 'However long it takes I'll be there when you come home – and I'll keep the business running. I promise you, Tom. I'll be there – and you will come home. You will!'

'It's time, Miss Pearce.' Constable Rogers coughed discreetly. 'I'll give you another minute or two.' He turned his back on us deliberately.

'Nellie . . . Nellie . . . '

Tom held out his arms and we embraced with a desperate feverishness that made us both weep.

'I love you, Nellie. I love you so much.'

'I love you, Tom. Don't worry. It will come right, you'll see.'

'You'd best go now, lass. Don't fret over me. You know what they say about a bad penny.'

I gave a choking laugh as I remembered the last time he'd said those words to me, then I kissed him again. The tears were building inside me as I followed Constable Rogers through to the front but at the last moment I turned and waved to Tom with a smile on my face.

'We'll take that statement now, Miss Pearce,' Constable Rogers said as he handed me a piece of paper. 'Check that and see if it's what you told me earlier. We want it as exact as possible, because you'll be questioned in court.'

I felt that he at least was on our side and it lifted my spirits as I read through what he had written. I made one or two small changes then agreed that it was accurate.

'I told you that Tinker said he would have his revenge on Tom but what he actually said was that he would have him.'

'Did he now? You're sure – only that sounds as if he meant to kill Tom?'

'I think he did. That's why he pulled the knife.'

He nodded. 'If we could prove that, it would be self-defence.'

289

'It was an accident. Tom was trying to get the knife away from Tinker and he fell on it. There must be a witness who can testify to that.'

'No one spoke up at the time.' Constable Rogers scratched his ear. 'I'll see what I can do but some folk won't talk to the police. You might do better yourself.'

'If I can find a witness . . . '

'I'll see he's heard.' He paused. 'I've known Tom since he was a nipper – and I know Tinker for what he was. If it was up to me I'd give Tom a medal, but it isn't. The law's the law even when it's a bit of an ass.'

'Yes, I know. Thank you, you've been very kind.'

'Get the best lawyer you can afford,' he advised. 'They're worth every penny they charge in a case like this.'

'Yes, I shall. Goodbye and thank you again.'

I smiled as I left but my heart was heavy as I cycled home and I felt like weeping with frustration. There must have been witnesses to the fight. The Black Boar was always busy with men drinking in the tap room, but often people preferred to stay out of something like this; they were afraid of getting involved, even though it only meant telling the truth. I had promised Tom we would get him out of that cell but we both knew he might have to stand trial for manslaughter if not for murder.

If he was found guilty his sentence might be several years in prison or worse . . . but that couldn't happen. I wouldn't let Tom hang for a crime he hadn't committed.

Somehow I would find a way to set him free.

Chapter Seventeen

'I didn't think you would come this evening,' Mrs Roberts said as she greeted me in the kitchens of the church hall. 'I'm delighted to see you, of course, but are you sure you feel up to it?'

'I needed to get away for an hour or two,' I replied. 'It's a week now since they moved Tom and I've heard nothing. I'm fretting at home so I thought I might as well come.'

The past few days had been like drifting through a nightmare. Ever since Tom's first fight with his father I had been living with a feeling of unease and now that the worst had happened I was so worried about him that I hardly slept, pacing the floor night after night as I tried to work out a way of helping him. At least while Tom had been held in the local cells I'd been able to visit and to send him some decent food in, but now there was nothing I could do for him and it made me restless. Nothing – except ask everyone who came to the shop if they had heard anyone say they'd witnessed the fight outside the Black Boar. So far no one had admitted to knowing anything.

'I've spoken to the vicar about a good lawyer,' Anne Roberts said. 'He thinks you should get a QC from London for Tom and he's writing to a friend of his for advice.'

'Will you thank him for me, please?'

People were being so kind but it all took so long. A week shut up in a remand home would seem like a year to Tom. It made me want to weep or scream with frustration every time I thought of him there.

'If you need money we could start a collection. Tom was

291

popular with people in the Dales. I'm sure they would give what they could to help him.'

'Thank you, but Tom has some savings and I have jewellery to sell. It was left to me by a friend and I think it may be worth quite a bit. I shall sell that to pay the lawyer.'

Tom wouldn't want people to collect for him unless the situation was desperate: he had too much pride.

'Well, if you change your mind . . . ' Anne Roberts smiled at me. 'We're going to be using some of your own recipes this evening, Nellie. I've tried several myself and they are very good – especially those vegetable and breadcrumb rissoles.'

'They are good,' I agreed. 'Which others have you tried?'

'Oh, most of them, but I thought we would demonstrate the boiled chicken with vegetables and dumplings tonight. Also one of your nourishing soups.'

'The soups are good value, especially when the cooking facilities are poor.'

'Our women have to manage as best they can when they're travelling. They come and go – but they seem to have their own means of getting a few eggs or a chicken. That's why I chose this particular dish.'

The small group of women had gathered round the long, scrubbed pine kitchen table and were already preparing vegetables and potatoes for the meal they were going to cook and take back to their families. I knew several of them by sight; they were regular visitors to Anne's little school and greeted me with friendly smiles.

'These are all meals you can prepare over a fire,' I said. 'The chicken dish can be made in an iron pot if you let it cook slowly, but I know most of you have access to an oven when you're on the farms so I'll show you three different ways of using the leftovers from the chicken. It can be delicious minced and folded in pastry or in a rich gravy with a few onions and of course there's always a tasty savoury pie . . . '

We began with three simple dishes but the questions started coming and I demonstrated a quick, easy crumble topping that needed only a little fat and could be used for both sweet and savoury dishes, many of which could be cooked in the clever ovens the women often built for themselves with large stones and banked with hot ashes.

It was when the evening was drawing to its close that one of the women approached me privately, out of hearing of the others. She glanced nervously over her shoulder, then spoke in hushed tones.

'You're Tom Herries's lass, aren't you?'

I nodded, my heart beginning to beat faster as I waited for her to go on. Somehow I knew that what she had to say was important.'

'My man saw it all. He says Tinker was drunker than usual. He pulled a knife on Tom and in the struggle he fell on the blade. 'Twas his own fault.'

'Would your man swear to that in court?'

She looked frightened, taking a step back as if she was on the verge of fleeing and shaking her head. 'He told me not to say. I just wanted you to know. He won't go near no court.'

'Not to save Tom's life?'

'He won't hang. It were an accident. He were only defending himself.'

'He might if no one tells the truth. They think Tom meant to kill him, they're saying it was murder.' I caught her arm. 'Please, Ruby. Please ask your man. Tell him Tom needs his help. Ask him if he will let me at least write his words down. If he made his mark . . . '

'He can write his name,' she said with a touch of pride. 'We all can thanks to Mrs Roberts.'

'Please ask him to come and see me or let me come to your van. Please, Ruby – for Tom's sake.' I was almost pleading with her now, my eyes stinging with the tears I was struggling to hold back. 'For my sake, too.'

'I'll ask for your sake,' she said. 'He'll curse me for telling you and maybe I'll get my ear smacked – but I'll ask.'

I knew better than to press her further, but my heart was just a little lighter. Now there was one witness and perhaps there might be others. I could only go on asking . . . praying that someone who was prepared to stand up in court would come forward.

It was nearly half-past eight when I cycled back to the shop.

I put my bike in the shed and let myself in at the kitchen door. Mary met me at the foot of the stairs and the look on her face told me that something had happened.

'Is it news of Tom?'

She shook her head, seeming strange. 'There's a visitor for you in the parlour,' she said in a whisper. 'It's Alice Simpson.'

'Alice is here?' I was surprised but pleased. 'I was going to write to her, to ask if she could sell those rings for me. She'll know where to get a better price for them than I would.'

'You go up, I'll put the kettle on.'

Mary was looking at me in an odd way again. I wondered about it as I walked upstairs but I was eager to see Alice. She might know of a good lawyer for Tom. I ought to have written to her at the start but I'd been so busy.

She was looking at one of my recipe booklets as I walked in and turned to me with a welcoming smile.

'May I buy some of these?' she asked. 'I know several people who would like to have a copy.'

'You can have as many as you like,' I replied. 'I'm so glad you came, Alice. I've been meaning to write. Have you heard about Tom?'

'Yes.' She hesitated, obviously uncomfortable and on edge. 'I was very sorry. It must be a worry. If I can help in any way . . .'

'You might be able to as it happens. I've some jewellery, diamond rings and a couple of brooches Mrs Jones left me. I was wondering if you could sell them for me in London. I need the money for a good lawyer. The vicar says we ought to have a Queen's Counsellor.'

'Yes, of course that would be best. I'll sell the jewellery with pleasure and I'll ask Gerald if he knows anyone who might take the case. He has influential friends and I'm sure he will help.'

She hesitated again and I sensed she was anxious to tell me something but did not know how to begin.

'Why did you come, Alice? It wasn't just a social visit, was it?'

'I had something to tell you but I'm not sure . . .'

The look in her eyes sent a shock winging through me like

294

the touch of a live wire and I sat down suddenly, my legs weak and my heart pounding against my ribs.

'This is something to do with Lucas.'

'I still can't believe it,' she said in a hushed, excited tone. 'If I hadn't spoken to him myself on the phone . . . '

'Lucas?' I whispered tremulously. 'You – you're telling me he's alive?'

'Isn't it wonderful? He's in London now but I'm sure he will come down as soon as he's free.' She stopped as she saw my face. 'What's wrong, Nellie? I thought you would be pleased.'

'Of course it's wonderful news and I am pleased he's alive but . . . '

I'd been swept up in such a maelstrom of emotions that I hardly knew where I was. For months I'd grieved for Lucas, my pain and distress so intense that I'd brought myself to the brink of self-destruction; I'd fought my way back to life for Samantha's sake – and now Alice was telling me that Lucas was alive. It was all a mistake.

'But things have changed.' Alice nodded as I stared at her, still too bewildered to order my thoughts. 'I spoke to your mother. She told me you were planning to marry Tom but surely now . . . ' She stopped and shook her head. 'No, of course you couldn't desert him. You must stand by him until this is all over but then . . . couldn't you . . . ' Her cheeks were flushed and her gaze dropped away in embarrassment.

'I've promised to wed Tom,' I said, unshed tears stinging my eyes. 'How could I let him down? I hurt him once before because of Lucas. How could I do it again?'

'Nellie.' Alice understood I was upset but she wasn't ready to give up just yet. 'I know how you feel, really I do – but you love Lucas, don't you?'

Our eyes met and this time mine fell first.

'I don't know. This is so sudden.' I got to my feet and walked to the window, my back towards her as I stared out at the street where darkness was falling softly around us. 'I went through hell when you told me he was dead. I wanted to die too but I had to live for Samantha's sake and now . . . I don't know.'

'But Lucas is alive. That must change everything.'

'Oh, yes,' I cried, turning to face her on a surge of anger. 'We must all jump when Lucas pulls the strings, mustn't we? He disappears for months on end without a word, then he's suddenly back and we have to do what he wants, no matter who gets hurt.'

'You're very bitter.' Alice was distressed, hurt.

'Don't you think I have cause?'

'Yes. Yes, I do. But I believe Lucas loves you in his own way. And you loved him once.' Alice got to her feet. 'I'm staying at Beaumont House tonight. The War Office is taking it over and I have to sign an inventory of the contents. I'll see you before I go back to London – and I'll sell the rings for you.'

'Oh, Alice,' I said sadly. 'Don't go like this. I don't want to quarrel with you. I'm just so worried about Tom . . .'

'Yes, I can see that.' She smiled and held out her hands to me. 'I was angry, too. I thought Lucas could have found a way to contact us long ago – but that's Lucas, my dear. He always was careless and he won't change.'

'You'll call again tomorrow?'

'Yes.' As she was about to turn away she stopped and took something from her bag. 'Your mother gave me a letter for you. I almost forgot.'

'Oh, thank you.'

I took it reluctantly. Why had Ma written to me?

'Until tomorrow then.'

'Yes.'

We moved towards each other, suddenly embracing fiercely. There were tears in my eyes as I went with her to the door and watched her drive away.

I was restless for most of the night. It was impossible to take in what Alice had told me. Lucas was alive. He was alive! It was shocking, wonderful, terrible news that rocked me to the core. A part of me wanted to shout it out loud but there was a tiny voice that whispered in my ear, warning me to be careful. I had loved Lucas so much that for a while I'd wanted to die rather than face the future without him, but the past months had changed things and I was no longer sure how I felt. During the long winter of my grief I had fought hard to become stronger and sometimes I felt the old Nellie had gone. I was different now: a woman, not an eager girl who had wanted only to please.

During one of my restless periods that terrible night I opened the letter Alice had brought and read the rather strange message from my mother.

'You'll not want to read this,' she began without preamble in her old style. 'I can't blame you if you hate me, Nellie. God forgive me I hated you from the day you were born, and after Sam died I hated you more than ever before – but now I've had time to think and I realize I was hasty. I shouldn't have thrown you out the way I did. Sam loved you and the lass. I don't suppose you'll want to, but you can come home sometimes. Bob misses you and the lass. Forgive me if you can, Rose.'

It was a strange, awkward, almost pitiful letter. I thought that perhaps she was lonely but I couldn't worry about Ma's problems now. I had too many of my own pressing down on me.

In the morning when Alice came I gave her the jewellery and told her I didn't want to see Lucas.

'There's no point,' I said. 'Please explain the situation to him, Alice. Ask him not to come.'

'If that's what you want.' She looked doubtful as she kissed my cheek. 'Perhaps it's for the best.'

'You warned me not to love him at the beginning,' I reminded her. 'It's time to let it go now, Alice. You know I'm right.'

We parted in sadness, then I turned and went into the shop.

Mary was standing on a pair of steps dusting some shelves. She had sensed the tension in me all morning and she didn't look round until I spoke to her.

'I'm going to try driving Tom's van,' I announced. 'You can manage here if I go out on his rounds, can't you?'

She swung round to face me, almost falling off the steps in surprise. 'You never mean it, Nellie? You can't drive, can you?'

'If Alice can drive so can I – it can't be that difficult.

297

Besides, I've seen Tom drive the van dozens of times. He showed me once but I wasn't bothered about learning then.'

'You'll need a licence, lessons . . . '

'I'll get whatever I need when I have to. I'm going out to the yard to try it now. Don't come, Mary. I'll feel better if no one's watching.'

She gave me a dubious look but I ignored it, going out to the back yard to stare at the van for a few minutes. It looked harmless enough just sitting there and Alice's news had made me restless. I needed something to occupy my mind. Learning to drive would be a challenge.

For two days I shunted the van backwards and forwards in the yard, learning how to move the gears and how to stop. Twice I bumped into the wall and managed to dent one side of the rear lights but gradually I got the hang of it.

Mary looked at me with troubled eyes as I loaded baskets and boxes into the back of the van the next morning.

'Be careful, Nellie. I wish you wouldn't do this.'

'I've got to keep the business going. I promised Tom.'

It was little enough to do. I was on edge, frustrated because we seemed to be getting nowhere in our search for the right lawyer.

'Tom wouldn't approve of this,' Mary said severely. 'Not unless you get someone to teach you how.'

She was probably right but I was feeling reckless. Thoughts of Tom and Lucas chased themselves round and round in my mind like puppydogs after their own tails until I was torn in two by conflicting loyalties. I couldn't bear to stay in the shop. Besides, I wanted to call on Ruby's man and see if he would sign a statement about what had really happened during that fateful fight and the family was camped too far out of the village for me either to walk or cycle there.

'I'll drive slowly,' I promised. 'Don't worry, Mary. I'll be careful.'

She watched from the shop doorway as I started the van then scrunched the gears sickeningly and lurched off down the street with several fits and starts before I finally found the right gear and got going.

Fortunately for me there was no traffic on the road as I

left the village and started down a long, winding track that led across the moors. Several of Tom's best customers lived in isolated cottages and I knew they would be pleased to see me, if only for a chat. It was unlikely that I would meet another car or even see anyone between customers so I couldn't do any real harm.

Going in one direction wasn't too bad, though I found it awkward when I had to turn the van round on narrow tracks. Once my back wheels hung precariously on the edge of a deep ditch but somehow I managed to get back to the shop in one piece late in the afternoon.

I was feeling exhausted but elated, especially with the results of my talk with Ruby's husband. It had taken a lot of pleading and several packets of Woodbines but in the end he'd put his name to a piece of paper.

Collecting my baskets I hurried towards the kitchen door, then my heart caught in fright as it opened and Constable Rogers came out. He was frowning as he strode to meet me.

'Been driving the van then?'

'Yes.' I bit my lip. 'It was only across the moors.'

'And through the village.'

'Yes, but . . . '

'No buts, young lady. Don't let me see you driving again until you've found a qualified driver to go with you. Come up to the station this evening and I'll help you fill out all the forms you'll need.'

'But who's going to teach me to drive?'

'I know one or two who might. Leave it with me. I want your word, Nellie Pearce.'

'All right,' I promised, knowing I was lucky to get off this lightly. 'Mary has been nagging me to do it properly, too.'

'That's settled then.' He nodded and smiled. 'I've a bit of good news. There's a farmer from over Hanlith way witnessed the whole of the fight. He's willing to swear he saw Tinker pull that knife . . . '

I waved the statement from Ruby's man under his nose in triumph. 'That makes two. Ned won't go to court but he's made a statement in his own words.'

'That's good, that's good, Nellie. At least we've got

299

something to show. All you need now is a clever lawyer and you'll soon have Tom home.'

'Do you really think so?'

'Two witnesses to back up his own statement – and your own – must help.' He put his helmet on. 'You remember what we've said about your driving!'

'Yes, I will. I promise. And thank you for coming to tell me the news.'

I hurried into the kitchen where Mary was waiting anxiously.

'Samantha's having a nap,' she said. 'I gave her her tea half an hour ago. I was beginning to worry with you out so late driving that van.'

'Well, I've promised to do it right,' I told her with a rueful smile. 'It was a pity Constable Rogers caught me just now – though I'm glad of his news.'

'It is good, isn't it?' Mary agreed. 'As for the driving, that's just as well in my opinion. What would have happened to Samantha if you'd had an accident?'

'I shan't. Don't scold me, Mary,' I begged. 'I could do with a cup of tea if there's one going?'

I had begun to unpack my basket. She watched as I opened a large white muslin parcel.

'What's that?'

'I bought it from a farmer who had just killed a bullock – it's part of the stomach and intestines.' I laughed as she looked disgusted. 'Don't pull a face, Mary. By the time I've finished with it you won't know what you're eating. I'm going to make some pies to sell in the shop and soup for us.'

'Haven't you done enough for one day?'

'I promised I would keep the business going for Tom and I shall. Even if it means working half the night.'

Mary shook her head at me and went through to the shop as the bell clanged loudly as if whoever had entered was impatient.

I finished my drink then got up to wash the cup. The meat I'd bought would need a thorough cleaning before it was fit to use and I'd just put it in the colander when I heard something behind me.

'Who was . . . ' I'd thought it was Mary but, as I saw the

300

man standing by the door, my heart stood still for one fraction of a second before racing wildly. I could feel the blood draining from my face and for a moment I could hardly breathe. 'Lucas . . . I asked you not to come.'

'Alice told me.' He glared at me as I wiped the blood from my hands and moved away from the sink. 'Of course I had to come, Nellie. I promised I would. Have you forgotten?'

How could I have forgotten? I gazed up at him.

'You promised a lot of things.'

'And now I've come back to keep my promises.' He took a step towards me. 'Come away with me, Nellie. I'm going back to America. I've done what little I can and I'm sick of this wretched war – and this country.' His eyes flicked towards the mess of raw meat I'd left in the sink. 'I've had enough of shortages and sacrifice. Things are better in the States. Let me give you and Samantha all the advantages you've never had. Let me make it up to you, Nellie.'

I was silent as his words died away. Once I would have given anything to hear him say them but now – now they made me angry.

'It's too late, Lucas. You left me once too often. How could I ever trust you again? How could I be sure you wouldn't just go off and leave me if you felt like it?'

'You're angry, but I couldn't tell you what was going on last time. I'm still sworn to secrecy about what really happened out there. Surely you understand that?'

'Yes, I understand. But what about afterwards? You must have escaped or something but you didn't try to contact any of us. You just let us go on believing you were dead,' I cried, the anger suddenly flaring out of me. 'You must have known what that would do to us – to me! Surely you could have sent a message somehow? Just to let us know you were alive . . . '

'It might have endangered others. There were reasons. Besides, I was ill for a while.' His eyes flashed with temper. 'You're being unreasonable. Don't you know there's a war on? I was working for my country.'

'Work! That's all that really matters to you, isn't it? It always has been, Lucas. You went off to America without a thought for me . . . '

301

'You know that isn't true.' He reached out for me, drawing me against him as his mouth took mine in a hard, punishing kiss that shocked me into silence. He gazed down at me, a gleam of triumph in his eyes. 'You're mine, Nellie. You'll always be mine. Whatever I do. Stop fighting me. You know you want to come with me so admit it. This is just one of your little tantrums.'

'You think that's all you have to do, don't you?' I touched my lips with shaking fingers as I recovered my breath. 'You think you just have to crook your little finger and I'll do whatever you want . . . no matter how much it hurts others.'

'You mean Tom Herries, I suppose?' He shrugged carelessly. 'What can you do for him that others can't? You've got someone serving in the shop and we can find him a decent lawyer . . . '

'I can't leave Tom just like that!'

'Why not? What is he to you?' Lucas's eyes narrowed suspiciously. 'You can't waste your life on a common chap like that.'

'How dare you! Tom is my friend, my very best friend. I won't leave him, Lucas. I can't.'

'You'll come if you love me,' he said harshly, his expression becoming cold and haughty. 'You owe it to me – and Samantha. She's my daughter. I can give you more than he ever will.'

'This isn't fair, Lucas. Don't use Samantha against me.'

'I love you, Nellie. I need you.' His voice had a note of pleading now. 'Please come with me. We'll find someone to help Tom. I promise . . . '

He was tearing me in two. A part of me longed to trust him, to fly to his arms and forget everything except how much I had once loved him, but there was another part of me, a different self who knew that I could not walk away from Tom when he needed me.

'No, Lucas,' I said softly. 'I won't come with you. Not now, not ever.'

'But I need you. I can't paint without you. Nothing I did in Switzerland was any good . . . '

'In Switzerland – how long were you there, Lucas?' A

prickling sensation had started at the nape of my neck. 'How long?'

'A few weeks.' His eyes fell before the accusation in mine. 'I know what you're thinking but I couldn't get home sooner.'

'You could have written!'

'I wasn't well. Nellie, please . . . '

'You were well enough to paint.'

He couldn't meet my eyes. For a few moments he had almost swayed me to his way of thinking but now I was furious.

'So I got wrapped up in my work. I'm selfish and thoughtless at times, but I love you. I need you, Nellie. I need you . . . '

'No, Lucas. You don't need me, not really – but Tom does. If I deserted him now I would never forgive myself.'

Lucas looked so angry that I thought he meant to strike me. 'You're in love with him, that's it, isn't it?' He glared down at me. 'You were seeing him years ago, when we were at the house . . . maybe he's Samantha's father?'

My hand flew out before I knew what I was doing. He recoiled as I struck him across the face, his eyes glittering.

'You just take that back, Lucas Harrington!'

The glitter died from his eyes though he was still angry. 'All right. I shouldn't have said that – but I meant what I said about you being in love with him.'

'That's not true!'

'Isn't it?' Lucas was smiling now, a smile that caught at my heart and made me gasp. 'I think it is, Nellie. You may not know it yourself yet, but I think it is true.'

'Lucas, I'm sorry for hitting you. I shouldn't have done that.'

'I deserved it. I've let you down too many times. I'm the one who should be sorry.'

'It could never have worked. We were from different worlds.'

'It might have worked if I'd taken you with me the first time. I was a fool.' He touched my cheek, a rueful smile curving his mouth. 'But that's my loss. Be happy, my dearest. If ever I can help you or Samantha . . . '

303

'Yes.'

I could hardly speak. My throat was tight with emotion. I watched as he walked to the door. For one long, poignant moment he stood looking at me with a mixture of regret and reproach in his eyes, then he was gone.

I was still standing there with the silent tears trickling down my cheeks when Mary came back.

'Oh, Nellie,' she said. 'Nellie love . . . '

'Don't!' I cried. 'Just leave me alone for a few minutes. I'll be all right. I just need a little time.'

She nodded, then went upstairs as Samantha began to call out. I turned back to the sink. Work: I needed to work. A dream had just died a very painful death but I would be all right.

I would be all right.

Chapter Eighteen

'Those pies were delicious,' Anne Roberts said as I got ready to leave after classes. 'Will you give me the recipe?'

I laughed and shook my head. 'Not this time. I need some secrets.' She would have had a fit if she'd known what was in them!

'What are you going to do about that lecture tour?' she asked, delaying me again. 'You won't just forget about it I hope?'

An official-looking letter had arrived for me that morning. I'd had the fright of my life when Mary brought it in, thinking it must be bad news, but it was an invitation from someone at the Ministry of Food asking me to lecture about my wartime recipes. I suspected that Alice had shown them to someone Gerald knew at the Ministry.

'I don't see how I could do it,' I said. 'It would mean travelling all over the country to various Women's Institutes and some schools. I can't expect Mary to do everything.'

Anne nodded, looking thoughtful. 'I suppose not. It's a shame, though.' She smiled at me. 'It was good news about Joe, wasn't it?'

'Wonderful,' I agreed. 'Mary hasn't stopped singing since she got his letter to say he is a prisoner but in good health.'

'At least she can look forward to him coming back when it's all over – and it has to end one day.' Anne shook her head as if to clear it of gloomy thoughts. 'How are you getting on with your driving?'

'When Constable Rogers said he would give me lessons I didn't think he meant it but he's taken me out three times

305

this week – and he's found a driver to go with me on the rounds.'

'Yes, Fred Thomas. I've seen you with him. He's a cantankerous old devil but he used to drive in London years ago so you'll be safe enough with him.'

'That's what Constable Rogers said.'

Everyone was being so kind. The takings at the shop had nearly doubled this last week and I was sure people were buying things they didn't need just to help out. They all asked how Tom was getting on though I wasn't able to tell them much; I'd written to him several times but as yet he hadn't answered and I knew he must be feeling very low.

I was thoughtful as I cycled home. Alice had sent me a cheque for five hundred pounds, offering to lend me more if I needed it.

'I've spoken to Gerald,' she'd told me in her letter. 'Don't worry, Nellie. I'm sure we shall soon have some news for you.'

It was more money than I'd expected for the rings and I wondered if Alice had sent a little extra. She wouldn't admit it if I asked her, of course. Anyway, I wasn't going to let pride stand in my way. We were going to need every penny for Tom's lawyer.

'Nellie . . . Nellie . . . '

I stopped pedalling and looked round as I heard the voice, then put my feet to the ground when I saw who was calling me.

'Bob – what are you doing here?'

'I came to see you,' my brother said and gave me a cheeky grin. 'Surprised to see me then?'

'Does Ma know you're here?'

'She thinks I'm staying with a friend.'

'Oh, Bob . . . '

'She ain't been well,' he said. 'She cries a lot and she misses you and Sammie.'

'She might miss Samantha but . . . '

'She talks about both of you,' he said quickly. 'She's changed, Nellie. She ain't like she was.'

'What do you mean?'

'She's nicer than she used to be.' He kicked at a stone on

the ground. 'She caught me talking to Jerry Herries the other day and instead of calling me over the coals she told me to bring him in for a bite to eat.'

I stared at him in astonishment. 'She never did!'

'Honest, Nellie. He's been sleeping rough and she told him he could have a bed with us if he agreed to have a bath once a week and started going to school with me.'

'And what did Jerry say?'

'He ran off but I reckon he'll come back when he's hungry enough. You should have seen him gobble up Ma's jam tart.'

'Yes, I'm sure. When you see him again, tell him I want to talk to him.'

'All right.' Bob kicked at the stone again. 'Will you come and see Ma? Please, Nellie?'

'Yes, in a day or two,' I promised. I supposed I ought to have gone after Alice had given me the letter. It wouldn't be easy to forget the way Ma had acted after Sam died, but I ought to try. 'Now you're coming back to the shop with me. In the morning I'll ask someone to take you home in Tom's van.'

'Have you heard anything about him?' Bob looked at me anxiously. 'They ain't going to hang him, are they?'

'No, we shan't let that happen,' I said, quelling the spasm of nerves his question had set off in my stomach. 'He didn't kill Tinker on purpose. They will have to let him go soon.'

I smiled at my brother as I got off the bike and wheeled it with him trotting at my side. Sometimes I felt close to despair but I mustn't let him see it. Almost three weeks had passed since Tom's arrest and despite everyone's efforts we seemed no nearer to getting him released. How he must be suffering shut up in that terrible place!

I put my bike in the shed and sent Bob on ahead to the kitchen. When I went in he was sitting by the fire stroking a ginger cat which Samantha had recently adopted. It had appeared out of nowhere and she was devoted to it.

'Have you seen Mary?' I asked. He shook his head and I turned to the sink to fill the kettle. 'She's usually got this boiling by the time I get in . . .'

'I think she's upstairs,' Bob said, scratching the cat behind

307

its ear and making it purr. 'I heard something when I came in but it's gone quiet now.'

I went to the bottom of the stairs and called. 'Mary . . . Mary, are you there?'

'Coming.' She clattered down the stairs, her face flushed. Her excitement was obvious as she caught at my arm. 'You'll never guess . . . it's Tom! He's upstairs waiting for you.'

'Tom?' I stared at her in disbelief and for a moment the room seemed to spin. 'But how . . . when . . . Tom?'

'Don't ask,' she said, laughing now. 'Go on – he's waiting for you.'

I ran up the stairs, my heart nearly bursting with relief and joy. I couldn't believe it. Oh, I couldn't believe it! I'd been feeling so down and now Tom was back – but was it for good?

He was standing looking out of the window but as I entered he turned round and his face lit up with pleasure. I noticed that he was a little thinner, then he took two quick strides towards me and I ran into his arms. We hugged and kissed, swift, eager kisses of welcome and relief.

'Nellie . . . Nellie love,' he cried and his voice cracked with emotion. 'I thought I might never see you again, never hold you . . . '

'Oh, Tom,' I whispered as I glanced up and saw tears in his eyes. 'We've all been thinking of you, praying for you.'

'It was only the thought of you believing in me that kept me going. It wasn't too bad until they moved me . . . but that's all over now. I'm home, lass. Home for good.'

'But how, Tom?' I brushed the tears from my cheek. 'Why did they let you go? We're still trying to find the right lawyer for you . . . '

'I thought you must know.' Tom frowned, then moved away, seeming to withdraw slightly. 'It was Lucas Harrington. He came to see me a few days ago, then he got me a QC – a Mr George Gregory. They tell me he's the best in the country. He presented the new evidence, persuaded the authorities that it was an accident while I was defending myself. They held a brief hearing in London then let me go. Said there was no case to answer and I was a free man. Mr Gregory says he'll fix it with the army and I won't have to go

308

back for a couple of weeks. Even then he thinks they may put me in a camp for training new recruits because of my arm still not being quite right. I'll probably be working in supplies or something like that.'

'I'm so glad, Tom . . . so very glad.'

He nodded but didn't say anything and I sensed he was holding back. Something was bothering him.

'What's wrong, Tom? Something is, I know that.'

He gave me his lopsided grin. 'You know me too well, lass.'

'You're not angry with me, are you?'

'How could I be – after all you've done for me?' He hesitated then said, 'Lucas is up at the house. He's leaving for London in the morning. Pack your things and I'll take you to him.'

'What are you talking about? Why should I want to go to him?'

'We travelled down together. He told me you'd refused to leave while I was in trouble. I know he's asked you to go to America with him – to marry him.'

'He asked but I turned him down.'

'For my sake. It was like you, Nellie – but I'm back now. I'm free. It's all over. You've kept your word. Now you're free to go to him. I'm releasing you from your promise to marry me.'

'You're . . . ' I glared at him. 'Sometimes you're that daft, Tom Herries! If you don't want me here just say so, but don't try to make up my mind for me.'

'Nellie?' Tom stared at me uncertainly. 'I know you said you would marry me but that was when you thought . . . '

'Yes, I thought Lucas was dead. I thought I still loved him but I don't.'

'Nellie?'

I moved towards him, smiling now. 'Ask me again, Tom. Ask me if I'll marry you. Ask me if I love you.'

For several seconds he couldn't speak. Finally he said, 'Nay, don't say it, lass. How can you? He's always been the one.'

'I loved Lucas when I was a young girl, Tom. I won't deny it. I loved him so much it broke my heart when Alice told me he was dead – but that girl died of her grief. I'm a woman now. The woman loves you, Tom. Lucas knows it – that's why he helped you. He's selfish and often unkind, but sometimes, just now and then, he can do something wonderful. I suppose that's why I loved him in the first place.'

'Nellie lass.' Tom reached out to touch my face in wonder. 'I've loved you for as long as I can recall. All I want is to spend the rest of my days with you but you have to be sure. It would break my heart if I thought you were secretly hankering for him.'

'I shan't,' I said softly. 'I promise you, Tom.'

We heard the kitchen door open and Bob called out a cheeky goodbye.

'Enjoy yourselves up there,' he yelled. 'Don't do anything I wouldn't.'

There was the sound of Mary admonishing him and then the back door slammed. Tom grinned as I looked puzzled.

'Mary's taken Bob off with her for the night. They'll be sleeping at my cottage. It was her idea. I couldn't talk her out of it.'

'Mary knows me,' I said and moved towards him. 'She's been such a good friend, Tom, but she knows I shan't need her this evening.'

'Nellie . . . Nellie love. I love you that much it hurts. I'll make you happy, lass. I swear it.'

'I'm happy now,' I said. 'Stop talking nonsense and come to bed.'

I woke to find Tom's side of the bed cold and empty but I wasn't worried. He would be up seeing to things, getting the van ready for his rounds, because that was his way.

Memories of the night just past brought a smile to my lips. After several hours of passion and loving closeness Tom would have no reason to doubt my feelings for him. If I had doubted them myself those last lingering doubts had flown in his strong, loving arms.

I stretched luxuriously, a feeling of well-being flooding through my body.

'You're awake then? I thought I'd let you lie awhile.'

I sat up as Tom came in, followed by Samantha. She was

still in her nightgown but her hair had been brushed and her face was clean.

'Mummy, Mummy,' she called and clambered on the bed. 'Dada home . . . Dada home.'

'You don't mind?' Tom asked. 'She asked me who I was so I told her . . .'

'You are her Dada now, Tom,' I said, and he nodded.

'Kettle's on the boil. Shall I bring the tea up?'

'I'll come down. There'll be no slacking just because you're home.'

He grinned at me. 'I've been looking at the van. I'd best teach you to drive it before you wreck it completely.'

'Get out of here!'

He laughed and dodged the pillow I threw at him. Samantha went into a fit of giggles and I spent the next five minutes tickling her and chasing her round the bedroom.

It was nearly half an hour later when I went down to the kitchen. Tom was sitting at the table eating a piece of toast and reading something.

'You didn't tell me about this,' he said, looking up.

'What – oh, the letter from the Ministry of Food. It's not important, Tom. I shan't go on the tour.'

'Why not?' he asked. 'I'm on leave for the time being and Mary will help out – your ma, too, I shouldn't wonder. It would be good for her, make her feel wanted. You should go, Nellie. Your recipes are good, just what folk need these days.'

'I suppose I could.' I looked at him. 'You wouldn't mind me being away? It might be for several days at a time.'

Tom got up and came to me. He gazed down into my eyes and the expression in his own made my heart leap.

'I'm that proud of you, lass,' he said softly. 'You've got a gift and it's something you can use to help others. I love you, Nellie Pearce, and I want you for my wife. That doesn't mean I want you tied to the house or the shop. You've a rare talent and you should use it.'

'I've thought I might like to teach cooking one day . . .'

'Then you'll do it,' he said. 'If you need to go away for training we'll cope.'

'What about children? You'll want your own, Tom.'

'We've got the little lass, the rest will come when it's time.'
He smiled and bent to kiss me on the lips. 'We've got the rest
of our lives, Nellie.'
'All our days.'
He was a good, fine man and I knew how lucky I was.
'I like the sound of that, Tom,' I said. 'I like it a lot.'

You have been reading a novel published by Piatkus Books. We hope you have enjoyed it and that you would like to read more of our titles. Please ask for them in your local library or bookshop.

If you would like to be put on our mailing list to receive details of new publications, please send a large stamped addressed envelope (UK only) to:

Piatkus Books: 5 Windmill Street
London W1P 1HF

PIATKUS

The sign of a good book